Individual Freedoms & State Security in the African Context

Individual Freedoms & State Security in the African Context

THE CASE OF ZIMBABWE

John Hatchard

LLB, LLM (LONDON)
of the Middle Temple, Barrister at Law
Senior Lecturer in Law, University of Buckingham
formerly Senior Lecturer in Law, University of Zimbabwe

BAOBAB BOOKS
HARARE
OHIO UNIVERSITY PRESS
ATHENS
JAMES CURREY
LONDON

James Currey
54B Thornhill Square, Islington
London N1 1BE

Baobab Books
PO Box 1559
Harare

Ohio University Press
Scott Quadrangle
Athens, Ohio 45701

First published 1993

93 94 95 96 5 4 3 2 1

British Library Cataloguing in Publication Data

Hatchard, John
Individual Freedoms and State Security in the African Context: Case of Zimbabwe
I. Title
346.8910285

ISBN 0-85255-366-8 (James Currey Cloth)
0-85255-365-X (James Currey Paper)

Library of Congress Cataloging-in-Publication Data

Hatchard, John.
Individual freedoms & state security in the African context : the case of Zimbabwe / John Hatchard.
p. cm.
Includes bibliographical references and index.
ISBN 0-8214-1031-8 (cloth). -- ISBN 0-8214-1043-1 (pbk.)
1. War and emergency powers--Zimbabwe. 2. Civil rights--Zimbabwe. 3. Human rights--Zimbabwe. 4. Zimbabwe--National security--Law and legislation. 5. War and emergency powers--Africa. 6. Civil rights--Africa. 7. Human rights--Africa. I. Title. II. Title: Individual freedoms and state security in the African context.
KTZ3709.H38 1991
342.6891 '085--dc20
[346.8910285]

92-30057
CIP

Typeset in Zimbabwe in 9/11 pt Palatino
by the Publications Unit, Legal Resources Foundation
and printed by Villiers Publications Ltd, London N6

Contents

Dedication

To My Mother and Father
Vera and Stephen Hatchard

Preface

This book started life as a short note on a preventive detention case in Zimbabwe. Its growth was a result of my realisation that states of emergency are a common phenomenon in Africa and that during them, governments enjoy frighteningly wide powers which significantly affect the lives of every citizen. Clearly, unbridled power cannot be tolerated and some safeguards are necessary. This book therefore examines the relationship between emergency powers and individual freedoms in Africa using Zimbabwe as a case study. I hope it will shed some light on the intricate relationship between the two and also promote greater national and international awareness of the problems and dangers posed by states of emergency.

I would like to thank James Currey for working to make this book available throughout Africa. Special thanks must go to Beverley Hargrove for her invaluable assistance in getting the manuscript typeset and ready for press.

To my wife Trinah I owe an enormous debt of gratitude. It was only due to her understanding and support during the research and writing that the book was finished. Thanks also to my children, Sam, Simbidzayi, Zohra and Prudie for letting me complete the project in peace and quiet.

Finally, I must thank my computer with whom I have sat for so many hours during the writing of the book. It has never failed me and has meticulously corrected all my spelling errors. May your cursor continue to blink for many years to come.

John Hatchard
Harare, Zimbabwe

1 Emergency Powers & Individual Freedoms: An Overview

Introduction

There comes a time in the life of almost every nation when a situation arises which threatens its security. Even in peacetime a government may legitimately declare a state of emergency and obtain additional powers in order to combat some grave danger. In this respect it is the international law equivalent of an individual's right to self-defence under the criminal law. Inevitably, the use of these powers has serious implications for individual freedoms which are often curtailed or abrogated as a result. In this book the term 'individual freedoms' covers those categories of human rights which are internationally accepted as requiring protection but which are often endangered by State action in times of national crisis. These are, the right to life and liberty, freedom of movement, association, and conscience, protection from torture and other inhuman treatment, and protection of the law.

This book is a case study of the relationship between individual freedoms and emergency powers in Zimbabwe and seeks to highlight some of the problems associated with the use of such powers in contemporary Africa. A study on Zimbabwe is particularly pertinent because the country was under a continual state of emergency for twenty-five years, during which time the question of the protection of individual freedoms was of considerable concern, both domestically and internationally. Originally introduced in the then white-ruled Rhodesia in 1965, the state of emergency was retained after independence in 1980 and was only finally lifted in July 1990. In view of the dangers posed to individual freedoms by emergency powers, the book examines in particular (i) the justification for the declaration/retention of a state of emergency; (ii) the scope of emergency regulations and their impact on individual freedoms; and (iii) what safeguards are necessary in order to protect those freedoms during a period of emergency. It is asserted that even if a state of emergency is justified, this does not necessitate or justify the complete abrogation or curtailment of the exercise of individual freedoms. Such justification must be considered in the light of the fact that the worst abuses frequently occur when the State has abandoned its commitment to individual freedoms in favour of protecting security interests. Throughout the book, a comparison with other African jurisdictions is made whilst the model which is proposed for the protection of individual freedoms during a state of emergency is one which is potentially applicable to the entire continent.

The relationship between individual freedoms and emergency powers is studied from a legal and political perspective and entails an examination of the role law has played, is playing and may play in this respect. These issues are particularly significant because emergency powers have been a central feature of many contemporary African nations and especially those characterised by executive, centralised, authoritarian regimes. A study of Zimbabwe is thus important because it remains a multi-party State with a constitution which provides for executive accountability, the protection of individual freedoms and an independent judiciary. If emergency powers can undermine individual freedoms in these circumstances, then this has grave implications for constitutionalism and the rule of law in other African States. In order to put the Zimbabwean situation in perspective, this chapter now provides an overview of states of emergency in both international law and domestic law in sub-Saharan Africa. The following chapter then examines the state of emergency in Rhodesia which was highly influential in the development of security laws in Zimbabwe.

States of Emergency in International Law

Given the variety of situations encompassed and the differing political circumstances in which the declaration is made, it is extremely difficult to define what constitutes a state of emergency. Indeed, according to the African Conference on the Rule of Law there is no way of defining a state of emergency or of reducing it to any criteria. The matter is further clouded in that many unproclaimed states of emergency exist when the ordinary law-making procedures are used to pass 'quasi' emergency laws in the shape of wide-ranging security legislation. However it is generally accepted that the only circumstances which justify a derogation of individual freedoms are those which threaten the life of the nation. The African Conference has noted that it is only possible to specify certain conditions without which a state of emergency cannot be proclaimed, the main one being that:

> the regular operation of authority [is] impossible, but that so long as a situation exists where the authorities can operate and the problems arising can be overcome, a state of emergency may not be declared.[1]

Whatever the definitional difficulties, it is important to seek practical parameters to the issue. In general there are at least five situations which can justifiably give rise to a state of emergency: (i) a state of war or preparations to meet its imminent outbreak. Here extremely wide powers are required and these will almost inevitably affect most facets of national life; (ii) armed internal rebellion or subversion. This situation is sometimes linked with (i) above but does not necessarily require the taking of such wide-ranging powers concerning, for example, external relations or restrictions on non-nationals; (iii) civil unrest on a localised scale. Here additional law and order provisions, applicable only to those areas affected by the unrest, are all that are normally required to deal with the threat; (iv) an economic emergency, notably one relating to problems of underdevelopment. Here the parlous state of the national economy may require the taking of emergency powers aimed at preventing the economic collapse of the country. The necessary powers are very different to those discussed above.[2] (v) natural disasters (*force majeure*). Here the government may need to take immediate steps to counter the problem by requisitioning transportation for example. Specific types of powers are necessary and these will almost certainly be of a temporary nature.[3]

The right of a State to derogate certain individual freedoms during an emergency situation is well established in international law. Article 4 of the International Covenant on Civil and Political Rights (ICCPR) states that:

> In time of public emergency which threatens the life of the nation and the existence of which is officially proclaimed, the State Parties to the present Covenant may take measures derogating from their obligations under the present Covenant to the extent strictly required by the exigencies of the situation, provided that such measures do

not involve discrimination solely on the ground of race, colour, sex, language, religion or social origin.[4]

Four elements are contained here: (i) the public emergency must be actual and imminent; (ii) its effects must involve the whole nation, although arguably the emergency may apply to events of a more localised nature; (iii) the continuance of the organised life of the community must be threatened; (iv) the crisis must be exceptional.[5] In this connection, the United Nations Human Rights Committee has emphasised that measures taken under the ICCPR are of an exceptional and temporary nature and may only last as long as the life of the nation is threatened. It has further noted that it is precisely during times of emergency that the protection of individual freedoms becomes all important and that this is especially true for those rights not subject to abrogation.[6] The term 'threatening the life of the nation' is particularly significant here. Its natural and customary meaning refers to an exceptional situation of crisis or emergency which affects the population and constitutes a threat to the organised life of the community of which the State is composed. In *Re Lawless*[7] the European Court of Human Rights found that such a situation existed in Ireland in July 1957 from a combination of several factors i.e. the existence on its territory of the Irish Republican Army (IRA), a secret organisation engaged in unconstitutional activities and using violence to attain its purposes; the steady and alarming increase in terrorist activities between 1956 and 1957; and the fact that the IRA was operating extra-territorially, thus seriously jeopardising relations between the Republic of Ireland and Northern Ireland. In contrast, in Greece in 1967, the European Commission on Human Rights considered that the threat of a communist take-over of the legitimate government by force; the state of public order; and a constitutional crisis did not constitute a public emergency threatening the life of the nation. This was because (i) there was no evidence of an imminent displacement of the lawful government by the communists; (ii) the presence of industrial unrest was similar to that in other European countries; and (iii) the Commission did not agree that there was an imminent threat of such political instability and disorder that the organised life of the community could not be carried on.[8]

Even if the declaration of an emergency is justified, it does not necessarily mean that the use of wide-ranging emergency measures is warranted. As the European Commission on Human Rights has pointed out, a link is required between the facts of the emergency and the measures chosen to deal with it. Thus, under the European Convention although individual governments may decide the scope of the emergency powers, the European Court of Human Rights may determine whether any action has gone beyond that which is strictly required by the exigencies of the situation. This provides a useful safeguard and ensures international publicity on the use of such powers. As is seen later, in practice, the real danger to individual freedoms is the wide-scale and excessive use of emergency powers in circumstances which have little to do with the reasons for the declaration of the emergency. This approach is substantially repeated in other regional documents such as the American Convention of Human Rights, the Council of Europe Convention for the Protection of Human Rights and Fundamental Freedoms (the European Convention) and the European Social Charter.[9] Whilst Zimbabwe has not ratified the ICCPR, the state of emergency was justified by the government in terms of Article 4 of the ICCPR and thus it is on this basis that the state of emergency in Zimbabwe will be examined.[10]

Zimbabwe has ratified the African Charter on Human and Peoples' Rights which provides for the protection of all individual freedoms and contains no specific power permitting a State to derogate from its obligations. However, several provisions contain 'clawback' clauses[11] i.e. provisions which permit a State to restrict certain individual freedoms in circumstances provided for in domestic law.[12] As Gittleman points out, such clauses restrict a State's freedom of action in that they limit the circumstances in which derogation may occur and also define rights which are never subject to abrogation.[13] Even so, such clauses are a poor substitute for the derogation provisions in the ICCPR in that they permit States to arbitrarily determine if and how its citizens may exercise their individual freedoms. In this respect, the African Charter arguably places too much emphasis on 'peoples' rights at the expense of 'individual' rights.[14]

States of Emergency in Domestic Law in Africa

In Africa, some States have attempted to specify the grounds for the proclamation of a state of emergency. In Ghana, section 26 of the Second Republican Constitution defined a state of emergency as one which was 'calculated to deprive the community of the essentials of life, or which renders necessary the taking of measures which are requisite for securing public safety, the defence of Ghana and the maintenance of public order and supplies and services essential to the life of the community'. In South Africa, a proclamation can be made if there is a serious threat to the safety of the public or maintenance of public order which cannot be brought under control by the ordinary law of the land.[15] The Namibian Constitution of 1990 provides that the President may only declare a state of emergency at a time of national disaster, during a period of national defence or a public emergency threatening the life of the nation or the constitutional order.[16] Other countries have attempted a more detailed analysis. In both the 1979 and 1989 Nigerian Constitutions the grounds for the declaration of a state of emergency are: war; a clear and present danger of or an actual breakdown of public order and public safety to such an extent as to require extraordinary measures to restore peace and security; the imminent danger or occurrence of any disaster or national calamity affecting the community; or any other public danger which clearly constitutes a threat to the existence of the Federation.[17] In Tanzania, the grounds include 'a definite danger of great magnitude, to the extent that peace will be disrupted and public safety will be endangered [so that] the situation can only be contained by resorting to extraordinary steps' and 'other dangers that are obviously a threat to the country'.[18] Although this terminology is uncomfortably vague, it is clear that domestic constitutions also recognise that the declaration or renewal of a state of emergency is restricted to extraordinary situations when the very foundations of society are threatened.[19]

The constitutional documents used by Britain for most of her former African colonies contained no criteria for the declaration of a state of emergency. Thus, for example, in Zambia, Sierra Leone, Kenya, Botswana and The Gambia, the President is empowered to proclaim a state of emergency without any need to fit the reasons into any constitutional formula. Even so, in practice the need to obtain the approval of the legislature for such action means that reasons justifying the introduction or continuation of a state of emergency are normally given.[20]

States of Emergency in Africa

One of the characteristics of the colonial period in Africa was the complete absence of individual freedoms for the indigenous population and the use of legal and political institutions to maintain white supremacy. As Read points out, in anglophonic Africa, colonial rule was essentially authoritarian and even the introduction of English law as the basis for local legal systems did not result in the colonial subjects enjoying the full rights of liberty, due process, free speech and the rest which the common law is said to guarantee an

Englishman himself.[21] In the post-1945 period in particular, the imperial powers often used emergency regulations in an effort to retain political and economic control and to stem the tide of African nationalism. For example, in 1952 in Kenya, and following the onset of the Mau Mau rebellion, a state of emergency was declared and emergency regulations ousted the jurisdiction of the courts in some cases, reduced judicial safeguards in others and imposed detention without trial.[22] The effect of the regulations 'was to place the person and property of the inhabitants of the Central Province utterly at the mercy of the administration and during the early years of the emergency, the administration showed little mercy'.[23] Similarly, during the prolonged struggle for Namibian independence, the South African authorities used a wide array of emergency powers against its political opponents. These included the widespread use of detention without trial and the imposition of curfews.

In contemporary Africa the colonial example has been widely followed. The use of emergency powers remains a common feature of national life and is frequently accompanied by abuses of individual freedoms. In recent years some eighteen sub-Saharan African nations have declared a state of emergency, namely: Ethiopia; Lesotho; The Gambia; Ghana; Kenya; Madagascar; Mauritius; Nigeria; Liberia; The Sudan; Somalia; Senegal; Sierra Leone; South Africa; Swaziland; Zaire; Zambia and Zimbabwe. Despite the sophisticated international and domestic safeguards, the tendency has been towards the use of states of emergency to entrench political power and to curtail the legitimate exercise of individual freedoms. For example, in Lesotho in 1970, Chief Leabua Jonathan and his ruling party were defeated in a general election. Unwilling to renounce power, he declared a state of emergency and detained without trial leading members of the successful Basotho National Party.

The problem is exacerbated in that some African countries, especially those without a justiciable Declaration of Rights, have passed 'quasi' emergency laws using the ordinary legislative process. In practice, these give the government the sort of powers normally associated with a state of emergency. For instance, in Tanzania, the Preventive Detention Act provides for indefinite detention without trial without any need to declare a state of emergency. The Ghanaian Preventive Detention Act 1958 was also part of the permanent legislation. In force until the overthrow of the Nkrumah regime in 1966, it was used to detain hundreds of political opponents. Other quasi-emergency measures have imposed severe restrictions on the freedom of information and introduced new 'crimes against the State'.[24] For example, in Botswana, the National Security Act 1986[25] prohibits the carrying out of acts which are considered prejudicial to the safety or interests of Botswana. This is punishable by up to thirty years imprisonment and is intended to counter acts of terrorism and sabotage in the country by South African agents. The Act also provides that 'Where it appears to a police officer of or above the rank of Sergeant . . . that the case is one of great emergency and that in the interests of Botswana immediate action is necessary, he may search [any premises] without a warrant.'[26] The terms of such legislation are very reminiscent of emergency laws. In reality, the use of such laws can also create a permanent 'state of emergency' or even martial law, without the need for an emergency declaration. In South Africa, in 1960, a declared state of emergency made under the Public Safety Act 1953, lasted some five months. It was not until July 1985 that it was renewed and this lasted only eight months. The last emergency proclamation was made in June 1986 and finally lifted in 1990. The draconian nature of the 'ordinary' security laws explains why the unbroken security crisis since 1960 was not countered by the constant use of emergency powers. For example, under the 'ordinary' law, citizens may be banned or detained by official decree for committing vague security offences, whilst powers of censorship, proscription of organisations and the control of meetings are also readily available. Under the Defence Act

1957, members of the South African Defence Forces may be employed for the prevention or suppression of terrorism or internal disorder in the Republic. There are also powers to requisition transportation, commandeer property and control access to ports and airports. An extensive indemnity for members of the South African Defence Forces is also permanently in place. In fact, Mathews argues that the 1986 declaration of a state of emergency was an 'inadvertent emergency' since it was only promulgated because amendments to the Public Safety Act were frustrated in parliament.[27] Whilst international criticism of the continued state of emergency was well founded, it should not be forgotten that it is only when the whole apparatus of state security laws is removed that the permanent 'state of emergency' will end.

Many African States have also experienced a military coup, with some, such as Ghana and Nigeria, having suffered a succession of such interventions. Emergency-style powers in the form of military decrees are frequently introduced following such coups and almost inevitably lead to the dismantling of the constitutional processes and restrictions on the enjoyment of individual freedoms. For example, following the 1984 military coup in Nigeria, the Constitution (Suspension and Modification) Decree No. 1 of 1984 provided for the suspension of much of the 1979 Constitution. The restricted definition of 'period of emergency' in section 41 and the safeguards for arrested or detained persons were suspended, thus in effect legalising the indefinite detention of persons.[28] In addition provision was made to oust the jurisdiction of the courts[29] and to set up military tribunals to try criminal offences.[30] A somewhat similar situation exists in Sudan. In 1989 the Revolutionary Command Council for National Salvation issued Constitutional Decree No. 2 which proclaimed a state of emergency throughout the country. This empowers the President of the Council, *inter alia*, to compulsorily acquire land; to control the movement of goods and persons; and to control workers, including the right to terminate the contract of any government employee. The ordinary law courts are prohibited from hearing any case involving actions taken under Decree No. 2 and are replaced by special courts. The Emergency Regulations 1989, which complement the decree, provide that any person violating any of its provisions may be punished with death or imprisonment for up to twenty years. The operative constitutional decrees do not contain any provisions protecting the rights referred to in the International Covenant on Civil and Political Rights. Neither is there a separate Bill of Rights to serve a similar purpose.[31]

Overview

The right and duty of a government to use emergency and security laws in times of national crisis is undeniable. However as Machan points out, national emergencies do not justify systematic abuses of individual freedoms any more than personal emergencies permit individuals to commit crimes.[32] Accordingly both international and domestic laws seek to lay down parameters to the declaration of a state of emergency in an attempt to safeguard individual freedoms. Thus measures taken during a state of emergency must be directly connected to the emergency situation, must be suitable to lessen or at least control the situation, must be utilised only in the absence of less drastic alternatives and must be accompanied by domestic safeguards against abuses.

In practice the real threat posed by emergency powers to individual freedoms is not so much their use *per se* as their abuse. In Africa, many governments have sought to use such powers improperly in order to entrench their own political power and to eliminate dissent. This is a continent-wide problem affecting countries with civilian governments of all political hues as well those with military regimes.[33] Preventing abuses of power by legal means is extremely difficult if a government is intent on unjustifiably maintaining power by every available means and is prepared to disregard any constitutional and other legal constraints in doing so. Nevertheless the political changes in 1989 and 1990 in Eastern Europe indicate that a new impetus for western-style democracy and the protection of individual freedoms is taking place. Africa is not excluded from these new 'winds of change' or, as President Mugabe has put it, 'gales of change'.[34] For example, in 1990 Zambia became a multi-party democracy after years of one-party rule and in October 1991 achieved a peaceful transition of power through free and fair elections. The new government of the Movement for Multi-Party Democracy then immediately lifted the state of emergency. In Cape Verde a peaceful change of government was also achieved whilst in Namibia one of the most enlightened constitutional documents ever seen in Africa came into effect in March 1990 bringing with it real hope for the effective protection of individual freedoms there. Francophonic Africa has also witnessed remarkable changes leading to a return to multi-party politics and the introduction of new constitutions designed to protect individual freedoms.[35]

The need then is to build on this platform by developing effective constitutional and legal frameworks in which an acceptable and realistic balance is struck between the needs of the State and the protection of individual freedoms. The intention of this book is to investigate how to achieve such a balance.

Notes

1. *African Conference on the Rule of Law 1961, Report on the Proceedings* p.162. This is also the view of Marks who states that an emergency situation is one which places 'institutions of the State in a precarious position and which leads the authorities to feel justified in suspending the application of certain principles': Marks, 1982, p.175.
2. This point is discussed in detail in Chapter 11.
3. For a brief but helpful examination of this point see Groves, 1961, p.1 and Rossiter, 1948, p.6.
4. Article 4(1). These are the generally recognised criteria for the declaration of a state of emergency and are thus an influential guide, even though Zimbabwe has not ratified the convention.
5. European Court of Justice in *Denmark, Norway, Sweden & Netherlands v Greece* (3321–3/67; 3344/67) Report: 5 November 1969.
6. GC 5/13, HRC 36, p.110.
7. Case 322/57; Judgment 1 EHRR 15. See also *X v Ireland* (493/59) CD 7, p.85.
8. See note 5.
9. See also Mangan, 1988, p.376, who argues that an emergency situation does not, by itself, justify systematic human rights violations and that a government must consider the magnitude of the emergency and whether the deprivation of human rights can be avoided.
10. It was also justified as being in accordance with Article 15 of the European Convention: see *Parliamentary Debates*, 13 July 1982. Zimbabwe finally ratified the International Covenants in 1991.
11. Higgins, 1978, p.281, states that a 'clawback' clause is one which 'permits, in normal circumstances, a breach of an obligation for a specified number of reasons'. Compare Hartman, 1981, at p.6.
12. For example, Article 6 provides for the right to liberty 'except for reasons and conditions previously laid down by law'. This enables the State to continue with detention without trial so long as this is provided for in its own domestic law.
13. Gittleman, 1984, p.157.
14. This point is also noted by Ojo and Sesay, 1986, p.99.
15. Section 2(1) Public Safety Act (South Africa).
16. Article 26(1).
17. Section 265(3). The section is extant despite the military coup and the suspension of much of the Constitution.
18. Section 32(2) Law of the Fifth Amendment of the State Constitution of 1984.
19. Some writers assert that a serious economic crisis should also be covered by an emergency proclamation. See, for instance, Mathews, 1971, p.39. This is discussed in a later chapter.
20. Although this safeguard was avoided in some countries, such as Zambia and Kenya, by the maintenance of a virtually perpetual state of emergency (see below).
21. Read, 1973, p.29. A similar point is made by Ghai and McAuslan, 1970, pp.407–8. The position elsewhere was similarly repressive and as one writer asserts, 'The savagery of Belgian colonialism portrays a picture of almost total human degradation, and within that context it is little wonder that the semblance of legality imported from Western civilization had little or no meaning.' Eze, 1984, p.18.
22. Emergency regulations also empowered the courts to impose the death sentence, see, for example, *Kuruma v R* [1955] AC 197.

23. Ghai and McAuslan, pp.159–160. Although Cameroon experienced a somewhat similar armed struggle, independence was still achieved through negotiation.
24. See Criminal Code 1960 section 183 as amended. For a full analysis, see International Commission of Jurists, 1983, p.105.
25. Act 11 of 1986.
26. Section 11(2).
27. Mathews, 1986, p.195.
28. Section 41 provided that emergency measures were only constitutional if 'reasonably justifiable for the purpose of dealing with the situation that exists during that period of emergency'. For a full discussion on the 1984 Decree see Ojo, 1987, p.254 *et seq*.
29. For instance, the State Security (Detention of Persons) Decree No. 13 of 1984 and Public Property (Special Military Tribunals) Decree No. 2 of 1984. See Ojo, 1987, p.261.
30. For instance, the Robbery and Firearms (Special Provisions) Decree No. 20 of 1984 and Recovery of Public Property (Special Military Tribunals) Decree No. 3 of 1984. See Ojo, 1987, p.265.
31. For a full account of the decree see United Nations document CCPR/C/45/Add.3 dated 28 February 1991.
32. See Machan, 1975, p.222.
33. It is not intended to assert that military governments are in any way an acceptable alternative to civilian governments. As Liebenow points out, the *modus operandi* of the military dictates against constant bargaining, open-ended discussion, and absence of closure that are requisites of a functioning democratic society. However at times, there is little difference between the actions of so-called civilian governments and their military counterparts. See Liebenow, 1986, p.261.
34. See text of speech given by President Mugabe at the opening of the Commonwealth Heads of Government meeting in Harare, Zimbabwe, October 1991.
35. See Reyntjens, 1991, p.29.

2 Constitutional Development & the State of Emergency in Rhodesia: An Overview

Constitutional Developments up to 1961

Zimbabwe (formerly Southern Rhodesia) was originally inhabited by descendants of the great southern migration which peopled most of Central and Southern Africa. A well organised Shona-speaking State developed with a tradition of self-government and independence going back to the Kingdom of Monomotapa (Munhumutapa). In about 1830 the Ndebele, an off-shoot of the Zulu nation, crossed the Limpopo River from the south and established a centralised State in the south-west. By 1888 Lobengula, the Ndebele king, claimed sovereignty over all the territory which now forms Zimbabwe.

In October 1889 Cecil Rhodes obtained a Royal Charter setting up the British South Africa Company (BSAC). This enabled the Company to exercise powers of government in its 'field of operations' i.e. immediately to the north of Bechuanaland, north and west of the Transvaal and west of Portuguese Mozambique. No northern boundary was specified. In 1890 Mashonaland was occupied by BSAC forces who founded the capital in Salisbury (now Harare) and in the following year the territory was declared a British Protectorate. In 1893 hostilities between the Company and the Ndebele led to the occupation of Matabeleland and the flight of Lobengula to the north. Attempts to capture him failed but reports of his death led the British to declare the Matabele kingdom at an end. As a result, in 1895 the entire territory was named Rhodesia. The first *Chimurenga* war, which took place between 1896 and 1897, was a countrywide rebellion against the occupation although there were essentially separate revolts in Matebeleland and Mashonaland. With considerable difficulty, the Company regained control of the country but the war was highly influential in the later freedom struggle.

Until 1923, the Colony of Southern Rhodesia, as it became known from 1898, was administered by the BSAC. By 1922 the settlers had obtained a majority in the Legislative Assembly over the representatives of the Company and were seeking a new constitutional structure. A referendum was then held to determine whether, on the termination of the Company's administration, the territory should be incorporated into the Union of South Africa or become a colony enjoying 'responsible government'. By a majority of 8,744 to 5,989 the latter option was chosen. It is unlikely that the number of African voters exceeded 60 (out of an estimated population of around 900,000).[1] Accordingly, under the terms of the Southern Rhodesia Constitution Letters Patent 1923, the country became a self-governing colony. Thus the overwhelming black majority found themselves governed under the loosest of imperial supervision by ministers responsible to a legislature elected by the local whites and under the day to day control of an adminstration staffed by locally recruited Europeans. As in all other colonial possessions, there were no entrenched protections of individual freedoms although Britain did retain some supervisory powers by means of the 'reserved clauses' which required imperial consent to legislation passed by the colony on certain matters, the most important of which being discriminatory legislation against Africans.[2]

African attempts to bring about political change started in earnest after the Second World War. In July 1947 Benjamin Burombo organised the African Workers' Voice Association, which was an important forerunner of African nationalist groups, and which undertook a campaign of civil disobedience designed to draw the attention of the British Government to the plight of the African population. In 1952 the organisation was banned but its work helped lead to the formation in 1957 of the first national party, the African National Congress. The party was headed by Joshua Nkomo, a former trade union official from Bulawayo. Following the declaration of a state of emergency in 1959 caused by nationwide civil unrest against government policies, the Congress was banned but was replaced by the National Democratic Party (NDP). This in turn was also banned and as a result, in 1961 the Zimbabwe African Peoples Union (ZAPU) was formed and headed by Nkomo. ZAPU itself was also banned in September 1962. Following dissatisfaction with the policies of ZAPU, in August 1963 the Zimbabwe African National Union (ZANU) was founded with Revd Ndabaningi Sithole as its President. Unlike previous nationalist organisations, ZANU was dedicated to national independence and liberation through armed struggle and accordingly launched the second *Chimurenga* war.

Between 1953 and 1963 there was some transfer of governmental and legislative power to organs of the Federation of Rhodesia and Nyasaland. However, even before Federation, demands were growing inside Southern Rhodesia for the removal of Britain's reserved powers and for the introduction of a new constitution. Britain made it clear that its acceptance of these demands depended upon the introduction of adequate forms of internal safeguards for Africans and a substantial increase in African representation in the Assembly. At the 1961 Constitutional Conference in London, representatives of the NDP agreed to proposals whereby Africans could expect to gain 15 seats in a 65 seat legislature. Although strong pressure from NDP supporters later led to a rejection of these proposals, the conference proceeded to draw up the 1961 Constitution of Southern Rhodesia which was only legally revoked in 1980 when the country gained formal independence.

The 1961 Constitution provided for considerable internal sovereignty over domestic affairs. The reserved powers under the 1923 Constitution were largely removed and the matter of the franchise now fell within the competence of the Southern Rhodesia Legislative Assembly. Above all there was the formal recognition by Britain of a constitutional convention that Parliament at Westminster would not legislate on any matter within the competence of the Assembly, including the amendment of the constitution, without the consent of the Southern Rhodesia Government. The document also contained an entrenched and justiciable Declaration of Rights and provided for a Constitutional Council to consider whether legislation or administrative action was inconsistent with the Declaration. However, suspension of the Declaration of Rights was permitted during a state of emergency with the result that many of the most basic rights were unavailable when they were most needed.[3] As a result the International Commission of Jurists declared that the restrictions in the document so undermined the Declaration as to make 'one wonder why the trouble was ever taken to put those human rights into the Constitution'.[4] The franchise provisions enshrined the principle of unimpeded progress to majority rule although in practice the educational and economic requirements for voting all but guaranteed a permanently subordinate role for Africans in Southern Rhodesian politics.

The UDI Period

Following the 1962 General Election which was won convincingly by the Rhodesia Front Party (RF), lengthy negotiations between the Rhodesian and British governments took place on the question of independence, which constitutionally could only be conferred by Britain. No agreement was reached and, following the declaration of a state of emergency in the country, on November 11 1965 Prime Minister Ian Smith and other ministers holding office under the 1961 Constitution purported to issue a Unilateral Declaration of Independence (UDI). The regime then purported to adopt the 1965 'Constitution of Rhodesia' which was similar to the 1961 Constitution with the only significant changes being those designed to remove the elements of subordination to Britain. The British government responded by making drastic modifications to the 1961 Constitution and declared void and of no effect any law passed or executive function performed by the illegal regime. The United Nations also imposed selective and then comprehensive mandatory sanctions against Rhodesia in a bid to end the rebellion. At first, the position of the judiciary was unaffected by UDI in that the judges were regarded as continuing in office under the 1961 Constitution. Indeed the 1965 document purported to continue their appointments without requiring any acknowledgment of the illegal regime. It was not until the case of *Madzimbamuto v Lardner-Burke*[5] that matters came to a head. Here the Privy Council in London upheld the right of the United Kingdom Parliament to exercise unfettered legislative power over Southern Rhodesia and to deny all legal validity to the actions of the Smith regime. As a result, a majority of the Rhodesian judiciary acknowledged the Smith regime as the lawful government in the country and recognised the 1965 document as the only valid constitution.

In 1970 the illegal regime purported to adopt the republican Constitution of Rhodesia which precluded any prospect of majority rule. A new franchise was adopted based on race which provided for eventual parity of African and European representation in the House of Assembly but which excluded the possibility of majority rule. The Declaration of Rights was made non-justiciable thus paving the way for considerable abuses of individual freedoms by the Smith regime in later years.

The proclamation of the Republic made prospects for a constitutional settlement bleak. There was also little sign that economic sanctions were working. In addition, negotiations between Smith and the then British Prime Minister Harold Wilson aboard the British warships *Tiger* (in 1966) and *Fearless* (in 1967) had proved fruitless. These were based on possible amendments to the 1961 Constitution so as to provide an independence settlement consistent with the British position of no independence until agreement on six principles namely: majority rule; guarantees against retrogressive amendments to the constitution; the unacceptability of racial discrimination; immediate improvement in the political status of the African population; no oppression of majority by minority or of minority by majority; and what was agreed had to be acceptable to the people of Rhodesia. No African representatives participated in the talks. However, with a change of government in Britain, agreement was reached in 1971 between Smith and the new Conservative Foreign and Commonwealth Secretary, Sir Alec Douglas Home. This was based on British acceptance of the republican constitution as the constitutional framework for legal independence subject to amendments which included a justiciable Declaration of Rights and changes in the franchise which enabled African representation to go beyond parity in the House of Assembly. Even so, majority rule was unlikely to be obtained for between thirty and fifty years. As an integral part of the agreement, a Commission headed by a British judge, Lord Pearce, visited Rhodesia to test African opinion. The African National Council (ANC), under the chairmanship of Bishop Abel Muzorewa, was established within the country in order to oppose these proposals. Although the Smith regime claimed that the Chiefs, who supported the plan (and were generally puppets of the government) spoke for the African majority, the ANC campaign to galvanise public opposition to the plan was entirely successful with the Pearce Commission concluding that it was not acceptable to the people of the country as a whole. In 1972 the ANC developed into a permanent political movement with Muzorewa as its President.

Settler response to the nationalist movement was the enactment of increasingly repressive security legislation. Restrictions on the freedom of expression were first instituted in the Sedition Act of 1936. This was followed by the Subversive Activities Act 1950 and the Public Order Act 1955. This legislation was later considerably strengthened. The Preventive Detention (Temporary Provisions) Act 1959 provided for detention without trial whilst the Unlawful Organisations Act 1959 gave the executive the power to ban nationalist organisations. Both statutes were used on many occasions against the nationalists. Perhaps the high point for repressive legislation came the following year. The Vagrancy Act 1960 allowed for the arrest without warrant of vagrants i.e. persons unable to show evidence of employment or visible and sufficient means of subsistence. Such a vague definition enabled the security forces to arrest at will virtually anyone they chose and almost invariably the power was directed against the non-white population. This was followed by the controversial Law and Order (Maintenance) Act 1960 which sought to consolidate the Sedition Act and Subversive Activities Act although in practice the effect was to greatly increase governmental powers. For example, the police obtained new powers such as the right to search premises without a warrant and without the permission of the owner, the power to declare a lawful meeting unlawful and to order persons there to disperse and the power to forbid any person, however eminent, from addressing such a meeting. The Bill met with considerable opposition especially from the Federal Chief Justice, Sir Robert Tredgold, who, foresaw (correctly) that it would compel the courts to become party to widespread injustice. The refusal of the government to amend the Bill led to his resignation.

This legislation was reinforced by the Emergency Powers Act which provided the Governor with wide-ranging powers to deal with any emergency situation.[6] Six declarations of a state of emergency were made prior to 1965, each lasting for three months. Then, following the declaration of a state of emergency in 1965, emergency powers were resorted to in an attempt to entrench white minority rule and to curtail African demands for a voice in the political development of their country. For the next fifteen years, the Rhodesian government used emergency powers to turn the country into an executive dictatorship and left few areas of public life unaffected. For example, in an attempt to counter international sanctions, emergency regulations provided for strict controls on the economic life of the nation and the Minister was empowered to make any order to control or regulate the production, sale, transport, distribution, or purchase of any goods when it appeared to him 'necessary or expedient'. Regulations also implemented additional security measures which gave the authorities powers further limiting freedom of movement, liberty and expression and providing for detention without trial. The permanency of the state of emergency was now a fact of life and as Chief Justice Beadle noted in the case of *Madzimbamuto*: 'Proclamations made for the maintenance of public order and preservation of the peace must be regarded as matters of everyday occurrence in the conditions presently existing in Southern Rhodesia.'[7]

In 1969, the Declaration of Rights was made non-justiciable on the ground that it could 'involve the judiciary in political controversy'.[8] Individual freedoms were thus reduced to a complete sham and 'state terrorism' became a reality. The illegal regime now faced an intensification of the armed struggle within Rhodesia by both ZANLA (the armed wing of ZANU) and ZIPRA (the armed wing of ZAPU) forces. The 'Battle of Sinoia' on 28 April

1966, when seven ZANLA guerillas died in a battle with Rhodesian security forces, is now seen as the start of the second *Chimurenga* war. However it was not until the early 1970s that the armed struggle started to have a significant impact on the country. Perhaps the crucial moment came in 1975 with the independence of Mozambique. From then on ZANLA forces were able to establish bases there from which guerrillas infiltrated into Rhodesia across the long common border. In the face of this escalation of the war, oppressive legislation increased. For example, the Indemnity and Compensation Act 1975 was designed to protect members of the Rhodesian security forces from all civil or criminal liability for any actions taken or to be taken. This effectively allowed them to operate with complete impunity. Emergency regulations were then used to impose collective fines on villagers suspected of assisting guerillas, to close clinics and scores of schools in the rural areas and to introduce the use of 'protected villages' which led to the forcible movement of thousands of civilians in the rural areas.[9]

There were no safeguards against this legislation. Being non-justiciable, the constitution provided no protection at all for individual freedoms for even the limited protections in the 1961 document had been eliminated in the republican constitution. With Smith's RF party having an overwhelming parliamentary majority, the legislature was largely subservient to the government with most members docilely doing as instructed. The judiciary did little to assist. Following the Madzimbamuto decision, a few judges had resigned,[10] but the rest remained to uphold and support the illegal regime. Indeed during the entire UDI period, no decision ever went against the State. Thus in practice the government had ensured that there were no restraints or safeguards on its freedom of action.

International efforts to find a settlement continued. In 1974, and following pressure from South Africa, the Smith regime agreed to release from preventive detention some of the leading nationalists including Robert Mugabe and Nkomo. Then in 1976 Smith was forced to concede the principle of majority rule and this helped bring about a constitutional conference in Geneva in October 1976 under British chairmanship and attended by all parties to the struggle. A coalition of ZANU and ZAPU called the Patriotic Front (PF) was created for the conference and, despite internal strains, the PF continued to operate until after the 1979 Lancaster House conference. The failure of the Geneva conference led to the intensification of the armed struggle with increasingly large areas of the country falling under the influence of the freedom fighters and with the government responding by the widespread and arbitrary use of the security laws against the civilian population.

In 1977 an Anglo-American bid to end the crisis foundered after Smith refused to accept the terms of the settlement which would have led to United Nations sponsored elections. Instead Smith pursued a policy of procuring an 'internal settlement' with several compliant African leaders, including Bishop Muzorewa of the now renamed United African National Council (UANC) and Revd Ndabaningi Sithole who had been ousted as leader of ZANU at a congress in Mozambique at which Robert Mugabe was elected the new party President. The object of the internal settlement was to provide for majority rule but with adequate 'safeguards' for whites. It was hoped that these changes would both induce many freedom fighters to abandon the armed struggle and lead to international recognition of the new regime thus leading to the lifting of sanctions and the attainment of legal independence.

In March 1978 the settlement was signed and was followed by a transitional period during which a constitution for the re-named Zimbabwe–Rhodesia was drawn up. The 'safeguards' contained in the constitution included reserving 28 seats for whites in the 100 seat National Assembly, thus ensuring that the RF could block any constitutional changes. A justiciable Declaration of Rights was included which purported to outlaw discriminatory laws and practices and to protect individual freedoms. In practice this was a fiction because, as the Declaration did not apply to existing legislation for an initial period of ten years, all the existing security legislation remained intact despite the fact that most of it contravened the Declaration. Crucially certain key provisions were also designed to ensure continued white control. Thus the retention of the white seats was guaranteed for a minimum of ten years and, even then, Parliament could only abolish such seats if a recommendation to this effect was made by a commission, the majority of whose membership was almost inevitably white. In addition, a system of commissions ensured white control over appointments to the judiciary, the public service, the police and the security forces. Thus although Muzorewa was now appointed Prime Minister, he had little real political power and played no part in the appointment of such key figures as the Chief Justice and defence force chiefs.

The internal settlement was unsuccessful largely because it failed to end the war in which the PF was clearly winning and because it did not gain any international recognition. In desperation the government proclaimed martial law and introduced draconian curfew regulations, secret trials and summary executions.

In May 1979 hopes were raised in Rhodesia of British recognition of the internal settlement when a Conservative government led by Margaret Thatcher was elected in Britain. However her administration sought a fresh constitutional settlement acceptable to all parties and to the international community. The framework for this came in August 1979 following the Commonwealth Heads of Government meeting in Lusaka, Zambia. The 'Lusaka Accord' recognised that it was the responsibility of Britain to grant legal independence to Zimbabwe on the basis of majority rule and welcomed the intention of the British Government to invite all parties to a constitutional conference in London. As a result the Lancaster House conference was held from 10 September to 21 December 1979 and was attended by the Patriotic Front led by Mugabe and Nkomo and a delegation from Zimbabwe–Rhodesia. After lengthy discussions, agreement was reached on an independence constitution, arrangements for a transitional period during which fresh elections would be held and for a cease-fire to be monitored by a military force of some 1,200 under British command. A British Governor, Lord Soames, was appointed to run the country for the period up to independence and on 12 December 1979, the day on which he reached Salisbury, the House of Commons in London was told that Rhodesia had returned to legality. The Southern Rhodesia Act 1979 was then passed which provided for the making of an independence constitution for Zimbabwe by Order-in-Council. The Act also provided for the running of Rhodesia until formal independence. Executive and legislative power was vested in the Governor to whom all officers and authorities, including the defence forces, were to be obedient. Although the state of martial law was terminated, the security laws and the state of emergency were retained.[11]

Overview

Whilst the right of a State to defend itself is undeniable, the history of Rhodesia illustrates the dangers attendant with the use of emergency powers. Here a self-induced state of emergency was used for fifteen years to enable a small ruling elite to retain political power against the wishes of the vast majority of the population. The state of exception truly became the state of norm. As a result an executive dictatorship was established. Wide-ranging emergency regulations and the like limited or excluded the exercise of individual freedoms such as freedom of movement, protection of the law and right to liberty. In addition, any safeguards against arbitrary rule were methodically eliminated. The legislature was either completely by-passed or merely used as a rubber-stamp. The constitution was manipulated so that the Declaration of Rights was rendered totally meaningless. After

1967, the loyalty of the judiciary to the Smith regime was such that not one judgment went against the State. By the elimination of any safeguards for individual freedoms, the Rhodesian government ensured that constitutional government was replaced by State terrorism. Then, through the use of emergency powers, the government was able to create an executive dictatorship under the guise of legality.

There are two clear lessons from the Rhodesian experience for other African States. Firstly, that there is a real danger of considerable governmental abuse of power during a state of emergency. As a result it is essential that states of emergency are retained only for a limited period and are justified in international law. Secondly, that some safeguards are essential in order to protect individual freedoms. This requires the development of a constitutional structure which is capable of protecting individuals at the time when such protection is most needed.

Ironically, the same Rhodesian legislation was inherited by the new majority government after independence and was retained virtually intact. In the following chapters, the justification for the retention of these powers, the manner of their use and the effectiveness of the constitutional safeguards are examined.

Notes

1. Palley notes that it was unlikely that the number of African voters had increased from 1914 when it was estimated that the number did not exceed sixty: Palley, 1966, p.211.
2. The powers were rarely used but probably acted as a psychological barrier to the introduction of legislation which might have met with the disapproval of Britain. See Palley, 1966, p.241.
3. Retrospective legislation concerning criminal offences, and prohibition on slavery, forced labour and inhuman treatment as well as the right to life were never liable to abrogation.
4. *Bulletin of the International Commission of Jurists, 'Southern Rhodesia: Human Rights and the Constitution'* No. 18, March 1964, p.44. On several occasions the government also sought to by-pass the Declaration. See, for example, the cases of *Nkomo v Lardner-Burke* (discussed in a later chapter) and *Maluleke v Minister of Law* 1963 (4) SA 206.
5. [1969] AC 645.
6. See Chapter 4 for a full discussion on this Act.
7. Above, 1968 (2) SA 284, at p.353.
8. See the Whaley Commission Report which was appointed to draw up the new constitution.
9. See Chapter 8 for details.
10. These included Justice Fieldsend who was later to return after independence to become the first Chief Justice of Zimbabwe.
11. Proclamation 11/80 SI 179/80 and Termination of Martial Law (Consequential Provisions) Order 1980 O 13/80.

3 The State of Emergency in Zimbabwe

The New Constitutional Structure

In order to appreciate the declared reasons for the state of emergency in Zimbabwe, a brief introduction to the new constitutional structure in the country is appropriate.

Perhaps the most remarkable feature of the Lancaster House conference was that the talks produced a settlement which led to a peaceful transition to majority rule. Thus on 18 April 1980 Zimbabwe became independent and was admitted into the United Nations and the Commonwealth with effect from that date. The new Constitution of Zimbabwe provided for a non-executive President with powers and functions resembling those of the British monarch, a Prime Minister and a Cabinet responsible to Parliament. The legislature was a bi-cameral body consisting of a popularly elected House of Assembly and an indirectly elected Senate which merely had a delaying power as regards the passing of legislation. The independence of the judiciary was also recognised. Individual freedoms were protected by a Declaration of Rights which was entrenched and made fully justiciable.

The settlement provided for the election of 80 common roll members to the 100 seat House of Assembly. The parties forming the Patriotic Front fought the elections separately. ZANU(PF) (as the party became known)[1] led by Robert Mugabe won 57 seats and accordingly he was appointed Prime Minister. ZAPU (now known as PF–ZAPU) led by Joshua Nkomo won 20 seats while the UANC won just three, thus underlining the fraudulent nature of the internal settlement.[2] The Rhodesia Front party won all the 20 seats reserved for whites. The make-up of the legislature was later radically altered with the abolition of the white roll seats, the establishment of a uni-cameral body, and the enlargement of the membership to 150. At all times, the ruling party enjoyed a commanding majority.

The indirectly elected President had largely ceremonial powers with political power being vested in the Prime Minister and a Cabinet made up of ministers appointed by the President acting on the advice of the Prime Minister. In only a strictly limited number of circumstances was the President able to act independently and these mainly related to the appointment or removal of the Prime Minister. The powers were only important in the event of a hung Parliament and the commanding majority of ZANU(PF) thus rendered them superfluous. This left the President as something of a figurehead although from time to time he was able to perform a useful advisory role.[3] The establishment of an executive President was always the goal of ZANU(PF) and in 1987 major constitutional changes[4] brought this about with Robert Mugabe being elected President.[5]

The Constitution provides that the President may proclaim at any time that a state of emergency exists or that a situation exists which, if allowed to continue, may lead to a state of emergency.[6] The proclamation may relate to the whole or part of the country. This action requires the approval of more than one half of the total membership of Parliament within fourteen days, failing which it ceases to have effect and the President must revoke it.[7] If the proclamation is approved, the state of emergency remains in effect for up to six months unless Parliament resolves that it should be for a shorter period. The legislature may also resolve that the state of emergency be extended for up to six months and that it should relate to a lesser area as it may specify.[8] In either case the President must comply with the resolution. There is no limit to the number of renewals of the emergency. Such a system is useful because it requires a public debate on the issue at regular intervals.

Justifying the State of Emergency

Following independence, fresh security problems beset the new administration. In response thereto it obtained a renewal of the state of emergency every six months until July 1990 when government decided not to seek its renewal. The reasons for the constant renewals are inter-related but for the sake of clarity are examined here under the headings of firstly, internal unrest and political instability and secondly, external security threats.[9]

Internal Unrest and Political Instability

According to the United States Department of State, the new government of Robert Mugabe 'inherited the country with western legal and political traditions'.[10] This overly simplistic assessment is far removed from reality. In the Rhodesia of Ian Smith, the sole aim of government with its framework of security, economic and social legislation and disregard of individual freedoms, was to perpetuate the domination of one small racial group. In its efforts to defend this privilege, the regime led the country into war-torn chaos. With an all-powerful executive and a compliant legislature and judiciary, human rights violations abounded.

Faced with this background, Robert Mugabe went to great lengths to allay fears of constitutional instability and to promote national reconciliation. Despite considerable misgivings over some aspects of the new constitution, he insisted that:

> We are prepared to work under a parliamentary democracy, as accepted by us in the Lancaster House Agreement. Even though we have the power with the Patriotic Front coalition, I do not think we want to make any major amendments. I think we want to try the constitution as it exists and see how it works. True, we had our reservations about certain clauses, but it is only fair that we give the constitution a fair trial.[11]

His first government was also one of national unity and included one white and five PF–ZAPU members, with Joshua Nkomo, the Party leader, getting the important Home Affairs portfolio.[12] Shortly afterwards an additional two whites were added. Perhaps uniquely, some of the very men who had helped mastermind the war against him, including Ian Smith himself, were allowed to retain their seats in Parliament.[13]

Despite rigorous adherence to the government policy of reconciliation, internal unrest and political tensions quickly materialised. The major contributory factor was the strained relationship between ZANU(PF), which was almost entirely supported by the majority Shona speakers and PF–ZAPU which enjoyed overwhelming support in Matabeleland. There is no consensus as to the causes of this antagonism but it probably originated from the split in the nationalist movement in 1963 which led to the formation of ZANU. After independence, the first strains appeared over the formation of the new Zimbabwe National Army. This always promised to be a very difficult undertaking given that at independence there were three separate and ideologically distinct forces. These comprised the 77,000 strong Rhodesia security forces, the Auxiliary Forces loyal to Muzorewa and the ZANLA (the military wing of ZANU) and ZIPRA (the military wing of ZAPU) forces. Perhaps not unnaturally, those troops not loyal to ZANLA were viewed with some suspicion by government. Many whites left the military with a good pension but tensions remained high amongst a number of ZANLA and ZIPRA forces particularly because it was not possible to enlist all former combatants into the new army. This led to allegations that a disproportionate number of ex-ZIPRA combatants were being demobilised, most of whom had little or no education and little chance of finding any alternative employment.

The mutual antagonism and suspicion between ZANLA and ZIPRA forces erupted into violence on 9 November 1980 in camps at Entumbane near Bulawayo in Matabeleland. In no time at all a mini-war was in progress involving all ranks. Small arms, machine guns, mortars, grenades and explosives were all employed, resulting in several hundred casualties.[14] Ironically, units of the National Army led by members of the former Rhodesia African Rifles and supported by the white dominated Air Force were deployed to restore order but for the first time after independence a curfew was imposed on the area. Early the following year further clashes occurred in several army barracks and again there were heavy casualties.[15] These incidents resulted in the defection of some former ZIPRA men from the army, adding strength to the burgeoning dissident movement. After that, at least publicly, tensions within the ZNA largely subsided.

In the early years, one of the main reasons for the continued state of emergency was the security problem posed by dissidents. From the earliest months of independence reports began to circulate concerning dissident activities in Matabeleland and the Midlands undertaken by former ZIPRA guerillas. These involved the destruction of property and attacks on the civilian population in the rural areas. The grievances of the dissidents were mixed but centred on dissatisfaction with the participation of the people of Matabeleland in government and the armed forces. The security problem was exacerbated by South African support for the dissidents. Zimbabweans in Matabeleland and in the Dukwe refugee camp in Botswana were recruited by South African agents and then trained at bases in northern Transvaal and supplied with weapons captured from Angola and Namibia. According to some reports the weapons were of the same type and bore similar serial numbers to those recovered from a captured MNR base in Mozambique. The South African trained dissidents later became known as 'Super-ZAPU'.[16]

In addition to the violence in Matabeleland attacks were made on leading government and ZANU(PF) members. Thus in December 1981 a bomb devastated the party headquarters in Central Harare killing 6 and injuring up to 150 persons. This was probably an attempt on the life of the Prime Minister who normally held a party meeting in the building at that time. In June 1982 further attacks were launched on the homes of both the Prime Minister and Enos Nkala. Nkala, an Ndebele and who was then Minister of National Supplies and later Minister of Home Affairs, was a close associate of Mugabe and a prominent opponent of PF–ZAPU.

Government continued to justify the state of emergency on the grounds of continued dissident activity and maintained that the dissidents owed allegiance to PF–ZAPU although this was consistently denied by Nkomo and other party leaders. However the dissident activity brought increasing strains on the government of national unity and this was further exacerbated by the discovery of large arms caches on property belonging to PF–ZAPU in Matabeleland. As a result of this find, in February 1982 Mugabe dismissed Nkomo and three other PF–ZAPU ministers from his Cabinet.[17] The remaining PF–ZAPU members resigned shortly afterwards. The following month Nkomo's two top military aides, Dumiso Dabengwa and Lookout Masuku, were arrested and charged with treason. The arrest of Masuku was particularly significant as he was the former Deputy Army

Commander in the new Zimbabwe National Army. Both were later tried for treason but were acquitted. They were immediately detained under a ministerial detention order and held until 1986.[18] Nkomo himself left the country for a time claiming that his life was in danger.

The dissident problem took on an international dimension when, on 23 July 1982, ten foreign tourists were seized by armed men on the road from Victoria Falls to Bulawayo. Three women and one man were released shortly afterwards but the other six men were abducted and never seen alive again. A letter sent by the kidnappers to the Prime Minister demanded the release of Dabengwa and Masuku, failing which the tourists would be killed. Tragically the victims were murdered shortly after their capture although it was not until some three years later that their bodies were discovered. The self-confessed leader of the gang, Gilbert Ngwenya together with Austin Mpofu were convicted of committing an act of terrorism and sentenced to death. Both freely admitted taking part in the kidnapping, claiming that their actions were politically motivated. In the Supreme Court, Justice Gubbay noted that the victims were all foreign tourists having nothing whatsoever to do with the political grievances which Ngwenya and Mpofu harboured against the government and were simply used as pawns in a misconceived political game. He added that 'The barbaric and inhuman act of the appellants, which was attended by far-reaching publicity, [has] shocked the peace-loving people of Zimbabwe and the whole civilised world. Many families [have been] caused immeasurable grief and worry and bore the terrible uncertainty of not knowing whether their loved ones were still alive.'[19] On 7 April 1986 both men were hanged in Harare Central Prison.

Dissident activity and the state of emergency continued and in January 1984 the scale of the security problem was set out by the Minister of Home Affairs. When seeking a renewal of the state of emergency, he informed the House of Assembly that in the previous six months there had been 75 murders committed by 'bandits', 284 armed robberies and 16 rapes. He also noted that some dissidents were being funded from South Africa. As regards the continued use of emergency powers, he noted[20] that 'the ordinary laws of the land do not allow the government to deal adequately with a situation where certain of our inhabitants are bent upon disrupting the peace and economic prosperity of the country'.

As a result of the continuing violence, relations between the two major parties remained extremely tense. The 1985 General Election did little to alter the political scene as ZANU(PF) again failed to win a single seat in Matabeleland where PF–ZAPU won all 15 seats capturing over 82 per cent of the popular vote. In contrast, in the rest of the country the ruling party won over 92 per cent of the popular vote, failing to win only one of the 65 seats available.[21] Accordingly the violence continued unabated in Matabeleland with the destruction of property and attacks on local peasants remaining commonplace. In January 1986 the Minister of Home Affairs told Parliament that during the second half of 1985, bandits had murdered 103 people, raped 57 women, committed 263 armed robberies and destroyed millions of dollars worth of property. Similarly disturbing figures were announced in 1986 and 1987. During this period there were also 96 contacts between the security forces and dissidents.[22] Amnesty International also noted that ZANU(PF) supporters were victimised.[23] Government run clinics and health centres were also regular targets for attack. For example, in September 1987, six paramedical staff were shot dead at a clinic whilst carrying out an immunisation programme for local children. The serious disruption of commercial farming was epitomised by the fact that by 1984 in the Kezi/Marula district of Matabeleland, an area of some 370,000 hectares, the security situation was so serious that only 11 commercial ranchers remained on their land out of a total of 53 at independence. These activities, together with a severe drought in the region between 1982 and 85, caused enormous suffering to the people of Matabeleland and posed a considerable security threat to the country.

The dissident problem was largely a political one and eventually steps were taken to find a political solution. In October 1985, meetings commenced between ZANU(PF) and PF–ZAPU with a view to a possible merger of the two parties. In April 1987 the talks collapsed with government once again asserting that an upsurge in dissident activity was directly attributable to PF–ZAPU. Pressure to merge was then stepped up as Minister of Home Affairs, Enos Nkala, amongst other things, banned any PF–ZAPU meeting or public rally, ordered the closure of its offices nationwide and then dissolved six PF–ZAPU dominated local authorities in Matabeleland North. The talks were later resumed and on 22 December 1987 an 'agreement of unity' was signed between the two parties. It was agreed that there was an irrevocable commitment to unity under the name of ZANU(PF) with Robert Mugabe becoming the First Secretary and President of the united party. Significantly, it was also agreed that 'both parties shall . . . take immediate vigourous steps to eliminate and end the insecurity and violence prevalent in Matabeleland'.[24] This was followed by the holding of joint rallies with high ranking officials of both parties explaining the agreement and ordering dissidents to stop fighting.

The effects of the Unity Agreement were dramatic as dissident related activity stopped completely and all dissidents gave themselves up. This confirmed the view that the problem required a political rather than a 'military' solution. On 28 April 1988 a free pardon was announced for all dissidents together with those involved in collaborating with dissidents and 'PF–ZAPU political fugitives from justice'.[25] In July 1988 the Minister of Home Affairs informed the House of Assembly that peace had returned to Matabeleland. He added that 'Former dissidents have now come out of the bush and are now receiving every possible assistance. The country can look forward to their complete integration into society.'[26] The new merged ZANU(PF) party then proceeded to win a decisive victory in the 1990 general election, winning 116 of the 119 seats contested.[27] Five PF–ZAPU members were then appointed to ministerial positions with Joshua Nkomo first being made a Senior Minister in the Presidents' Office and later a Vice-President.[28]

A fresh political challenge emerged in 1988 in the shape of the Zimbabwe Unity Movement (ZUM). In July 1988 the government came under unprecedented criticism from some back-bench members of Parliament over allegations of corruption and an attempt to forcibly introduce a one-party state. As a result, in October 1988 Edgar Tekere, a founder member of ZANU(PF) and its former Secretary-General, was expelled from the party. Students at the University of Zimbabwe in Harare then joined in protests against government corruption and some 1,000 barricaded themselves into the university in protest at Tekere's expulsion. Their protests were vindicated as in April 1989 a Judicial Enquiry chaired by Mr Justice Sandura (the Sandura Commission) and set up by Mugabe to enquire into the corruption allegations found that a number of government ministers had behaved improperly in obtaining cars and profiting from their resale. Tekere then moved to set up ZUM. Strong pressure was exerted to prevent the new party establishing itself and supporters were harassed and some detained by the security forces. In a clear reference to ZUM, in January 1990 the state of emergency was renewed with the Minister of Home Affairs giving as one reason the fact that 'certain political parties' were training young Zimbabweans outside the country with the aim of having them return to commit destabilising acts. No evidence was ever produced to support the assertion. The attempt to justify the continued state of emergency on these grounds did the government no credit. In reality it was a clumsy and illegitimate attempt to intimidate ZUM members and to use emergency powers to prevent the exercise of legitimate political rights.

External Threats

During most of the first ten years of independence, the spectre of white-ruled South Africa lay heavily across the whole of southern Africa. The Pretoria regime continued to view black African nations with hostility, regarding them as willing tools of communism or as evidence of an inevitable breakdown of normal life once black majority rule was attained. The only options Pretoria appeared prepared to consider were those which would sustain white privilege in the face of the allegedly communist inspired 'total onslaught'.[29] Thus it was not surprising that South Africa constantly sought to destabilise the entire southern African region. As Weisfelder notes[30], destabilisation was a deliberate policy using overt and covert forms of intervention to build up stresses on weaker governments to prompt them to desperate expedients. He continues:

> By disrupting economic activity, undermining political and administrative institutions, accentuating ethnic, regional or religious antipathies, and augmenting existing fears and suspicions, destabilization contributes to political decay and inability to meet basic human needs.[31]

At the centre of the region lies Zimbabwe. Mugabe's policies of socialism and national reconciliation raised the prospect of a non-racial State north of the Limpopo River which could challenge South African domination of the region. As the most economically advanced State in the Southern Africa Development Coordination Conference (SADCC)[32] and the hub of the regional transport system, Zimbabwe was the centre for the re-routing of traffic away from the traditional routes via South Africa. Having failed to install Muzorewa as Prime Minister, the Pretoria regime resorted to a variety of tactics aimed at destabilising Zimbabwe. Many of the security problems which faced Zimbabwe were the result, at least in part, of this policy and these formed a further basis for the continuation of the state of emergency.

Some of the most serious security incidents involved attacks on strategic installations. For example, on 16 August 1981, explosives placed in the armoury at the Inkomo Barracks near Harare destroyed over Zimb $35 million worth of armaments. On 25 July 1982 seven Hunter fighter jets, a Cessna F.337 and a recently acquired British Aerospace Hawk Mk 60 jet fighter were destroyed in a raid on the Zimbabwe Air Force base at Thornhill near the Midlands city of Gweru.[33] In addition, South African support for dissident elements in Matabeleland led the then Minister of Home Affairs to assert that 'If there were no South Africa, there would be no dissidents in this country today.'[34] There were also a series of South African inspired attacks on targets belonging to the African National Congress, the South African liberation movement.[35] In August 1981 Joe Gqabi, the ANC representative in Zimbabwe was gunned down outside his Harare home. South African agents then made a series of attacks on ANC targets causing death and destruction amongst the civilian population. One extraordinary incident involved Odile Harington, a South African national, who was sent by Pretoria to spy on ANC members in Zimbabwe. She was swiftly detected whilst trying to send information out of the country and confessed to acting with the intention of assisting in the elimination of all liberation movements fighting against South Africa. She was charged with giving information intended to be useful to an enemy. At her trial, a certificate from the Minister of Foreign Affairs was received on the question of whether the information was for an 'enemy'. It stated:

> The ANC, its members, offices and premises in Zimbabwe have been subjected by South African agents to frequent attacks by bombs and other devices resulting in wanton destruction of property and the lives of innocent defenceless people. Clearly, any acts of sabotage, bombing or destruction of lives and property of the ANC and its members are not in the interests of Zimbabwe. Above all Zimbabweans have been

killed and their property destroyed. The Zimbabwean Government views any military action against the ANC in Zimbabwe as violating . . . the integrity and sovereignty of Zimbabwe . . . South Africa has by these acts of sabotage and destabilisation, cross border military incursions, assassination of people in Zimbabwe and bombing of property in Zimbabwe made herself at least a potential enemy.[36]

Zimbabwe consistently denied that it allowed the ANC to use its territory for military action against the Pretoria Government.

A further aspect of the destabilisation campaign within Zimbabwe concerned the use of whites, many thousands of whom had chosen to remain in the country. Some were recruited by South Africa as spies. For example, Geoffrey Price was the director of close security in the CIO (Central Intelligence Organisation) with responsibility for the protection of the Prime Minister and his Cabinet colleagues. In March 1982 he hurriedly left Zimbabwe after allegations that he had headed a spy ring. Government then moved to confiscate his property alleging he was 'an enemy of the State'. Two other white CIO officers, Hartlebury and Evans, were also detained on suspicion of spying for South Africa.[37] The problem for Government in this area was made clear by the Minister of Home Affairs:

Zimbabwe is a young country with State apparatuses that manifest weaknesses. In all honesty, we have to admit that our apparatuses are further weakened by the presence of individuals disloyal to Zimbabwe and loyal to both Rhodesia and South Africa.[38]

In early 1988 three whites from Bulawayo were detained in connection with sabotage attacks. South African agents, acting with local white Zimbabweans, then attempted to free the men but were foiled by the security forces. Even so, the incident increased concern as to the loyalty of white Zimbabweans and as the Minister of Home Affairs noted:

The majority of the saboteurs being used are members of the white community who were serving in the security services in the Smith era. These saboteurs also recruit blacks who used to work with them during the Smith regime.

He added that potential agents were promised large amounts of foreign exchange by Pretoria in exchange for their co-operation.[39]

The problem of destabilisation was a continuing one and, according to the Government, even in 1990 'the ever present threats and naked aggression by South Africa' were reasons for the continued state of emergency.[40] There is no doubt that there was a policy of destabilisation by South Africa against Zimbabwe. But was a state of emergency necessary to combat it? Threats alone did not constitute any justification. Further, isolated acts of terrorism are better viewed as criminal activity requiring criminal sanctions rather than such a danger to the security of the nation that a continuous nationwide emergency becomes necessary. The suggestion of some that the continued presence of South Africa merited in itself a perpetual state of emergency was a quite untenable argument.[41] Based on the information disclosed by government and the other wide-ranging security legislation available, it is difficult to support the view that South African actions justified the continued state of emergency.

Events in Mozambique also had a destabilising effect on the country. This was due to the activities of the Mozambican National Resistance Army (RENAMO) which was waging a civil war against the government there. RENAMO was originally established in 1974 by the Rhodesian CIO as the result of an agreement made with the Portuguese secret service, the General Directorate of Security. The intention was to establish an internal resistance movement designed to destabilise Mozambique following the departure of the Portuguese and thus counter the efforts of the new black majority government, headed by President Samora Machel, which was committed to assisting the Zimbabwe freedom struggle. The plan was unsuccessful but in 1980, RENAMO was 'transferred' to the control of South Africa.[42] It has continued to embroil Mozambique in a bloody and most brutal conflict.[43] As early as 1981 the activities of RENAMO began to affect Zimbabwe. Due to her close relationship with Mozambique, the rebels declared 'war' against Zimbabwe and proceeded to mount a well organised campaign of economic sabotage, wanton destruction of property and the killing and maiming of civilians, mainly in the northern and eastern border areas of Zimbabwe. For example, between July 1987 and July 1988 there were over three hundred reported incidents of armed robberies, rapes and abductions by RENAMO bandits. 'Bandit related' killings also occurred. Thus as the people of the eastern region sought to enjoy the fruits of independence, they and their property were once again subjected to violence and destruction.[44] Many abandoned their homes and moved to safer places. By the end of 1989, the border areas were still being infiltrated by RENAMO 'bandits'[45] resulting in constant reports of violence and destruction.[46] With the ending of the dissident problem in Matabeleland, the threats posed by RENAMO became one of the principal reasons for the continued state of emergency.[47]

The RENAMO problem was one over which Zimbabwe had little control. Its 'special relationship' with Mozambique, built up as a result of the assistance given to ZANU during the war years, meant it willingly gave both political and military support to the Mozambican government. The scale of the RENAMO activities in parts of Zimbabwe was undoubtedly a serious security threat and required a firm response. However, even if this justified the use of emergency powers, it did not justify a nationwide declaration as the problem was effectively confined to one part of Zimbabwe.

Overview

The International Commission of Jurists has rightly noted that during a state of emergency, the real challenge is to prevent the abuse of emergency powers.[48] In an effort to do this, it was seen in Chapter One that Article 4 of the ICCPR permits the derogation of certain freedoms only during a period of 'public emergency which threatens the life of the nation'. Without such a limitation, declarations of a state of emergency can turn into an instrument of oppression and tyranny. As Elias points out, this is the fundamental difference between totalitarian regimes like Hitlerite Germany or Franco's Spain and the liberal democracies of the Western world. In the latter there is an anxious concern on the part of everyone for a return to normality once the temporary emergency is removed. In the former, the individual becomes ruthlessly subordinated to the over-riding claims of the State, a mere cipher without rights but only duties.[49] It follows that the declaration of a state of emergency is a matter of international concern and the justification for such action must be subject to careful scrutiny.

In 1980 the Government of Zimbabwe pledged itself to national reconciliation and proved by its later actions that it was prepared to accept a pluralistic society. This is something the Rhodesian regime was never prepared to do. Further, the government always enjoyed the support of the vast majority of the population – unlike its predecessor. The country also faced considerable security problems during these years. Whether these justified the continued state of emergency is debatable. Although Zimbabwe has not ratified the ICCPR, ministers justified the continued state of emergency in terms of Article 4 on the basis that national life was 'threatened by the internal subversion of dissidents and the evil designs of external powers'.[50] Thus it is appropriate to use the Article 4 provisions to test the situation in Zimbabwe.

In January 1990 the state of emergency in Zimbabwe was renewed for the 49th consecutive time since its proclamation in 1965. Its renewal on nineteen consecutive occasions after independence was based on a bewildering variety of grounds. The earlier discussion shows that there was no justification for a continuous nationwide state of emergency based on security grounds. Indeed, it is argued later that in some respects the use of emergency powers actually exacerbated the situation. In reality, there is little doubt that the state of emergency was retained because the use of such powers was a very convenient way of governing. Thus, according to one account, in government circles, some argued that as the security powers did not affect the lives of most people, the state of emergency should be retained in order to deal with urgent problems as and when they arose.[51] The conclusion therefore is that, based on the reasons given by government, the continued nationwide state of emergency did not comply with the requirements of Article 4 and was not justified in Zimbabwe.

The use of 'quasi' emergency legislation was (and even after 1990) remains a cause for concern. Thus the Law and Order (Maintenance) Act and the Public Order Act still remain intact.[52] In addition the Presidential Powers (Temporary Measures) Act 1986 also offers government another option for executive rule. Although a 'permanent' statute, it bears a striking similarity to the Emergency Powers Act in that it permits the President to make regulations dealing with urgent situations that arise or are likely to arise when he considers it necessary or expedient to do so 'in the interests of defence, public order . . . economic interests or the general public interest'. He/she is also empowered to modify or amend statutes.[53] Unlike the EPA, the regulations have a limited life, expiring after 180 days, although Parliament can always incorporate them into permanent legislation. They cannot be replaced with substantially identical regulations until after a period of six months. In fact the Act itself poses a clear threat to individual freedoms. The potential problem became clear when the first regulations were made shortly before the 1986 Non-Aligned Conference in Harare.[54] Concern about the poor condition of some buildings in the country and the unfavourable impression that this might have on visiting dignitaries, led the President to make regulations empowering any local council to order property owners to demolish, repair or repaint any building or generally improve the look of the premises. Any failure to comply entitled council employees to enter and complete the work at the owner's expense. In order to accomplish this aim, the regulations also amended the Urban Councils Act.[55] Their validity was never challenged but they probably contravened the constitutional right to protection from arbitrary entry.[56] Arguably they also contravened the constitutional ban on 'forced labour' as this covers all work which is extracted from any person under the menace of a penalty and for which the person has not offered himself voluntarily.[57] The temporary nature of the regulations is welcome, but the scope of governmental powers is still enormous. Its objectionable features mean that it has no place in the legislation of the country.[58]

Detention without trial was a common manifestation of emergency powers. However its use is not dependent upon a continued state of emergency. The Emergency Powers Amendment Act 1986 enables the President to make regulations providing for preventive detention during a period when the House of Assembly (now the Parliament of Zimbabwe) has resolved that a situation exists which may lead to a state of emergency and which requires the use of preventive detention.[59] Whilst much of this legislation is itself objectionable, it serves to emphasise the powers of government and further undermines the justification for the continued state of emergency.

The problem of the 'perpetual' state of emergency also requires attention. The African experience is that in some States, citizens are forced to live in virtually a perpetual state of emergency with laws being made by the executive which have little or no connection with the reasons for the original declaration. Some countries, such as Kenya and Zambia, which have ratified the ICCPR, have clearly failed to honour their commitment to the convention in this respect. It is widely recognised that a state of emergency is a temporary expedient.[60] Mathews asserts that there must be some control over and limitation upon, the renewal of public emergencies so that a perpetual emergency is not created by the indefinite renewal of emergency powers.[61] A useful approach is found in the International Law Association Minimum Standards which state that save in the case of war or external aggression, the 'duration of the emergency shall be for a period of fixed term established by the constitution'.[62] If there is a real commitment to normal constitutional rule on the part of African States, then there is no place for a perpetual state of emergency. Whether there are any effective safeguards on the declaration and renewal of an emergency is a key issue for discussion in the later chapters.

A related issue is whether the declaration of an emergency is justiciable, i.e. can the courts declare that there are no grounds for such action. The courts in both Zambia[63] and Nigeria[64] have declined jurisdiction in the matter. In Sierra Leone the Supreme Court has interpreted a similar constitutional provision to that in Zimbabwe as conferring on the President sole, unquestionable and unchallengeable power to determine the matter.[65] In view of the sensitive political nature of the issue, this is probably a realistic approach. However, the High Court in Lesotho has held that the 1988 Declaration of a State of Emergency and the emergency regulations made thereunder were null and void because they were not made in accordance with the procedure prescribed by the Emergency Powers Act 1982.[66] It remains to be seen whether, if the occasion arose, the courts in Zimbabwe would follow the lead of Lesotho on this issue.

Notes

1. The name was changed from ZANU to distinguish it from the so-called 'authentic' ZANU headed by Revd Ndabaningi Sithole. Sithole was the former leader of ZANU but was replaced by Robert Mugabe.
2. See Baker, 1983, p.45 and Cliffe, 1984, p.44. For a discussion on the 1979 and 1985 General Elections as well, see Sithole, 1986, p.75.
3. Former President Banana himself has pointed out that the Prime Minister generally sought his views on practically every major issue and added that 'contrary to the popularly held view that I was just a ceremonial president, I was deeply involved in the affairs of state'. *Moto*, May 1988, p.4. Indeed he played a crucial role as a unifying force at a time when there was considerable political tension between the two major parties. His continued efforts at reconciliation are freely acknowledged as being instrumental in bringing about the Unity Agreement.
4. In December 1987 the Constitution of Zimbabwe Amendment (No. 7) Act abolished the post of non-executive President and introduced an executive presidency. Former President Banana was well provided for, being given an attractive pension and other benefits. See Presidential Pension and Benefits Act 1987. For a full assessment of the changes see Hatchard and Slinn, 1989, p.117.
5. Mugabe was elected by an electoral college of all members of the House of Assembly and the Senate. In future, the President will be elected in a national election.
6. Originally such a declaration was made on the advice of the Prime Minister. After the establishment of the executive President in 1987, this requirement fell away.
7. Section 31J(2) and (3). Originally the House of Assembly carried out this function until the establishment of the uni-cameral Parliament in 1987
8. Section 31J(9), Constitution of Zimbabwe.
9. Other reasons relating to threats to the national economy are examined in Chapter 10.
10. United States Department of State *Country Reports on Human Rights Practices for 1981*, p.317. Report submitted to the Committee on Foreign Affairs, February 1982.
11. *Time*, 17 March 1980.
12. Nkomo was from Matabeleland in the west of the country and had been a lay preacher and social worker. He first came to prominence as the Secretary of the Railway Workers Association in Bulawayo and then played an

important role in the organisation of opposition to the formation of the Federation of Rhodesia and Nyasaland. He became head of ZAPU at its inception.
13. In 1987 Smith was eventually suspended from the House of Assembly. In 1980 the original Rhodesia Front parliamentary membership also included P.K. Van der Byl who was one of the architects of UDI and a high ranking Minister during that period.
14. For a full account of the incident see the discussion by Justice Gubbay in *Commercial Union v Fawcett Security* [1985] 2 ZLR 31.
15. An enquiry into the incidents was ordered by the Government headed by a black High Court Judge, Justice Dumbutshena. His report was never published. According to Mubako this was mainly because it was of poor quality and of little use. (Interview with Mubako, a former Minister of Home Affairs, May 1989). This assertion is hard to accept given the abilities of the judge and it was probably concealed for political reasons.
16. See Lawyers Committee, 1986, pp.20–25; Hodder-Williams, 1983 and Weitzer, 1984, p.529.
17. Prior to this, Nkomo was switched from Minister of Home Affairs to Minister of State (Public Service). This was seen by PF–ZAPU as a way of excluding him from participation in security matters.
18. Masuku was fatally ill and died on 6 March 1986 – less than one month after his release. There is nothing to link his death (from a form of meningitis) with his period in detention.
19. *Ngwenya & Mpofu v The State*, Unreported, Supreme Court of Zimbabwe SC 63/86 at p.3. Justice Gubbay was noting the words of the trial judge when assessing sentence.
20. *Parliamentary Debates*, 18 January 1984.
21. This was won by G.M. Sithole in Chipinge for ZANU (Ndonga) which is headed by Ndabaningi Sithole.
22. *Parliamentary Debates*, 22 January 1986. There are several reported cases of murder/robbery by dissidents. See e.g. *S v Ndlovu*, Unreported, Supreme Court of Zimbabwe SC 177/88 (attack on Silobini Business Centre at Esigodini), *S v Dube*, Unreported, Supreme Court of Zimbabwe SC 15/88, *S v Ncube*, Unreported, Supreme Court of Zimbabwe SC 30/85 and *S v Ndlovu* 1988 (2) ZLR 465 (SC).
23. Amnesty International News Release AFR/46/06/86.
24. Paragraph 9 of the Agreement.
25. Clemency Order No. 1 of 1988: General Amnesty GN 57A/1988. See *Government Gazette*, 3 May 1988.
26. *Parliamentary Debates*, 12 July 1988. Moves to re-integrate former dissidents into society have taken place with the establishment of co-operative farm ventures. Sadly, lack of expertise and capital have seriously undermined their commercial viability.
27. Two seats were won by ZUM and another by ZANU(Ndonga). The final seat was later won by ZANU(PF).
28. In a further effort to illustrate the benefits of unity, Mugabe appointed Dumiso Dabengwa as Deputy Minister of Home Affairs. This was significant because it brought him into a security related Ministry, which, following Nkomo's brief period as Minister of Home Affairs, was the first time that a former ZAPU supporter had been involved in security matters at that level.
29. Geldenhuys, n.d., pp.2–10.
30. Weisfelder, 1984, p.116.
31. At p.116.
32. See Chapter 10 for a full discussion on SADCC.
33. There have also been South African incursions into Zimbabwe. For example, in August 1982 three white South Africa Defence Force personnel were shot dead by Zimbabwean security forces in the Sengwe district in southern Zimbabwe. The incursion was admitted by the SADF although it was maintained that it was not done under specific orders.
34. Interview in *The Herald* (Zimbabwe) 17 February 1986.
35. Attacks also took place in Gaberone, Botswana; Maseru, Lesotho; and Maputo, Mozambique.
36. *S v Harington*, Unreported, High Court of Zimbabwe HC-H-651-87. Harington was found guilty as charged and sentenced to twenty-five years imprisonment. An appeal against conviction was later dismissed by the Supreme Court although the sentence was reduced to twelve years: *S v Harington* 1988 (2) ZLR 344 (SC); 1989 (2) SA 348 (ZS). In 1990 she was released and returned to South Africa.
37. There is little doubt as to the involvement of the officers and the trial judge set out at some length the subversive activities undertaken by them (see *Evans & Hartlebury v Minister of Home Affairs*, Unreported, High Court of Zimbabwe HC-H-485-84). In 1986 two senior customs officers Austin and Harper were also detained on suspicion of being South African spies. It is not clear as to whether this was in fact justified. (See further Chapter 7).
38. *Parliamentary Debates*, 16 January 1983.
39. *Parliamentary Debates*, 12 July 1988
40. For example, the Minister of Home Affairs informed Parliament that destabilisation tactics were expected to increase as more South African Defence Forces personnel were withdrawn from Namibia following its attainment of independence in 1990: see *Parliamentary Debates*, 25 July 1989. This again shows a misunderstanding of the nature of emergency powers as the Minister was referring to a future threat. Thanks to the rapid changes within South Africa, this threat never materialised.
41. See *Parliamentary Debates*, 21 January 1988 and 12 July 1988.
42. See the account by Flower, 1987, p.300 *et seq*.
43. In 1984 the Nkomati Accord was signed between Mozambique and South Africa which purported to end the involvement of the latter in RENAMO activities. Regrettably this did not materialise
44. At the end of 1988, the border areas most affected were Mukumbura, Rushinga, Chikombedzi and Gonarezhou: see Address to Parliament by His Excellency The President *Parliamentary Debates*, 7 December 1988.
45. See speech by President Mugabe *Parliamentary Debates*, 27 June 1989.

46. Between July 1987 and July 1988 there were 80 murders; 78 abductions; 34 sightings of bandits and 14 contacts. A total of 248 bandit related incidents led to a loss of property amounting to Zimb $65,312,170: see the speech of the Minister of Home Affairs *Parliamentary Debates*, 25 July 1989. A later destabilisation report released in October 1989 revealed that between 15 June 1987 and April 1989, 335 Zimbabwean citizens were murdered by RENAMO inside Zimbabwe, 280 were wounded and another 667 were forcibly abducted and forced to carry stolen goods. According to the report, 446 of those abducted are still missing and presumed dead. See the speech of T. Maluleke, MP, *Parliamentary Debates*, 8 November 1989.
47. See, for example, the statement by the Minister of Home Affairs *Parliamentary Debates*, 20 January 1987.
48. International Commission of Jurists, 1983, p.414.
49. *African Conference, 1961* p.162. See also Rossiter, 1948, p.8.
50. Minister of Home Affairs *Parliamentary Debates*, 13 July 1982.
51. Interview with Mubako, May 1989.
52. For a similar view as regards South Africa, see Mathews, 1986, p.193 *et seq*.
53. For example, the Presidential Powers (Temporary Provisions) (Parastatals Commission) Regulations 1988 SI 86/88 amended the Parastatals Commission Act 1987.
54. Presidential Powers (Temporary Measures) (Urban Property Renovation) Regulations 1986 SI 198/86.
55. Chapter 214.
56. Section 17, Constitution of Zimbabwe.
57. Section 14, Constitution of Zimbabwe. There is an exception in that during a state of emergency, forced labour may be required if reasonably justified for dealing with that situation. Tidying urban areas hardly falls into this category.
58. In 1987 the Presidential Powers (Temporary Measures) (Dissolution of District Councils: Matabeleland North) Regulations SI 279A/87 removed all local councillors from six district councils. This was apparently another move against alleged supporters of dissidents. The Presidential Powers (Temporary Measures) (Modification of Medical, Dental and Allied Professions Act) Regulations 1987 SI 191/87 amended the provisions of the Act.
59. This is in no way to support the use of preventive detention in a non-emergency situation.
60. For example, the delegates to the African Conference concluded that the declaration of a public emergency should only be effective for a specified and limited period. See generally *African Conference*, Proceedings of Committee 1, pp.96–113.
61. Mathews, 1971, p.39.
62. International Law Association Minimum Standards of Human Rights in a State of Exception, section A 1(3)(b). For an analysis of the rules see Carty, 1986, p.60. See also 'Study of the Implications for Human Rights of Recent Developments Concerning Situations Known as States of Emergency' United Nations Document E/Cn.4/Sub2/1982/15 paras 112–116.
63. 'It is not open to the courts to debate whether it is reasonable for there to be in existence [a state of emergency]' *per* Justice Baron in *Kapwepwe & Kaenga* [1972] ZR 248, at p.251.
64. *Williams v Majekodunmi* [1962] 1 All NLR 324. Although the court left open the question of a declaration made *male fides*. See also *Adegbenro v Attorney-General* [1962] 1 All NLR 431. The Federal Court of Malaysia has also held that the validity of an emergency proclamation is not justiciable: *Ningkan v Government of Malaysia* [1970] AC 379.
65. *State v Osman* [1988] LRC (Const) 212, at p.220.
66. *Law Society of Lesotho v Minister of Defence* [1988] LRC (Const) 226. Following this judgment, the Emergency Powers Act 1982 was repealed and replaced by the Emergency Powers Order 1988, No. 4 which retrospectively declared a state of emergency to the date of the original proclamation.

4 Implementing Emergency Powers

Operation of the Emergency Powers Act

Following the declaration of a state of emergency, the Emergency Powers Act comes into operation. Its purpose is:

> ... to prevent a state of emergency degenerating into a state of anarchy and to do this by conferring extraordinary powers on the President to deal with it, and, for the same purpose, it is permissible during a state of emergency ... to make laws which derogate from certain of the fundamental rights contained in the [constitution]. When a state of emergency exists, the Government is obliged to do everything in its power to bring it to an end and to avoid the ultimate step of introducing martial law.[1]

During a period of public emergency the President may make emergency regulations having nationwide or local effect which appear to him necessary or expedient for, amongst other things, public safety; the maintenance of public order; the maintenance of any essential services; and the preservation of the peace.[2] The only term which is defined is 'essential service'. This includes, hospital services; transport and distribution services; electricity, water and sanitary services; communications and 'any other service declared by the President, by notice in the *Gazette* to be an essential service for the purposes of the Act'.[3] This means that in practice an essential service is any 'service' if the President so determines. For example, a person detained under a thirty day detention order[4] on the grounds that he was suspected of violating the exchange control laws applied for a writ of habeas corpus.[5] In the Supreme Court, Justice Beck agreed that his first impression was that the reasons for the detention order did not fall within any of the areas detailed in the Emergency Powers Act.[6] He added that the concept of exchange control laws seemed entirely remote from the wording of any of the various purposes enumerated in the Act. But he continued:

> [Counsel] has drawn our attention to the Emergency Powers (Declaration of Essential Service)[7] which declared that 'finance, commerce and industry' are to be included within the phrase 'an essential service' for the purposes of the Exchange Control Act. That declaration is still extant ... Clearly, the effect of that declaration is to bring the concept of the nation's finance, and hence the protection of its foreign currency reserves for which, in turn, Exchange Control laws are designed, within the ambit of ... the Act, which both refer to 'the maintenance of any essential service'.

It was also contended that the investigation of a criminal complaint is something very different from the purposes contemplated in the Emergency Powers Act. Thus it was improper to detain an individual merely to facilitate the investigation of a criminal charge concerning, in this case, exchange control violations. It was further argued (quite correctly) that the ordinary criminal law already provided for adequate investigatory powers and that this was strengthened by the ministerial power to deny bail.[8] These arguments were rejected by the court because:

> Once it is appreciated . . . that an offence against the Exchange Control laws is such a matter for which it has appeared to the President to be necessary and expedient to make regulations for the maintenance of the country's financial interests, including regulations which empower the police to arrest and detain persons suspected of having contravened such laws, the submission, so it seems to me, loses all its force. How can it be said that the investigating officer has used his power of detention for an improper purpose in this case when he is using it to investigate suspected Exchange Control offences and when he is specifically and lawfully authorised to do so in relation to offences of this kind?[9]

The drafters of the Act were clearly intent on covering every possible eventuality. This is again shown by the fact that the Act specifically states that emergency powers regulations may make provision for a range of actions including: detention without trial; deportation of aliens; control of movement of persons within the country; control of business and industry; compulsory acquisition of property and the searching of premises.[10] This list is supplemented by a presidential power to make such regulations as appear to him to be necessary or expedient, whether or not they relate to any of the matters specified in the Act. The almost limitless width of these powers ensures that unless in violation of the constitution, few emergency regulations are *ultra vires* the Act. For example, the validity of a power conferred on a subordinate court by emergency regulations to pass the death sentence was confirmed because of 'the plain and wide language used' in the Act.[11]

The most far-reaching provision of the Act provides that the President may, by regulation, amend or suspend any law or declare the application of any law with or without any modification.[12] The accepted use of regulations and other subordinate legislation is to permit a minister to take certain action derived from powers devolved by Parliament and contained in an enabling Act. Accordingly any other action is *ultra vires*. However the Emergency Powers Act provides for what may be termed 'legislative' regulations which permit the minister to legislate by regulation without the need to follow the parliamentary process. This 'Henry VIII' style clause is a major deviation from the accepted use of regulations and is a provision which can effectively lead to rule by the executive. However, this did not prevent the regular use of the power because at least fourteen statutes were amended or modified following independence.[13] When a statute is affected by emergency regulations it 'shall, with effect from the expiration or repeal of such regulation, have effect as if such amendment, suspension or modification had never been made'.[14] This means that any repeal is prospective and rights and duties affected by regulations become legally enforceable again once they are revoked. For example, the obligation of a lessee to pay a higher rent is nullified during a period when regulations provide for a rent freeze. However, the higher rent becomes payable when the regulations expire or are repealed although the lessor remains unable to recover the higher rent payable during the validity of the regulations. It would be absurd if the repeal had retrospective effect so that the regulations were deemed never to have existed.[15]

As is seen in the following chapters, the Emergency Powers Act was reinforced by other security legislation, most notably the Law and Order (Maintenance) Act 1960, which remained virtually unaltered from Rhodesian days and which was frequently used. Such legislation remains in force despite the ending of the state of emergency.

Overall, the Emergency Powers Act enabled government to impose limits and controls on almost every aspect of national life, thus giving it the flexibility to respond to any emergency situation. A particular danger that it posed was that it enabled Ministers to make emergency regulations concerning matters which had little or no connection with the reasons for the state of emergency. Indeed, as is noted in later chapters, of the one hundred or so emergency regulations made in the period 1980–1990, several had no connection at all with the reasons for the emergency whilst many other had an extremely tenuous connection. The misuse of such powers meant that the Act represented a classic recipe for 'constitutional dictatorial rule'.

Implementing Emergency Powers: The Organs of State Security

The actions of government agents, and in particular members of the security forces, during periods of emergency often pose a real threat to individual freedoms. Enforceable constitutional protections to counter any unlawful actions are particularly important in developing countries which are especially prone to indiscipline in such forces. The danger is often amplified when, during a state of emergency, government security organisations and/or the military obtain greatly enhanced investigative powers. In this respect, Zimbabwe was no exception. In this section the organisation and operation of the security forces is examined, whilst the use of their powers *vis à vis* individual freedoms is examined in the following chapters.

Prior to 1988, the operational activities of the security forces were dealt with by an 'inner Cabinet' consisting of the Prime Minister (who was also Minister of Defence), the Minister of Home Affairs and the Minister of State (Security) in the Prime Minister's Office. The Minister of Home Affairs remained responsible for issuing indefinite detention orders, although in practice the decision to detain was normally made with the consent of the Prime Minister and after consultation with the Minister of State (Security). With the establishment of an executive presidency, the arrangements were altered by the President so that his advisers included a separate Minister of Defence, the Minister of State for National Security in the President's Office and the Minister of Home Affairs.

The Defence Forces

As Commander in Chief of the Defence Forces, the President appoints both the Commander of the Army and Air Force although in doing so he must consider the recommendations of a Board consisting of the Chairman of the Defence Forces Service Commission, the retiring Commander of the relevant branch of the service and a Permanent Secretary appointed by the President.[16] The President may remove a Commander after consultation with the Cabinet. Following the retirement of Peter Walls in 1980, the post of Army Commander was entrusted to Solomon Mujuru (formerly known as Rex Nhongo) who was the second highest ranking officer in ZANLA.[17] He built up an efficient force which saw action in both Matabeleland and Mozambique. With major security problems facing the country, army strength remained at around 50,000 up to 1990,[18] with the vast majority being former ZANLA guerillas. The Air Force was almost entirely a white preserve during the pre-independence period and played a major role in attacks on freedom fighters in Mozambique and Zambia which resulted in the loss of many thousands of lives. Some of these men remained in the service after independence to form the nucleus of the new force. Strenuous efforts were made to train new pilots both to replace those who left and due to doubts over the loyalty of some white officers.[19] The result of these challenges was that defence force spending was a considerable drain on the national exchequer accounting for an average of around 15 per cent of the total national budget up to 1990.

The security forces made frequent use of emergency powers in their operations against dissidents in Matabeleland and RENAMO rebels. In so doing serious human rights violations occurred, particularly against civilians in Matabeleland. Although some allegations were undoubtedly true, it should not be overlooked that the security forces themselves suffered frequent casualties during the struggle to maintain peace and to protect vital transport links.

Concern over the cost of maintaining a large standing army has now led to approval being given for the setting up of a National Service scheme. Amongst other activities, a long term objective of the scheme is intended to include military training designed to form a nucleus of well trained young people to enable the regular army to be greatly reduced in size.[20] In view of the rapid changes taking place in South Africa together with the possible settlement of the civil war in Mozambique, such a reduction is now a real possibility.

Central Intelligence Organisation

The Central Intelligence Organisation (CIO) is the most important intelligence gathering agency being controlled from the Office of the President. Created in 1963 as the successor to the British directed Federal Intelligence Security Bureau, the CIO was deliberately kept independent of British influence, presumably with possible future Rhodesian independence in mind. During UDI, the CIO dealt with external security leaving the Special Branch of the British South Africa Police to handle internal security matters. In 1982 the CIO absorbed the functions of the Special Branch and now covers all aspects of security. At independence, as the government did not wish to dismantle such an important body, several former officers under the Smith regime, including Ken Flower, the head of the organisation and one of the main organisers of the Rhodesian intelligence services during the UDI period, were retained. Flower remained in charge until his resignation in June 1981.[21] The new officers were (mainly) ZANLA ex-combatants and by 1988, the total manpower was given as 1,007.[22] The CIO played a crucial role in maintaining state security and scored some notable successes, particularly in countering the activities of South African agents. Regrettably it also built up a reputation for indiscipline and the use of harsh interrogation techniques against detainees and civilians in dissident affected areas.[23] Not surprisingly, there is little information concerning its activities. Indeed, government sought to protect members from legal liability through the use of indemnity regulations although later, several CIO officers were convicted of criminal offences arising out of field operations.[24]

Zimbabwe Republic Police

The Zimbabwe Republic Police (ZRP) is the immediate successor of the British South Africa Police (BSAP) and has the general tasks of preserving internal security and maintaining law and order.[25] It is headed by a Commissioner of Police who is appointed by the President after considering recommendations from an advisory board.[26] The President may remove the Commissioner from office after consulting the Cabinet, in which case he/she must also inform Parliament.[27]

In common with other colonies, the BSAP was used primarily to protect white interests and was universally unpopular with the African population. Indeed the initials BSAP were commonly said to stand in Shona for *Baba, Satani Ari Pano* meaning 'Father, Satan is Here'.[28] All senior posts were held by whites and Africans were unable to progress from the lowest ranks. Prior to independence the force was used as a vanguard against African nationalism so that, as a result, it made constant use of the security legislation. Thus, not surprisingly, by 1980 relations between the police and the majority of the population were in a deplorable state. Efforts were immediately made to transform the ZRP into a 'peoples' force' in which all racial and other discriminatory practices were outlawed. Indeed the new police motto *Pro Lege Pro Populo Pro Patria* summed up the approach. There were also drastic personnel changes. The vast majority of the white officers left the service immediately after independence and were replaced by 3,500 inexperienced ex-combatants. An accelerated promotion scheme was also introduced by presidential directive. Even so, the top echelon on the ZRP, unlike the army, still consists mainly of former BSAP officers.[29] An attempt was made in 1984 to bring in one ex-combatant at the deputy commissioner level. The scheme, which was devised by the then Minister of Home Affairs, was approved by the police and the Prime Minister but the President advised against it and after further consideration by Robert Mugabe, it was dropped.[30]

A shift from the pre-independence authoritarian attitude of the police towards the development of a peoples' force was dependant upon a minimum of political interference. Some emphasis was certainly placed on the development of goodwill and co-operation between citizens and the force. For example, in March 1985 Robert Mugabe told a police passing-out parade that 'The people must view the police as allies in fighting counter-revolutionaries, bandits and criminals of all sorts and hues.' He went on to tell the recruits, most of whom were former guerrillas, that during the liberation struggle they had learnt that without first winning the support of the people, understanding their grievances and living amongst them, they would not have gone far in fighting colonialism. Although the situation had changed, Mugabe emphasised that the strategy remained relevant and effective in the continuing struggle for national consolidation.[31] The constitutional 'independence' of the Commissioner of Police was also noted by the Supreme Court where Justice Gubbay stated that the incumbent was 'a free agent in so far as the administration and command of the police force is concerned. In those spheres he brooks no interference and is answerable only to himself'.[32]

Members of the force are also statutorily barred from actively participating in politics and this includes doing 'any act whereby the public or any member thereof might reasonably be induced to identify him with an organisation or movement of a political character'.[33] In practice the ZRP faced considerable political pressures which made it extremely difficult to retain the confidence of the public in its impartiality. The force falls under the Ministry of Home Affairs and policies concerning its role varied according to the particular Minister in office. For example, Simbi Mubako (1984–85) sought to allow the police to operate on a more 'traditional' basis with relatively little overt political interference. In contrast, Herbert Ushewokunze (1982–84) and Enos Nkala (1985–87) were both intent upon using the police to further the political aims of the ruling party. The point is well illustrated by the appointment of Nkala following the 1985 General Election. This was widely seen as the result of a government decision to bring increased pressure on PF–ZAPU in an attempt to reduce its support and to force it into unity talks.[34] On several occasions in 1985 it was alleged that ZRP officers failed to respond expeditiously when government supporters attacked suspected political opponents. The most highly publicised incident occurred immediately after the 1985 elections when in July 1985 several hundred houses in the Harare area belonging to supporters of opposition parties were ransacked and their occupants evicted over a 48-hour period by women and youth members of ZANU(PF). Observers noted that the police were seemingly unwilling to commit themselves and took no steps to end the violence for a considerable time.[35] As Wrobel wryly concluded: 'The police are not credited widely with having intervened whenever necessary to stop intimidatory actions by ZANU(PF) cadres'.[36] On other occasions it was intimated that loyalty by police officers to the government meant loyalty to the ruling party. Some Members of Parliament also asserted that Shona speaking officers were deliberately sent to Matabeleland in order to intensify the campaign against dissidents. In addition, police stations were used both to torture and to hold detainees with Stops Camp in Bulawayo being particularly notorious.[37]

Although little is known about its activities, the Police Internal Security and Intelligence Unit (PISI), a division of the Ministry of Home Affairs, also gained a most dubious reputation for detaining and torturing suspected dissidents.[38]

The Peoples' Militia

This body, which is open to all Zimbabweans between the ages of 18 and 50 years, was formed in June 1982 'to bring into existence a strong base for territorial defence' alongside the regular army. Its approved establishment is 3,500 and new recruits receive 12 weeks training before being stood down until needed. Up to March 1988 a total of 22,029 had been trained.[39] The original idea of the militia was based on village defence and the collection of information of a security nature for the security forces. However, with the continued unsettled security situation these roles were expanded to include guarding strategic installations, providing escort services to private transport companies which operated through Mozambique and giving protection to farmers in areas of unrest.

Overview

It is essential that a government has adequate powers to enable it to combat an emergency situation. In this respect, the Emergency Powers Act is similar to other statutes in Africa being designed to cover every possible eventuality. The real danger is that, in practice, the powers can be utilised for improper purposes with emergency regulations being used to by-pass the legislative process and to establish an executive dictatorship. This is a point which is examined in the following chapters. Similarly, security forces often need additional powers in an emergency situation. Once again the danger is that these organs are used by government to repress the population rather than to free it from the perceived threat to its security. In order to assess the position in Zimbabwe, the powers of the security forces and their use in practice are also examined in the following chapters.

Notes

1. MacDonald ACJ in *S v Hove* 1976 RLR 127 at pp.131–32
2. The other situations cover (a) making adequate provision for dealing with any circumstances which (i) have arisen or, in his opinion, are likely to arise whether such circumstances relate to the maintenance of any essential or other services or otherwise; and (ii) in his opinion, will interfere with the peace, order and good government; or (b) making adequate provision for terminating the state of emergency (section 3, Emergency Powers Act).
3. Section 2, Emergency Powers Act.
4. Section 53, Emergency Powers (Maintenance of Law and Order) Regulations 1983. This section is discussed in detail in a later chapter.
5. *Stubbs v Minister of Home Affairs*, Unreported, Supreme Court of Zimbabwe, 1981.
6. See *Pakai v Salisbury City Council* 1940 SR 189 at p.191
7. Rhodesia *Government Notice* 798A of 1965. See also Emergency Powers (Maintenance of Essential Services) Regulations 1989 SI 160A/89 which are discussed in Chapter 10.
8. See Chapter 8.
9. At p.3.
10. Section 3(2), Emergency Powers Act.
11. See note 7 above.
12. Section 4(2).
13. For a full discussion of this topic see Allen, 1965, p.169 *et seq*.
14. Section 5, Emergency Powers Act.
15. *Zimbabwe Township Developers v Lou's Shoes* 1984 (2) SA 778. The section is an illustration of the old common law rule that if an Act of Parliament which repeals a former statute is itself repealed by an Act which contains nothing in it that shows that the legislature intended that the former law be repealed, such law will, by implication, be revived by the repeal of the repealing statute.
16. See section 99, Constitution of Zimbabwe.

17. The commanding officer, Josias Tongogara, died shortly before independence in an automobile crash in Mozambique. Some doubts were expressed as to whether this was an accident although Ken Flower states that he investigated the whole matter and was satisfied the cause was an accident. See Flower, 1987, p.252.
18. Figure quoted by the Acting Minister of Defence, *Parliamentary Debates*, 15 August 1989.
19. See the case of the Air Force 6 discussed in later chapters.
20. See the statement of the Minister of Defence, *Parliamentary Debates*, 21 September 1988.
21. Until his death in 1987, he remained a 'special consultant' to Mugabe.
22. Minister of Labour, Manpower Planning and Social Welfare, *Parliamentary Debates*, 4 August 1988.
23. See, for example, the treatment of the Air Force 6 which is discussed in Chapter 5.
24. Officers from the security forces have frequently benefited from presidential amnesties. For example, in one such amnesty eighty-eight members of the police, army, CIO and ZANU(PF) Youth League convicted or accused of crimes in connection with anti-dissident activities were pardoned. In 1988 a CIO officer sentenced to death for shooting a prisoner whilst in the process of interrogating him was also pardoned.
25. Section 93, Constitution of Zimbabwe.
26. The Board consists of the Chairman of the Police Service Commission, the retiring Commissioner of Police (if available) and a permanent secretary appointed by the President. If the appointment is not consistent with any recommendation made by the Board, the President must inform Parliament as soon as is practicable: section 93, Constitution of Zimbabwe.
27. Section 93(5), Constitution of Zimbabwe. In fact in 1986, the removal of the then Commissioner of Police on disciplinary grounds was preceded by the holding of an independent Commission of Inquiry.
28. For an amusing account of the relationship see Shaidi, 1988, pp.76–77.
29. That is, the Commissioner of Police and his four top subordinates. By 1989 this position had not altered.
30. The affair illustrates the influence of the non-executive president over governmental affairs even though he had no constitutional power to override the Prime Minister. (Interview with Simbi Mubako, May 1989).
31. Text of speech delivered at the passing out parade of the Zimbabwe Republic Police in Harare, March 1985.
32. *Commissioner of Police v Rensford* 1984 (1) ZLR 202 at p.208.
33. See section 35, Police Act.
34. For example, in September 1985 Nkala was quoted as saying that he intended to 'wipe out' PF–ZAPU and stated that the recent violence was 'just warning lights to say we are coming, and have not yet opened full blast to deal with the dissidents leadership . . . We should also hit the dissidents at their very roots and that root is ZAPU and ZAPU leadership'. (Quoted in *The Times* (UK) 29 September 1985.
35. *The Guardian* (UK) reported that 'an officer at a nearby police station said they were ensuring that no-one was injured but were not taking any action to stop the illegal removals'. (9 July 1985). *The Times* (UK) also reported that 'the police are well aware of the evictions but have taken no action'. (9 July 1985). See also the Lawyers Committee, 1986, p.46.
36. See Wrobel, 1986, p.29.
37. See Chapter 8 for details.
38. See, for example, Amnesty International News Release AFR/46/36/85. Pisi is also an Ndebele word meaning 'hyena'– a much feared animal in Africa.
39. Minister of Home Affairs, *Parliamentary Debates*, 21 September 1988.

5 Constitutional Safeguards of Individual Freedoms

Introduction

The immense powers contained in the Emergency Powers Act clearly have the potential to undermine, or to at least seriously affect, the exercise of individual freedoms. A State which permits no limits upon executive action is a dangerous place indeed. Thus it is a cardinal rule that although security powers are needed to combat threat to the nation, constitutionalism is never excluded as a result. Just as safeguards are required on the declaration of the state of emergency itself, so protection for individual freedoms is needed against the arbitrary use of emergency powers. In this chapter, the protection of such freedoms in both international and domestic law is examined.

International Protection of Individual Freedoms

The establishment of the United Nations in 1945 was a major step towards the international protection of individual freedoms. Amongst other things, its Charter requires Member States to take joint and several action to achieve 'universal respect for, and observance of, human rights and fundamental freedoms for all'.[1] In 1948 the Universal Declaration of Human Rights was adopted and this sets out a general catalogue of human rights and fundamental freedoms. On the assumption that the Universal Declaration did not impose sufficiently binding obligations, the UN Commission on Human Rights drafted the International Covenant on Civil and Political Rights (ICCPR) and the International Covenant on Economic, Social and Cultural Rights (ICESCR). Both were designed to be legally binding on Member States. The former deals essentially with the legal rights of individuals whilst the latter deals with rights relating to living standards, the family, employment, health, education and the like. Some commentators have argued that rights under the ICESCR take priority over other rights. This is on the grounds that in developing nations, in particular, civil and political rights have little value or importance if people are starving or dying through lack of adequate primary health care.[2] This is the wrong approach, for the Covenants themselves do not place rights in any hierarchical order and are thus all equally worthy of protection. Indeed the UN General Assembly has confirmed that all human rights form an indivisible whole.[3] This integrated approach is confirmed in the African Charter on Human and Peoples' Rights. This was adopted at a meeting of the Heads of State and Government of the Organisation of African Unity in Nairobi on 26 June 1981. It is now in force following its ratification by a simple majority of OAU members, including Zimbabwe in June 1986. The document recognises that it is essential 'to pay particular attention to the right to development and that civil and political rights cannot be dissociated from economic, social and cultural rights in their conception as well as their universality and that satisfaction of economic, social and cultural rights is a guarantee for the enjoyment of civil and political rights.'[4] Thus the Charter clearly establishes that civil and political rights as well as economic rights are essential to the well-being of every society and are the goal for every African nation. The Charter specifically protects individual freedoms and requires States to undertake to adopt legislative and other measures to give effect to them.[5] This means that whatever ideological perspective a State may claim, it has the responsibility to protect individual freedoms. Even so, whilst the international recognition of individual freedoms is crucial as setting the standards, it is in the domestic law of each nation that the most important practical safeguards are found.

Safeguards of Individual Freedoms in Domestic Law

There are a variety of approaches to the protection of individual freedoms in domestic law. One is the enactment of piecemeal legislation designed to deal with particular rights which are considered in need of protection at that point in time, backed up by case law developed by the courts. This is the approach adopted in the United Kingdom. The effectiveness of this system is increasingly being questioned for, with no formal constitutional guarantees, individual freedoms remain at the mercy of the executive.[6] This is well illustrated by the British prevention of terrorism legislation which provides for, *inter alia*, a lengthy period of judicially unsupervised detention;[7] the detention of a suspect without access to a legal representative; and restrictions on the movement of individuals within the United Kingdom, including United Kingdom nationals.[8]

A second approach is the establishment of a set of fundamental principles upon which the nation is founded. These have no more than a persuasive effect being mere expressions of intent. For example, the Constitution of Malawi enumerates six principles upon which the Republic is founded. Amongst them is the recognition of 'personal liberties enshrined in the United Nations Universal Declaration of Human Rights, and of adherence to the Law of Nations'.[9] The constitutional committee which recommended this procedure based its objection to an entrenched Declaration of Rights on the grounds that (i) the laws of Malawi already provided an elaborate code for the protection of individual freedoms against public or private interference; and (ii) since Malawi was a full member of the United Nations, it was committed to the observance of the UN Declaration. Regrettably, as this approach has no enforcement provisions a determined government can pass laws which render nugatory such freedoms. Indeed, a constitutional amendment in 1968 added a proviso to the principles that 'nothing contained in or done under the authority of any law shall be held inconsistent with or in contravention of the principles to the extent that the law in question is reasonably required in the interests of defence, public safety, public order or the national economy'. The government remains the sole judge of when to apply the proviso. The resulting catalogue of abuses of individual freedoms bears witness to the failure of this approach.[10] In Tanzania, the 1984 constitutional document[11] also includes a statement of values and social justice to which the Republic adheres, with the main object of the Government being the well-being of the people. Further, the authority of the State and all its instruments must direct all their activities and policies towards the task of ensuring that all other human rights are respected and cherished.[12] As with the first approach, this procedure means that there is little or no protection of individual freedoms, so that citizens are effectively at the mercy of the State.

The third approach is the implementation of an entrenched and fully justiciable guarantee of individual freedoms. This is in the form of a Declaration or Bill of Rights enshrined in the national constitution. The supremacy of the constitution then ensures that other laws are subordinate to those freedoms. The Declaration normally consists of a statement of basic rights followed by a clarification of their scope in practice. This makes it possible to formulate attainable freedoms backed up by an effective procedure for dealing with alleged violations. Ideally clear and unambiguous meanings are needed for key terms with limitations and exceptions being explicitly stated. In practice this is extremely difficult to achieve. In Westminster-style constitutions, for example, exceptions on the vague grounds of 'public safety' or 'defence' abound. To counter this problem, the judiciary is given a key role of determining the scope of such freedoms. This means that even in times of emergency, the courts can consider the validity of emergency regulations *vis à vis* constitutional rights. Of course, certain rights, for example freedom from inhuman treatment, remain non-derogable under any circumstances. The British adopted this third approach for the Constitution of Zimbabwe on the grounds that this was in line with the independence constitutions of most of its other former colonies. Perhaps wisely, the fact that similar constitutional documents elsewhere on the continent had lasted but a short time after independence was overlooked.[13]

The Declaration of Rights in Zimbabwe

The Declaration of Rights is entrenched, fully justiciable and contains a detailed list of rights and freedoms. In this respect the document is in sharp contrast to the so-called 'constitutions' devised during the UDI period when individual freedoms were given no exercisable protection. The Declaration opens with a statement of general principles i.e. that 'every person in Zimbabwe is entitled to the fundamental rights and freedoms of the individual, that is to say, the right, whatever his race, tribe, place of origin, political opinions, colour, creed or sex, but subject to respect for the rights and freedoms of others and for the public interest, to each and all of the following, namely: a) life, liberty, security of the person and the protection of the law; b) freedom of conscience, of expression and of assembly and association; and c) protection for the privacy of his home and other property and from compulsory acquisition of property without compensation.'[14] Any limitations are designed to ensure that the enjoyment of such rights and freedoms do not prejudice those of others or the public interest. Individual freedoms, i.e. the rights to life, liberty, association, conscience, and free movement, protection from torture and the protection of the law, are then detailed. These are discussed in subsequent chapters when the impact of emergency powers upon them is fully considered.

The Supreme Court has original jurisdiction to hear cases involving individual freedoms and the process ensures a speedy determination of the matter.[15] As Justice Baron has noted, a favourable judgment obtained at the conclusion of the normal, and sometimes very lengthy, judicial process is of little value to the litigant. Even where speed is not of the essence there are obvious advantages to litigants and to the public to have an important constitutional issue decided directly by the Supreme Court without protracted litigation.[16] This is a useful power which the Supreme Court has utilised to good effect on several occasions.[17] For example, in the leading case on the rights of those detained without trial, there were only seventeen days between the decision of the High Court and that of the Supreme Court. The comment of the High Court judge that 'in cases involving the liberty of the subject there is need for a decision to be given speedily' was entirely apposite.[18]

The extent to which individual freedoms are enforceable during a state of emergency is of critical importance. Some commentators have argued that such freedoms have no place when a nation, and a developing nation in particular, is faced with critical security, economic or social problems. It is said that in such a situation, a nation must, above all, safeguard its security. Accordingly, the State and its agents must have the freedom to combat the danger using every means possible including the power to abrogate individual freedoms. Even Western democracies have severely curtailed individual freedoms during times of emergency. A useful example of this approach is found in the speech of Herbert Ushewokunze, the then Minister of Home Affairs, when seeking parliamentary approval for an extension of the state of emergency in 1982. Having condemned all efforts to hamper the activities of the security forces, he then roundly attacked the judiciary for deciding a case against the government stating:

> The efforts of the police are not being complemented by the courts. A lot [of people] now say what purpose is achieved by sending people to court where the justice dished out leaves one dumb-founded. It appears the courts are sowing seeds of a revolt against government and encouraging the growth of the dissident element which is spreading in Matabeleland.[19]

A related argument was developed in 1965 by the Presidential Commission in Tanzania which noted that developing nations lacked both the tradition of nationhood and a strong basis for internal security. As a result, it considered that a Declaration of Rights was not appropriate for Tanzania because 'it limits in advance of events the action which government may take to protect the nation from the threat of subversion and disorder'.[20]

Such views overlook the harsh reality that complete executive freedom frequently leads to serious human rights violations. In this context, individual freedoms are not an 'all or nothing' commodity for it is nowhere asserted that all such freedoms are enforceable at all times. Whilst some are never subject to abrogation under any circumstances, it is firmly established that others are liable to abrogation or derogation during a period of public emergency. This approach is reflected in the Constitution of Zimbabwe which states that the right to life, the protection from torture and inhuman treatment and the protection of the law are never liable to abrogation or derogation. However, the right to liberty, association, and movement are subject to limited derogation in the event of a public emergency.[21] Thus provided the law in question is for the purpose of dealing with any situation arising during the emergency 'nothing done by any person under the authority of such law shall be held in contravention of [these rights] unless it is shown that the action exceeded anything which, having due regard to the circumstances prevailing at the time, could reasonably have been thought to be required for the purposes of dealing with the situation'.[22] The constitution further provides that the right to free movement, assembly, conscience, expression, and association are subject to qualification by any law which is made in the interests of defence, public safety or public order. Such limitations only apply if they are reasonably justifiable in a democratic society. Even here, such vague limitations can render nugatory these rights unless there is a constantly vigilant judiciary prepared to interpret the provisions realistically.[23]

It is also argued that a Declaration of Rights can do positive harm. Emergency situations require swift action designed to respond to the consistently changing security picture. This is inevitably jeopardised if the government response is delayed or prevented by individuals using the Declaration to contest the measures in the courts. The case of Colin Bickle supports this view. Bickle, a white Zimbabwean, unlawfully flew his light aircraft from South Africa to an airstrip on his farm in Zimbabwe. He brought with him a South African agent who was involved in anti-ANC activities in both Zimbabwe and Botswana. The use of white owned property in Zimbabwe from which to mount South African organised attacks against the ANC and other targets prompted the Government to make emergency regulations providing for the State control of such property. This was on the basis that the constitutional right to the protection of property was subject to the 'vesting or administration of any property belonging to or used on behalf on an enemy'.[24] However, in 1983 the Supreme Court held the confiscation of the property was unlawful because South Africa was not an 'enemy State'.[25] The decision was both surprising and controversial given the fact that the two nations had no diplomatic relations; had held no meetings at ministerial level or above since 1980; and that South African agents had carried out several attacks on Zimbabwean territory. Dismay in government circles was wholly understandable and the decision potentially endangered public security.[26] It is quite unacceptable for the Declaration to become a vehicle to delay and frustrate legitimate government activities in this manner. However, the rule of law requires governments to operate in a lawful manner and for the courts to grant redress to those adversely affected. Bickle's case neatly illustrates the difficulty of balancing the interests of the State and individuals.[27]

It is further argued that the protection of individual freedoms is a preserve of the elite and excludes the majority of the population who have neither the education nor the financial resources to benefit from it. Indeed in Zimbabwe, constitutional cases are brought, almost invariably, by influential or wealthy individuals. In reality, this is really an argument attacking the judicial system as a whole for few would disagree that the object of any such system is the protection of the rights of all citizens. The fact that presently it is only open to a privileged minority merely expresses the hope that in due course it will become open to all.

Interpretation of the Constitution

In order to give full scope to individual freedoms, a realistic approach to the interpretation of the Constitution as a whole and the Declaration of Rights in particular is necessary. It is now established that in Zimbabwe its interpretation is based on the principle that:

> Respect must be paid to the language which has been used and to the tradition and usages which have given meaning to that language. It is quite consistent with this, and with the recognition that rules of interpretation may apply, to take as a point of departure for the process of interpretation a recognition of the character and origin of the instrument, and to be guided by the principle of giving full recognition and effect to those fundamental rights and freedoms with a statement of which the Constitution commences.[28]

Thus a benevolent albeit realistic interpretation of constitutional rights is required,[29] for 'a court which is over-active in striking down legislation can destroy the exalted instrument it is trying to bring to life . . . and can cause the Declaration, which is meant to be a charter of freedom to become a clog upon the wheels of government. That must be avoided for the sake of the Constitution itself and for the sake of the stature of Parliament as the highest law-making forum of the nation.'[30] In the United States the approach to such interpretation has been thoroughly canvassed. Black[31] notes that there is a presumption in favour of the validity and constitutionality of every Act of the legislature until the contrary is shown and all doubts are resolved in favour of the validity of the Act. If it is fairly and reasonably open to more than one construction, that which will reconcile the statute with the constitution and avoid the consequence of unconstitutionality must be adopted. The United States courts have also held that when the validity of an Act is in question, it is a cardinal principle that the court must first ascertain whether a construction of the statute is fairly possible so as to avoid the issue.[32] Accordingly, a statute is only unconstitutional if it is clearly proved to be so and a judge should only so declare if he/she has a clear and strong conviction as to its incompatibility with the constitution. In Zimbabwe, the Supreme Court has followed this approach:

> [A] litigant who asserts that an Act of Parliament or a regulation is unconstitutional must show that it is. In such a case the judicial body charged with deciding that issue must interpret the Constitution and determine its meaning . . . If one possible interpretation falls within the meaning of the constitution and others do not, then the judicial body must presume that the lawmakers intended to act constitutionally and uphold the piece of legislation so interpreted. This is one of the senses in which the presumption of constitutionality can be said to arise. One does not interpret the Constitution in a restricted manner in order to accommodate the challenged legislation. The Constitution must be properly interpreted adopting the approach accepted above. Thereafter the challenged legislation is examined to discover whether it can be interpreted into the framework of the Constitution.[33]

This is important because many of the individual freedoms contained in the Declaration of Rights are subject to derogation by any provision which is 'reasonably justifiable in a democratic society'. Here the Supreme Court held that the onus lay on the challenger to prove the legislation was not reasonably justifiable. This was based on the adoption of the realistic view that[34] 'a Legislature, elected by universal adult suffrage and liable to be defeated in an election, must be presumed to be a good judge of what is reasonably required or reasonably justifiable in a democratic society. But situations can arise even in such societies in which majorities oppress minorities and so the Declaration of Rights prescribes limits within which rights may be restricted. It is only in cases where it is clear that the restriction is oppressive that the Court will interfere.'[35]

The meaning of the term 'in a democratic society' is somewhat vague given that countries of differing ideological perspectives claim to be democracies. At the international level, both the Siracusa Principles and the Limburg Principles state that while there is no single model of a democratic state, a society which recognises and respects the human rights set out in the United Nations Charter and the Universal Declaration may be viewed as meeting this definition.[36] This means that a society, whether developed or developing, is considered democratic only if certain minimum standards are maintained.[37] The Supreme Court in Zimbabwe has also considered the meaning of the term.[38] Here Justice Gubbay referred to the view of Justice Magus in the Zambian case of *Patel*[39] that the term 'democratic society' had been appended to the constitution by the draftsman more for its emotive and ideological appeal than for any real regard for what it conveyed. He pointed out that the determination of what is reasonably justifiable in any democratic society is an objective test but even so, the term was ambiguous because it meant different things to different persons. Thus there is no single immutable standard which constitutes a democratic society but that the emphasis should be on whether the derogations imposed on the entrenched freedoms were reasonable.[40]

The first major case involving the interpretation of the Constitution of Zimbabwe arose in 1982 following the detention of Dumiso Dabengwa and Lookout Masuku. An order made under section 43 of the Emergency Powers (Maintenance of Law and Order) Regulations prohibited the men from communicating with their lawyers.[41] It was argued that as the Constitution was the supreme law in Zimbabwe, section 43 contravened the right of detainees to have access to their lawyers contained in Schedule 2 of the Constitution. Similar provisions to section 43 had appeared in all the emergency regulations since 1967. This was significant because at that time the constitution contained a 'saving' clause which provided that certain pre-independence laws (including section 43) remained valid for five years after independence despite being inconsistent with the Declaration. The State therefore argued that section 43 overrode the provisions of the schedule because despite the fact that the schedule was placed physically at the end of the Constitution, it was actually part of the Declaration by virtue of section 25 of the constitution. This reads:

> Notwithstanding the foregoing provisions of this Chapter, an Act of Parliament may in accordance with Schedule 2 derogate from certain provisions of the Declaration of Rights in respect of a period of public emergency.

This contention was based on the proposition that the schedule could have no existence independent of section 25 and must therefore be regarded as part of the Declaration. The Supreme Court rejected this approach holding that although the schedule was dependent upon the existence of section 25 'it is clear that [it] affords a separate right which is enforceable in time of a public emergency'. Whilst acknowledging that there was some ambiguity in the constitution, it added that in this particular type of case 'the structure of the constitution is so clear as to leave no room for ambiguity'. Here the court was at pains to point out that in interpreting the constitution, full recognition must be given to fundamental rights and freedoms. In the event, the court held that Schedule 2 existed independently of the Declaration and thus the order issued under section 43 contravened the constitution and was invalid. This is an extremely important decision for, as the court recognised, it is contrary to any true concept of justice that a detained person is denied the right of access to his legal representative. Further, the right is a special one, of value only to those whose rights are suspended during an emergency situation. To allow the suspension of that right renders the provision entirely nugatory.

The interpretation of the constitution is a complex undertaking, especially when matters of state security are involved. However, the bottom line is that it is quite unacceptable to subject individual freedoms to such severe limitations and restrictions during a public emergency as to render them meaningless. Thus there must be 'limits to the limits'. To achieve this, several principles are employed elsewhere. Firstly, the principle of 'proportionality'. Originally developed by the French Conseil d'Etat, this is widely used in Europe. It refers to the constitutional limitation on the power of the State in legislation as well as administrative action. Interference with constitutional rights is only possible if (a) permitted by the Constitution; (b) capable of achieving its purported objective; (c) necessary to achieve such purported objective in the sense that no lesser form of interference is available; and (d) reasonable or proportional in the sense that the purported objective of such interference is as such lawful, adequate, necessary and of superior or equal weight, when balanced against the affected right. These questions are asked in relation to the facts of every case and every right when there is a limitation and a challenge. Thus Orucu asserts that the proportionality principle is the ultimate test for justice and a requisite concretisation of the rule of law and is thus immanent in the concept of basic rights.[42]

A second principle is that of the 'core of rights'. This is based on the assumption that a right is meaningless when it is impossible for a person to exercise it either directly or indirectly. Thus the scope of the right must be both clear and not undermined by the deprivation of some other right. Rights are thought of as clusters of primary and concomitant rights. For example, the fundamental right to leave and enter the country of one's citizenship is a primary right. A concomitant right is that of obtaining a passport, without which the primary right is infringed. In effect there is a 'guaranteed core' of rights together with their concomitant rights which are not subject to abrogation.[43] This principle appears as part of a constitutional norm in the Federal Republic of Germany which states that a law 'cannot touch the core of a right or a freedom even on such grounds as public interest, general morality, public order, social justice and national security'.[44] Where the core starts or ends is judicially determined in every case.

A third principle is that of rationality or proximity. This concerns the power to abrogate a right in the interests of national security. The Zambian case of *Kachasu*[45] provides a useful example. Here the validity of regulations requiring schoolchildren to sing the national anthem and salute the national flag were challenged as an infringement of the constitutional right to freedom of conscience. The regulations were upheld on the grounds that the applicant had not established that they went beyond what was reasonably required in the interests of public safety or public order. The court considered that in order to maintain national security it was essential to have national unity. To counteract the danger of tribalism and sectionalism in the country it was necessary to instill in the nation a consciousness of national unity and national allegiance and thus the regulations were required in the interests of public safety or public order. As Mubako rightly notes, the decision meant that it was very difficult for an individual ever to challenge successfully any measure which the authorities claimed was in favour of public security.[46] A hypothetical example based on the Constitution of Zimbabwe will highlight the point. Suppose regulations permitted the government to compulsorily acquire land of wealthy landowners on the grounds that because of the acute disparity of incomes in the country, it was in the interests of public safety that steps were taken to produce economic equality. Without such action, there was a fear of a political crisis leading to civil disorder and the possible violent overthrow of the government. Are the regulations valid because the constitution provides that the right to protection from deprivation of property is subject to any law which authorises the taking of any action in the interests of state security?[47] It is argued that the property in question remains subject to constitutional protection. This is because the relationship between the impugned legislation and the relevant derogation provisions must be rational or proximate and here the purpose of the regulations is merely to promote economic equality. As Basu notes, constitutional rights are 'susceptible of restriction only to prevent grave and immediate danger to interests which the State may lawfully protect'.[48] Thus there are many situations which may ultimately affect national security but unless there are 'proximate tendencies' constitutional rights are not subject to abrogation. In practice it is difficult for a court to judge the question of proximity with any certainty. But a value judgment is required in order to balance State interests and individual freedoms. On this basis, the decision in *Kachasu* was certainly wrong.[49]

Interpretation of Emergency Powers Legislation

The protection of constitutional rights is also affected by the approach of the courts to the interpretation of emergency powers legislation. This is well illustrated by the Zambian case of *Rao v Attorney-General*.[50] Here the Supreme Court considered whether it was permissible for the State to detain without trial any person suspected of being involved in 'economic crimes' such as illegal trafficking in and smuggling of semi-precious stones, rhino horns and drugs. Regulations derived from the Preservation of Public Security Act provided for detention without trial on grounds of 'public security'. According to the legislation, this 'includes securing the safety of persons and property, the maintenance of supplies and services essential to the life of the community [and] the prevention and suppression of violence, intimidation, disorder and crime . . .' A majority of the Supreme Court of Zambia held that crimes which tended to cripple the economy of Zambia should be treated as a threat to public security and thus they fell within the scope of the regulations. According to Chief Justice Silungwe, as the word 'crime' in the definition of 'public security' appeared in its own right, the intention of the legislature was to make provision, in appropriate cases, for the 'prevention and suppression of . . . crime'. He added that the inclusion of the word 'includes' served to indicate that the definition was not exhaustive, and so, anything which was shown to fall within the spirit and intendment of the enactment was within the ambit of the definition. The effect is that by a liberal interpretation of the words 'includes' and 'crimes', the court gave the executive sweeping new powers of detention over matters which were purely criminal in nature. This is surely erroneous because when regard is had to the intention of the legislature, it becomes clear that 'economic crimes' could not conceivably fall within the ambit of the legislation. In fact the Act itself was passed in 1960 primarily in order to combat civil disorder during the struggle for Zambian independence and was intended to deal with matters such as civil unrest, political violence, unlawful assemblies and the like. Economic crimes of the type alleged in Rao were quite unknown at that time and thus could not possibly be part of the 'mischief' with which the statute was concerned.

The decision in Rao means that in Zambia the constitutional right to liberty was liable to curtailment by the use of emergency powers even when the matter involved a purely criminal issue. As well as being unsound in law, such a decision also calls into question the very independence of the judiciary itself.[51] It emphasises the need for judges to take a restrictive approach to the interpretation of emergency powers legislation. The extent to which the judges in Zimbabwe have succeeded in this task is considered in succeeding chapters.

Overview

It is essential that individual freedoms are given adequate constitutional protection, especially during periods of public emergency. Of course, in practice the operation of even the most liberal constitution depends upon the courts being prepared to interpret it in an enlightened manner.[52] The Declaration of Rights forms the cornerstone of this protection and if judges are so minded, they can develop the document into a genuine safeguard for individual freedoms, especially if there is a willingness to apply international human rights norms to domestic human rights.[53] Certainly the adoption of clear principles of interpretation can provide an invaluable framework for approaching this task. As the legal system in Zimbabwe is based on roman-dutch law,[54] the courts are in a better position to follow these approaches than their common law counterparts and it is hoped that they are influential in future constitutional cases.

Notes

1. Chapter 1, Article 3 of the United Nations Charter.
2. See, for example, Chirkin 1985, pp.146–156.
3. The Preamble to the ICESCR itself states that in accordance with the Universal Declaration 'the ideal of free human beings enjoying freedom from fear and want can only be achieved if conditions are created whereby everyone may enjoy his economic, social and cultural rights, *as well as his civil and political rights.*' (my emphasis).
4. Preamble to the Charter.
5. Article 1.
6. See especially the views of Lord Scarman, 1974, p.45 and 1987, p.129–33. He asserts that a Bill of Rights would give the citizen aggrieved by an infringement of his/her rights immediate access to a national court where relief from or a remedy for the infringement could be obtained.
7. This type of provision was held to contravene the European Convention of Human Rights by the European Court of Human Rights: see *Brogan v United Kingdom The Times*, [30 May 1988]. Nevertheless, the UK government has refused to comply with the ruling and has issued a notice of derogation under Article 5 of the Convention.

This was reiterated by the Government in November 1989.

8. See Parts II and IV Prevention of Terrorism Act 1989. For an analysis of the provisions see Hatchard, 1990, p.270. For a general account of the area see Bonner, 1985.

9. Section 2, Constitution of Malawi.

10. See, for example, the highly critical report of Africa Watch on Malawi in 1990.

11. Law of the Fifth Amendment of the State Constitution 1984.

12. Sections 8 and 9 of the Constitution of Tanzania.

13. For example, in 1984 a Bill of Rights was introduced into the new Constitution of Tanzania in 1984 for the first time. This became entrenched in 1988. The Namibian Constitution also contains an impressive and wide-ranging protections of fundamental human rights and freedoms: See Hatchard and Slinn, 1990, p.137 and Cottrell, 1991, p.46. These developments hopefully herald a return to the inclusion of a meaningful Declaration of Rights in other African constitutional documents.

14. Section 11, Constitution of Zimbabwe.

15. Section 24, Constitution of Zimbabwe.

16. Baron JA in *Mandirwhe v Minister of State (Security)* [1981] ZLR 61.

17. This procedure only applies to cases where rights under the Declaration are involved. This means that cases relating to detention without trial originate in the High Court as the Declaration does not apply to detainees.

18. *Dabengwa & Masuku v Minister of Home Affairs*, Unreported, High Court of Zimbabwe HC-H-180-82 *per* McNally J.

19. *Parliamentary Debates*, 13 July 1982.

20. *Report of the Presidential Commission on the Establishment of a Democratic–One Party State*, Dar es Salaam, 1965, pp.31–32. See also Martin, 1974, pp.38–45. The Tanzanian Constitution proceeded without a Declaration. But see now note 13.

21. Section 25, Constitution of Zimbabwe.

22. Schedule 2(1), Constitution of Zimbabwe.

23. See the following section for a full discussion on this point.

24. Section 16(8), Constitution of Zimbabwe.

25. *Bickle v Minister of Home Affairs* 1983 (2) ZLR 400. This was based on the recognition that Zimbabwe and South Africa retained commercial air links and were major trading partners. The word 'enemy' was said to mean 'an enemy State with whom Zimbabwe is at war either by reason of a declaration of war or by reason of armed conflict between the State and Zimbabwe on such a scale as to amount to a state of war'. In the later case of *Harington v The State* 1988 (2) ZLR 344 the Supreme Court sought to distance itself from the earlier decision and held that the word 'enemy' includes a potential enemy. The interpretation given to it in Bickle was said to have 'a limited and restrictive meaning, consonant with the protection of the property rights of the individual' (*per* Chief Justice Dumbutshena at p.354). On such a controversial issue, it is surely preferable for the courts to seek the guidance of the executive in the form of a certificate from the minister which is placed before the court: see the views of Justice McNally in *Hartlebury* 1985 (1) ZLR 1.

26. The decision was subject to severe criticism. See in particular Gutto and Makamure, 1985, p.119 where they accused the Supreme Court of betraying the people of Zimbabwe. In 1984 the Emergency Powers (Property Restriction) Regulations SI 257B/84 provided that the Minister of Home Affairs could appoint a supervisor to administer property subject to a property restriction certificate. This was issued against any person whose actions were considered prejudicial to security and who had left the country. Such a certificate was issued against property belonging to Bickle.

27. Regulations were then made which provided for the appointment of an administrator to administer any property which was made the subject of a restriction order. Control of certain property owned by Bickle (as well as property owned by PF–ZAPU) was then vested in an administrator: see Emergency Powers (Property Restriction) Regulations 1984 SI 257B/84; Emergency Powers (Property Restriction)(Amendment) Regulations 1984 (No. 1) SI 295/84; Emergency Powers (Property Restriction)(Amendment) Regulations 1984 (No. 2) SI 365/84.

28. Lord Wilberforce in *Minister of Home Affairs v Fisher* [1979] 3 All ER 21. This was adopted in Zimbabwe in the cases of *Minister of Home Affairs v Dabengwa and Masuku* 1982 (1) ZLR 236; 1982 (4) SA 301 and *Zimbabwe Township Developers v Lou's Shoes* [1986] LRC (Const) 328.

29. See Gubbay JA in *Ncube v The State* [1988] LRC (Const) 442, 459. See also *Minister of Home Affairs v Dabengwa* 1982 (1) ZLR 236, pp.243–4 and *Zimbabwe Township Developers (Pvt) Ltd v Lou's Shoes (Pvt) Ltd* 1984 (2) SA 778, pp.782–3.

30. *Smith v A-G of Bophuthatswana* 1984 (1) SA 196 at p.201. In the Zambian case of *A-G v Thixton* [1967] ZR 10 Chief Justice Blagden noted that 'when fundamental rights of liberty are concerned, the courts should be slow to place an interpretation on the relevant provisions which would have the effect of denying these rights to the subject' (at p.16).

31. See Black, 1911.

32. *Crowell v Benson* [1931] 285 US 22 at p.62 *per* Chief Justice Hughes.

33. *Zimbabwe Township Developers v Lou's Shoes*, above.

34. Chief Justice Georges in *Zimbabwe Township Developers v Lou's Shoes*, above.

35. Perhaps not surprisingly, the Supreme Court has held that the burden of proof lies on the person alleging a breach of the Declaration of Rights: see *Fikilini v Attorney-General* 1990 (1) ZLR 105.

36. The Siracusa Principles on the Limitation and Derogation Provisions in the International Covenant on Civil and Political Rights were drawn up in 1984 by an eminent group of international lawyers. In 1986 a further meeting was held at which the Limburg Principles were established which reflected what was considered to be the present state of international law on the topic.

37. Compare the approach of the court in the Zambian case of *Kachasu v A-G* [1967] ZR 145 where it was said that when a court applied the test of what was reasonably required in Zambia, then, so long as Zambia remains a democracy 'that which is reasonably required in Zambia must be reasonably justifiable in a democratic society'.
38. *Commissioner of Taxes v C.W.(Pvt) Ltd*, 1989 (3) ZLR 361 (SC); 1990 (2) SA 245 (ZS).
39. [1968] ZR 128 at p.129.
40. He approved the Canadian decision of *Federal Government of Germany v Rauca* 141 DLR (3d) 412, at p.424 on this point.
41. *Dabengwa & Masuku v Minister of Home Affairs*, above n.28.
42. Orucu, 1986, p.45.
43. An extraordinary example of this type of reasoning appears in the Indian case of *Olga Tellis v Bombay Municipal Corporation* (1986) AIR 180 (SC). Here it was held that the right to life included the right to a livelihood because no person can live without the means of living. If the right to a livelihood is not treated as part of the constitutional right to life, the easiest way to deprive a person of his right to life is to deprive him of his right to a livelihood.
44. Article 19/2.
45. [1967] ZR 145.
46. Mubako, 1983–84, p.125.
47. See section 16(8)(b) Constitution of Zimbabwe.
48. Basu, 1983, p.97 *et seq*.
49. The High Court of Zambia did not follow the decision in the later case of *Patel v A-G* [1968] ZR 99.
50. [1989] LRC (Const) 527.
51. See also the critical comment on the case by Mbao, 1989, pp.124–5.
52. This in itself is a challenge given the propensity for many governments to interfere in operation of the judiciary. The matter is fully explored in Chapter 12.
53. A point urged by Dumbutshena, 1990, p.311.
54. Section 89, Constitution of Zimbabwe.

6 Detention Without Trial & the Right to Personal Liberty

General Features of Detention Without Trial

Preventive detention (or detention without trial) enables the executive or its agents to detain an individual without recourse to the judicial process. This action is usually justified on the ground that the person poses a threat to 'public safety or public security'. Detention powers are used in two ways. Firstly for investigative detention. Here the security forces may detain a person for a specified period without bringing him/her before a court. Secondly, for indefinite detention. Here an executive order provides for the detention of any person for an indeterminate period. Despite the serious consequences associated with it, the ICCPR recognises that a State may utilise preventive detention during a period of public emergency,[1] and there are also several arguments to support this approach:

1. The State has the right and duty to employ its best efforts to protect society against those who threaten its security. This is especially so in times of emergency when the people of the nation join together as one 'community' to protect it against internal or external enemies. As the former President of Tanzania, Julius Nyerere, points out:

> Our Union has neither the long tradition of nationhood, nor the strong physical means of national security which older countries take for granted. While the vast mass of people give full and active support to their country and its government, a handful of individuals can still put our nation in jeopardy and reduce to ashes the efforts of millions.[2]

2. The criminal law is not always a suitable vehicle for the detention of individuals because its objective is to punish convicted offenders. The objective of preventive detention is to permit the executive to hold a person on suspicion of being a potential threat to State security. As a former Minister of Home Affairs in Zimbabwe, Herbert Ushewokunze has noted:

> The technique of preventive detention involves trying to identify those with a propensity to act so as to threaten state security, and to put them away until the danger dissipates. I would mis-use preventive detention if I used it to punish a person for an act already committed. Only the criminal law serves that purpose. I do not and will not use preventive detention to substitute for a criminal conviction. To imprison a person because we suspect his propensity to endanger security constitutes the very limit of imprisonment for suspicion alone. I must – and I do – constantly remind myself of this, and of the fallibility of all human suspicions, none more so

than when the suspicion consists of an estimate about whether a person will act in a security threatening way in the future. Even so Parliament has declared that we live in times of emergency. It has declared that in these times we cannot afford the usual value judgment that better a hundred guilty men go free than that one innocent go to prison.[3]

3. The criminal justice system is not always capable of handling a security threatening situation. For example, the continued existence of widespread unrest, subversion or politically motivated crime may require the use of preventive detention in order to prevent the breakdown of law and order.[4]

4. In security related cases, the evidence against the detainee may be so sensitive or secret that the State is not prepared to divulge it, even to the courts. Indeed Mugabe himself used this to justify the re-detention of some individuals following their acquittal by the courts.[5]

5. Widespread intimidation of prosecution witnesses often makes it impossible to secure a conviction.[6]

Despite the inherent dangers to individual freedoms which accompany the use of preventive detention, arguably its use is justified in the most extreme circumstances. For example, if a popularly elected government utilises its constitutional power to detain as a last resort and for a short period and only when its use is necessary for dealing with an emergency situation. In practice, this is rarely the case for the African experience shows that detention without is trial is primarily used by governments in order to prevent the exercise of individual freedoms.

Detention Without Trial in Africa

The use of preventive detention laws in sub-Saharan Africa is prevalent. In recent years at least thirty-seven nations have employed it in some form.[7] In some jurisdictions, preventive detention is employed only during a declared emergency situation. In others the detention without trial forms part of the ordinary law and needs no special procedure for its introduction. Thus in Tanzania the Preventive Detention Act 1962 permits the President to order the detention of any person where it is shown to his satisfaction that such person is acting in a manner prejudicial to the security of the State.[8] The law remains in full operation and, in 1985, was extended to cover Zanzibar as well.[9] In South Africa, regulations made under the Public Safety Act 1953 empower the Minister of Law and Order to order the indefinite detention of any person, whilst members of the security forces may detain any person for up to thirty days. These provisions are reinforced by the Internal Security Act 1982 which provides for three types of detention: (i) detention of State witnesses. Here the Attorney-General may order the detention of potential prosecution witnesses in certain security cases if of the opinion that they have material evidence to give and that there is a danger that they may abscond or be tampered with or intimidated. He may also order the detention of a witness 'in the interests of justice'.[10] The judiciary is expressly precluded from ordering the release of any person held under such an order; (ii) investigative detention. Here a senior police officer may detain any person without warrant if he has reason to believe that that person has committed a crime of terrorism or subversion or is in some way involved in such activities;[11] (iii) preventive detention. This provides for indeterminate detention following the making of a ministerial detention order.[12]

Many African nations remain the target of international criticism over their use of detention laws. For example, following the 1986 declaration of a state of emergency in South Africa, mass arrests occurred with more than 20,000 people being detained under the emergency regulations by the end of the year. A significant proportion were young people, including children as young as eleven or twelve, some of whom were detained for several months. The remainder were mostly community and political workers; students and teachers; and trade union members. All were protesting against the iniquitous apartheid regime. Indeed, during the 1980s states of emergency, at least 40,000 people were detained.[13] In Kenya in 1986, fears of a plot against the Moi government by the group *MwaKenya* led to the detention of many government critics including lawyers, students and intellectuals. Contrary to the terms of the legislation, the names of the detainees were never published. Preventive detention is still commonly used to silence government critics. In Malawi, preventive detention is described as a 'consistent and vicious government policy, designed not only to quash all dissent, but also to prevent any internal challenge to the authority of the ageing President Banda. Preventive detention is used simply to eliminate all political opposition.'[14] Similarly, in Uganda, detentions were used during the second Obote government as part of a policy of State terrorism.[15]

In Liberia, the serious riots at Easter 1979 over a proposed increase in the price of rice were attributed by government to an attempt by the opposition Progressive Alliance of Liberia to overthrow it. As a result, Congress granted the President emergency powers for one year. This resulted in the suspension of habeas corpus and the imposition of detention without trial.[16] The University of Sierra Leone was closed by government on the grounds that it was a 'base for subversive ideas and ideologies'. In February 1988, violence erupted in Dakar and other towns in Senegal following allegations of widespread electoral malpractice. A state of emergency was declared in the Dakar region and a 21.00 to 06.00 hours curfew imposed. Schools and the university, which were perceived as centres of discontent, were closed and 300 persons detained, including several leading members of opposition parties. A request by President Diouf for an indefinite extension of the state of emergency was later approved by the National Assembly.[17]

One of the best chronicled situations is that of Ghana between 1958 and 1966. Fear of legitimate political opposition to the Nkrumah regime led to the passing of the Preventive Detention Act 1958. As in Tanzania, the operation of the Act was not dependent upon a declared state of emergency. It permitted the Minister to order the detention of any Ghanaian citizen if 'satisfied' that this was necessary to prevent that person 'acting in a manner prejudicial to the defence of Ghana . . . or the security of the State'. The power was used extensively and many opposition leaders and dissidents were detained including several former Cabinet Ministers who were allegedly implicated in a coup plot.[18] Estimates of the numbers detained under the Act range from several hundreds to many thousands.[19] The late Dr Busia, an ardent opponent of Nkrumah and later Prime Minister of Ghana, singled out five objectionable features of the Act: (i) it empowered the President, solely in his discretion to deprive any subject of his liberty, virtually for life; (ii) the courts in Ghana held that the discretion was absolute; (iii) the President in the exercise of this absolute discretion, was not answerable to parliament, or any court or tribunal; (iv) a detainee was denied the right of facing his accusers or putting his case; (v) there was no provision or protection against the indiscriminate abuse of the powers conferred by the Act.[20] The Act was repealed in 1966 following the overthrow of Nkrumah but it vividly demonstrates the dangers attached to the use of preventive detention.[21]

In Rhodesia, detention without trial followed a similar pattern to that of other African nations. The Preventive Detention (Temporary Provisions) Act 1959 enabled the Governor to order indefinite detention with a view to preventing a detainee from acting in any manner potentially dangerous to public safety or public order. Following an abortive attempt to extend the validity of the Act for a further five years,[22] the government resorted to the Emergency Powers Act. Following the declaration of a state of emergency in 1965,[23] emergency regulations were made which provided for detention without trial when this was 'expedient in the public interest'.[24] In February 1966 the state of emergency was renewed[25] and a fresh set of regulations (the 1966 regulations)[26] provided for the continued detention of those held under the earlier regulations.[27] Their legality was then challenged in *Madzimbamuto v Lardner-Burke*.[28] Here the Rhodesian courts concluded that the Smith regime was the *de facto* government exercising control in Rhodesia and that the extension of the state of emergency, the issuing of the 1966 regulations and detention without trial were all measures which could be enforced. As a result, the detention laws were used extensively against African nationalists, with Robert Mugabe, Joshua Nkomo, Edgar Tekere and Simon Muzenda, amongst others, being detained between 1964 and 1974.[29] Others fared even worse. Enos Nkala was detained between 1964 and 1974 and from 1976 to 1979 whilst Maurice Nyagumbo was first detained in 1959 and from then until 1979, was never a free man for longer than twelve months at a stretch. In all he was only out of prison for thirty months during the whole of this period.[30] The actual number of those detained during the UDI period remains uncertain. According to government figures, in 1969 there were 142 detainees[31] whilst in 1972 there were 77 with the number rising to 90 by the following year.[32] According to Christian Care this figure rose to 432 in 1974 and 582 by 1975 when all detainees were due for release under the Kaunda/Vorster settlement plan. This was never fully implemented as the Smith regime stopped the process due to continued 'terrorism' in the country. In 1977 Amnesty International alleged that there were over 1,000 detainees whilst by 1979 over 7,000 indefinite detention orders were reportedly made under the martial law regulations.[33] It is clear that 'preventive detention was used to imprison people whose only danger to the State lay in their burning desire for justice'.[34] Thus the illegal regime used the detention laws on a wide scale in an attempt to protect a tiny white elite. In addition, the absence of any justiciable constitutional rights ensured that detainees effectively had no legal protections at all.

In Africa, the reality is that the use of preventive detention is generally unjustifiable. It is largely used by unscrupulous governments to entrench political power. Politician opponents, journalists, students, intellectuals and trade unionists and other government critics are frequently the subject of detention orders whilst mass detentions of those demonstrating against government policies also occur. In these circumstances, the use of preventive detention is indefensible being a clear violation of international human rights protections. It is against this background that the detention laws in Zimbabwe are examined.

Detention Without Trial in Zimbabwe

The Declaration of Rights protects the right to personal liberty and provides that any person who is unlawfully arrested or detained is entitled to compensation. In addition, any person arrested or detained upon reasonable suspicion of having committed or being about to commit a criminal offence and who is not released must be brought, without undue delay before a court.[35] The courts have consistently defended this right for as one judge has noted:

> Since time immemorial the liberty of the individual has been regarded as one of the fundamental rights of man in a free society. Long before Magna Carta codified the

> principle almost eight hundred years ago, man has pursued and jealously guarded his right to freedom of person. In the words of Thomas Jefferson 'The God who gave us life gave us liberty at the same time.' Revolutions have been staged and wars have been fought in the name of freedom. This includes Zimbabwe's own long and bitter struggle. The protection of this right is enshrined in the Constitution and the courts will certainly play their part in preserving this right against all infringements, and all attempts to erode or violate the principle involved.[36]

As a result, on several occasions the courts have awarded heavy damages against the State for the breach of the right. For example, in July 1980 John Makomberedze, a Zimbabwe citizen, was detained by members of the Zimbabwe intelligence services and later 'dumped' across the border in Mozambique with no formalities regarding his deportation or extradition. He was given no reasons for this action and his repeated requests for access to his legal representative were consistently refused. Some twenty months later he was released by the Mozambican authorities still without knowing the reasons for his detention. On his return to Zimbabwe, he found his family broken up and his business interests in ruins. The High Court upheld his claim for Zimb $50,000 damages, and condemned the authorities noting that their actions constituted an extremely serious breach of his constitutional rights.[37] Similarly, an elderly Harare lawyer, Denis Granger, brought an action for damages following his detention by four CIO officers. He said he was taking photographs at the scene of a road traffic accident when he was approached by the officers who started to rock his car shouting 'kill the spy'. He said he was abused and assaulted. At the trial, the CIO officers claimed they suspected he was a foreign agent but, as the trial judge pointed out:

> It is difficult to understand how anyone could believe that an enemy agent would stand in the middle of a four lane highway in broad daylight to photograph a vehicle while it is still so far away that the vehicle itself could hardly be identified, let alone its number plate or occupants.[38]

Granger was awarded Zimb $1,200 damages for the 'undisciplined and unreasonable behaviour' of the CIO officers. Despite such judicial pronouncements, the constitutional right to personal liberty is limited in that it does not apply to those detained without trial.

Although all political detainees were released at independence, the detention laws were retained in essentially the same form as before.[39] A 'section 17' order provided for the indefinite detention without trial if 'it appears to the Minister of Home Affairs that it is expedient in the interests of public safety or public order'.[40] The Minister could amend or revoke an order at any time but had restricted power to re-detain.[41] This did not give the Minister a complete discretion for even though section 17 was cast in a subjective form, in the exercise of his discretion the Minister was required to consider objective facts when determining whether reasonable grounds justifying detention existed.[42]

A 'section 21' order permitted a police officer without a warrant to detain any person for up to thirty days without charge or appearance before a court.[43] This was considerably in excess of the period for detention under the ordinary criminal law.[44] The grounds for detention were those under section 17 together with the power to detain any person who failed to satisfy a police officer as to his identity. This additional power did not specifically relate to security matters and enabled the police to detain any person in circumstances not connected with public safety or public order. Regrettably, there was no requirement to catalogue the use of section 21 orders and there is thus no information concerning detention practices. As regards re-detentions, similar restrictions as in section 17 orders applied. One related issue which was never resolved in Zimbabwe concerns the date of the commencement of a detention order. The Kenyan courts have held that it commences on the date of the service of the relevant order and not on the date of the original arrest. If this is correct then it means that any detention under a fourteen-day investigative detention order does not become illegal if a person is held in excess of that period so long as the order itself has not expired. In this case, a writ of habeas corpus is the only remedy.[45] If this is correct, then a detaining authority can hold any person for a far longer period than provided for in the legislation. Clearly some clarification on this point is necessary in the relevant regulations.

A 'section 53' order permitted a police officer without warrant to arrest and detain any person for up to thirty days if he reasonably suspected such person of any of the following: (a) he has acted or is about to act in a manner which is prejudicial to either the public safety or public order or the termination of the state of emergency; or (b) he has committed or is about to commit any offence under any law relating to either the preservation of public safety or public order or exchange control. This was an unusual provision being found in the 'General' part of the regulations which dealt with a miscellany of matters including controls on information relating to terrorism;[46] destruction of official notices relating to public safety;[47] and censorship of publications and movies[48] and was thus physically quite separate from sections 17 and 21.[49] The only immediate explanation for this is that the section was inserted into the regulations as an afterthought. There was also a certain overlap with section 21 although section 53 dealt with two new areas namely exchange control and the termination of the state of public emergency. The protection of the former is important because of the serious economic damage that contravention of the laws can cause. However, as this is a criminal matter for which the Exchange Control Act already provides severe penalties for any proven contravention, the use of the detention laws in this connection was seemingly quite inappropriate. As regards the latter, it is not clear as to what additional activity was envisaged which was not covered by section 21. In practice, thirty day detention orders were routinely made under section 21.[50]

The Use of Detention Orders in Zimbabwe

There was no legal obligation imposed on the detaining authorities to reveal the number of detainees or the reasons for their detentions and up to 1989 government made it clear that it had no intention of doing so. It is strange that so many African countries are reluctant to reveal this information. Logically one would expect them to be anxious to publicise it so as to act as a deterrent to others and to justify its actions to the international community. Continued silence on the matter or mere blanket denials imply, rightly or wrongly, that such governments have something to hide. For example, a report by the Lawyers Committee on Human Rights in 1987 alleged that several thousand Zimbabweans were detained without trial, often for far longer periods than the regulations permitted. The government strenuously denied the allegations but made no attempt to substantiate its case. One wonders why.

Information on detentions in Zimbabwe is thus available only from non-official sources. In 1985 it was claimed that up to 3,000 people were detained with the average figure being 800–1,200. Most were released after a few weeks.[51] After that, numbers decreased significantly. In late 1989, the Minister of Home Affairs, at last revealed that there were only 12 ministerial detainees,[52] and by the ending of the state of emergency in July 1990 only a handful of foreigners suspected of involvement in South African destabilisation activities remained. Section 21 detentions remained common right up to 1990 with its use being justified as being in the interests of State security 'which is paramount'.[53] As a result the police and CIO continued to detain people almost daily.[54]

Many detainees were political opponents or critics of the government. For example, Bishop Abel Muzorewa, the leader of the UANC and former Prime Minister, was detained for several months under a section 17 order apparently suspected of involvement with anti-government activities sponsored by South Africa.[55] Many members of PF–ZAPU were detained following the 1981 attack on the homes of the Prime Minister and Enos Nkala. These included Vote Moyo, the National Organising Secretary of the party, who was seized as he left the House of Assembly in Harare. He was never charged but was detained without trial until March 1986. Other prominent PF–ZAPU detainees were five members of Parliament who were detained following the 1985 General Election. They included Sydney Malunga, who was a long-term detainee of the Smith regime, and Edward Ndlovu. Both were originally charged with conspiracy to overthrow the government but Ndlovu was never brought to court whilst Malunga was never convicted.[56] In November 1985, virtually the entire membership of the PF–ZAPU controlled Bulawayo Town Council were detained and were reported to be 'helping police with their enquiries'. Six were held for several months although none were ever formally charged. At this time, many other party supporters were also detained for short periods. The Catholic Commission for Justice and Peace also reported that nearly 200 employees of the Bulawayo Town Council were detained for short periods during August and early September 1985. Many arrests were allegedly made by officers of the Police Internal Security and Intelligence organisation. Much of this activity had political overtones. Although ostensibly part of government's response to the dissident menace, the activity was also linked with attempts to pressurize PF–ZAPU into entering into the unity talks. Other notable detentions were those of veteran politician George Marange and other PF–ZAPU supporters from Beit Bridge in 1984 following the murder of a prominent ZANU(PF) supporter, Senator Moven Ndlovu. Marange was held until February 1986 whilst 14 other detainees were not released until the following year. Government also used the detention laws against several Zimbabwe Unity Movement activists following the 1988 launching of the party.

Trade unionists and other government critics were also subject to detention. Thus in 1985 nine trade union officials were held for a time, apparently on ideological grounds.[57] In October 1989 Morgan Tsvangirai, the Secretary-General of the Zimbabwe Trades Union Congress was detained by the CIO shortly after issuing a statement criticising the closure of the University of Zimbabwe and the arrest of student leaders. The reasons given for his detention were that the statement was allegedly 'highly subversive' and that he had been recruited by South Africa in 1988 in order 'to create turmoil in the labour movement'. Tsvangirai was released six weeks later, an implicit admission by government that these allegations were utterly groundless. Unrest at the University of Zimbabwe also led to the detention of several students. In 1988 student demonstrators were detained following protests at alleged corrupt activities by government officials – a charge later confirmed by the Sandura Commission.[58] Continued criticism of government policies and support for Tekere and the Zimbabwe Unity Movement also led to the detention in October 1989 of more students and a university law lecturer. All were released after a short time.

Detention orders were also made against human rights activists. In 1986, Nicholas Ndebele, the acting director of the Catholic Commission for Justice and Peace was detained following the publication by the Commission of a report on the torture of detainees which was in similar terms to that of an Amnesty International report. Government irritation at the regular critical Amnesty reports and suspicion that the

Commission had supplied the information was behind the detention although both bodies later confirmed that they had obtained their information from separate sources. The High Court ordered the release of Ndebele but he was briefly re-detained by the police along with Michael Auret, the Chairman of the Commission. Both were then released, apparently on the express instructions of Robert Mugabe.

The detention laws were also used to re-detain persons acquitted by the courts in security related cases. For example, in December 1981, two CIO officers, Colin Evans and Philip Hartlebury were charged with unlawfully passing intelligence information to South Africa, including information on Joe Gqabi the ANC representative in Harare who was later murdered. They were both acquitted by the High Court due to the inadmissibility of their confessions but immediately afterwards served with section 17 orders. Their importance as South African agents was later revealed when a ministerial statement disclosed that Pretoria had made several attempts to trade prisoners or foreign spies for the men. The most controversial re-detentions were in the case of the Air Force 6. Here six senior white Zimbabwe Air Force officers were charged with involvement in a devastating sabotage attack on the Thornhill air base in Gweru. They were all acquitted following a holding by the trial judge that their alleged confessions were inadmissible.[59] The officers were then given some twenty minutes with their relatives in the courtroom before being served with ministerial detention orders. News of their re-detention raised considerable interest both nationally and internationally with the Western press leading an outcry against the action. For example, in Britain *The Guardian* commented:

> This executive interference with the judiciary not only begs several questions but also compounds the damage done to Zimbabwe's standing by the detentions and the repression in Matabeleland. The great reservoir of goodwill at the birth of Zimbabwe in uniquely difficult circumstances evaporates before our eyes for easily avoidable reasons. It has been argued that those who came through a particularly savage war of independence are hardly likely to be gentle with the former race-enemy, or with internal opposition. But that is not the stuff of which national reconciliation, Mr Mugabe's promise on achieving power, is made. The only apparent difference now between detention by decree as practised in Zimbabwe and the apartheid state next door is one of quantity rather than quality.

The British Government also criticised the action with the then Prime Minister, Margaret Thatcher, writing to her Zimbabwean counterpart questioning the decision to re-detain the men. Quite naturally Mugabe reacted strongly pointing out that Britain was seeking to interfere with the internal affairs of an independent State. *The Herald* in Harare supported this stand, noting that:

> It comes as a great shock to all Zimbabweans who cherish their hard-won independence and sovereignty to learn of the underhand methods employed by Britain to try to compel Zimbabwe to free the detained air force men who, after rebelling against the Queen yesterday, are today celebrated heroes in the hearts of Margaret Thatcher and her colleagues. These arm-twisting tactics, coming as they did from people who are supposed to be 'civilised', can only be condemned as being 'frantic, impolitic and highly emotional'.

This reaction is interesting. Although many nationalists were detained for lengthy periods during the UDI period with no access to a lawyer and no constitutional protection, there was little outcry from Western countries. Whether this implies some racial bias is debatable but one wonders if the response would have been quite so forceful if the accused in the Air Force 6 case had happened to be black.

The Government of Zimbabwe responded to the criticisms of the detentions by taking a full-page advertisement in the British newspaper *The Observer*.[60] Entitled 'Zimbabwe on Trial' it included a statement by the Minister of Legal and Parliamentary Affairs putting the government side of the affair and making a 'plea for perspective and rationality after the Air Force 6 trial'. It pointed out that the detention laws were preserved in the Lancaster House Constitution and could have been used without holding the trial at all. In addition, it was said that the detention orders were made because of the serious political and military implications of the sabotage together with intelligence reports and other evidence which furnished the belief that the officers were involved in the action. Consequently, this was a case where not to detain would have gravely threatened the interests of the State. Such an approach begs several fundamental questions. Should preventive detention be used as a failsafe against the possibility of an acquittal at the trial? Based on the earlier discussion, including the views of the former Zimbabwean Minister of Home Affairs, Herbert Ushewokunze, the answer is surely in the negative. The fact that the result of the judicial process does not meet with the approval of a government can never justify the use of detention powers. Again, it is not clear why the intelligence reports referred to by the minister were not placed before the court. If they were so incriminating, then it was surely imperative to produce them, particularly in view of the paucity of other admissible evidence. One can only conclude that either the reports did not support this view or that government did not trust the courts with the information. Again, the ineptitude of the authorities ensured that the case was never properly investigated and thus the truth of the allegations was never actually considered at the trial. Even so, the use of detention laws to cover up gross inadequacies in the investigation of a case is quite wrong. Finally, perhaps the most telling point of all in this particular case is that within a short time all six men were released from detention. Quite why they had lost their high security status is not clear.

In some cases, detention orders were openly used as a replacement for the ordinary criminal justice process. Indeed in 1983 one of the reasons given by the Minister of Home Affairs for the renewal of the state of emergency was that 'inexperienced [police] officers were having to deal with experienced criminals' and thus needed the detention laws.[61] Perhaps the most notable example of this involved a prominent businessman, Sampson Paweni. In March 1984 he was arrested by CIO officers in connection with a massive fraud involving millions of dollars of government money. The matter was extremely sensitive as it was clear that certain high-ranking government officials were also involved in the racket. Paweni was granted bail but he and three other men were almost immediately served with detention orders alleging that they had engaged in acts of economic sabotage. How far economic activities justify detentions 'in the interests of public security or public order' is debatable.[62] It appears that apart from exchange control offences, detentions on the grounds of suspected unlawful economic activities do not, without more, fall within the scope of the regulations. In reality the detention order was made solely in order to assist police investigations and thus constituted a totally improper use of the detention powers.[63] Another example of this activity involved Charles Haruperi, who was involved with Paweni. He was charged with conspiracy to defraud but released on bail by the court. He was then served with a section 21 order, alleging for the first time that he was involved in acts prejudicial to State security. His application for release was upheld, the High Court rightly taking the view that the detention order was merely a pretext to keep him in custody to facilitate an investigation into a criminal offence.[64]

Overview

Preventive detention is a serious abrogation of the right to personal liberty and its use is understandably and rightly denounced by many commentators. The fact is that a detention order forces detainees (and their families) to live through an indefinite ordeal which can have the most deleterious effects upon all concerned.[65]

The use of detention laws in Zimbabwe raises some important issues for other African states. Firstly, the continued availability of preventive detention laws tends to make their use irresistible to government and its agents and thus open to potential abuse. The detention without trial of political opponents and critics was conveniently justified on spurious security grounds whilst in reality it was frequently used for political gain or to silence critics. This view is reinforced by the fact that the detainees review tribunal frequently recommended the release of detainees on their first appearance before it. Even in the more relaxed period following the unity agreement, students, trade unionists and political opponents were detained merely for criticising government policy and the corrupt practices of some leaders. This despite the fact of proven corruption on the part of several Cabinet ministers by the Sandura Commission.

Secondly, the courts can play a crucial role in the protection of the rights of detainees. Thus by holding that detaining authorities did not have an unfettered discretion over the decision to detain, the Minister of Home Affairs (or other detaining authority) was required to consider objective facts in order to arrive at the conclusion that reasonable grounds existed which justified detention. This was vital if the detention laws were not to become a political tool of the ruling elite as evidenced in Ghana and Malawi.

Thirdly, the circumvention of legal procedures by the re-detention of persons acquitted by the courts threatens the rule of law. Indeed any action of this nature flies in the face of the principle that the judiciary has the exclusive authority to decide all issues of a judicial nature.[66] Unless there is fresh evidence of a threat to national security, government must abide by a decision to acquit an individual and refrain from using its detention powers.

Fourthly, the use of detention orders by the police in purely criminal cases similarly brings into question the earlier statement of the former Minister of Home Affairs, concerning the basis of the decision to detain. Any diminution in the operation of the criminal justice system is quite improper and government was clearly wrong to permit this activity to continue. Such a policy also leads to a reduction in police efficiency and an increase in police abuse of power in that the need to carry out a proper criminal investigation prior to making an arrest is sometimes replaced by a wholesale rounding up of 'suspects' using the detention laws.

There is no doubt that the use of preventive detention in Zimbabwe in 'non-emergency' situations was a direct challenge to the rule of law and the constitutional right of freedom of the person. In 1989 the government sought to play down the use of the detention laws claiming that the only detainees were those connected with the South African commando raids into the country and accordingly it was the only 'government in Africa without political detainees of our own people'.[67] Of course, this claim was quite erroneous for there are some African countries, such as Botswana, which do not have preventive detention laws at all, and in any event, there was no time between 1980 and 1989 when this claim was accurate. With the ending of the state of emergency, the detention laws lapsed. Hopefully they will not be used again.

The lesson for Zimbabwe in particular and Africa in general is that the dangers attaching to the use of preventive detention generally far outweigh the justifications for its use. Of course, it is important not to lose sight of the fact that Zimbabwe did face acute security problems and that, in the words of the United States Supreme Court: 'the exigencies of the moment may properly evoke actions which calm hindsight . . . might perhaps view differently'. Even so, the experience of Zimbabwe shows that the use of detention laws severely limits the exercise of individual freedoms and accordingly must be used only in the last resort.

Notes

1. Article 4 permits derogation of the right to liberty enshrined in Article 9.
2. See Nyerere, 1967, pp.298–9.
3. *Moto*, July 1983, no 14, p.14.
4. In *Lawless v Ireland* 2 EHRR 25, the European Court of Human Rights found that a law which provided for detention appeared to be a measure strictly required by the exigencies of the situation. In doing so it had regard to the fact that the ordinary law had proved unable to check the growing danger which threatened the State; that the ordinary criminal courts, and even the special criminal courts and military courts, could not succeed in restoring law and order; and that the assembling of the necessary evidence to convict persons involved in IRA activities was meeting with great difficulties caused by the military, secret and terrorist character of the organisation and the fear it created among the population.
5. This is more important when there is a trial by jury. In most African countries, including Zimbabwe, juries are not used in criminal cases.
6. This point was also recognised in *Lawless* (above).
7. See, for example, *Amnesty International Annual Report 1987*.
8. Section 2(1). The State Security Act in The Sudan has somewhat similar provisions: Al Naim, p.159. This is a particularly valuable article because the author was himself detained under the Act and gives a first-hand account of life as a detainee.
9. Preventive Detention (Amendment) Act 1985 and see Peter, 1990, p.25.
10. Section 31, Internal Security Act 1982.
11. Section 29, Internal Security Act 1982.
12. For a full discussion see Rudolph, 1984, pp.22–39.
13. Webster and Friedman, 1989, p.21.
14. See Howard, 1986, p.152 *et seq*.
15. See Lule, 1982, p.67.
16. Dissatisfaction with the Tolbert government led to the April 1980 coup which toppled the regime.
17. The emergency decree was suspended on 21 May 1988 and shortly afterwards a wide-ranging Amnesty Law was promulgated which applied to all infractions committed in connection with the February elections.
18. In Parliament, President Nkrumah declared that 'the only people who need be alarmed about the Preventive Detention Act are those who are attempting to either organise violence, terrorism or civil war or who are acting as fifth columnists and for some . . . interested in subversion in Ghana. The Bill has been deliberately drafted so that the government can deal resolutely and without delay with any attempt to subvert the State by force. The government is determined not to be caught unprepared . . . by subversion either from within or without. In order to preserve due process of law it may on occasions be necessary to have specific powers.' *Parliamentary Debates*, 14 July 1958. A catalogue of the abuses perpetrated under the 1958 Act is set out in International Commission of Jurists, 1983, pp.103–4.
19. International Commission of Jurists, 1961, p.66.
20. The International Commission of Jurists also criticised the Act on similar grounds: see ICJ report (above).
21. For further examples of the problem in Africa see Skelton, 1980, p.319 and *Amnesty International Annual Reports 1980–90*. For a general review see Duchcek, 1973, especially p.176; and Ebiasah, 1979, pp.269 *et seq*.
22. In March 1964 the Governor assented to the Preventive Detention (Temporary Provisions) Amendment Act 1964 which purported to amend the earlier Act by extending its validity from five to ten years. The Constitutional Council (the fore-runner of the Senate Legal Committee) made an adverse report on the grounds that the new Act was contrary to the terms of the 1961 Constitution. This report did not prevent the continued utilisation of the Act and the detention of many nationalist leaders. It was not until Joshua Nkomo successfully challenged its validity that government finally accepted defeat, see *Nkomo v Minister of Justice* 1964 RLR 520.
23. Proclamation 51 of 1965.
24. Emergency Powers (Maintenance of Law and Order) Regulations 1965. They were issued in response to increased threats to internal security from African nationalists and not in anticipation of UDI: see Young, 1969, p.276.
25. The Emergency Powers Act was amended to give government the power to declare a state of emergency on the additional grounds of 'interference with the maintenance of any essential service' and external threats to the 'peace good order and good government of Rhodesia'.
26. Emergency Powers (Maintenance of Law and Order) Regulations 1966 RGN 71/66.
27. In addition a new section was introduced into the 1965 Constitution, ironically in Chapter 7 entitled the 'Declaration of Rights' which increased the power of the Minister to permit detention in the interests of 'defence'. This word was not defined and was severely criticised as being a guarantee against the protection of liberty, being frighteningly wide in its scope for arbitrariness. See Austin, 1968.

28. 1966 RLR 756 (GD); 1968 RLR 203 (AD).
29. Although living in dreadful conditions at times, Mugabe succeeded in obtaining three university degrees, including a law degree, during this period. These were in addition to the three university degrees he already held. For an insight into the conditions of detainees at this time see Niesewand, 1973, p.180 *et seq*.
30. See Nyagumbo, 1980, p.120 *et seq*. After independence he held several key ministerial posts including Minister of Mines and later Senior Minister of Political Affairs in the President's Office. In 1989 he was dismissed from the government for illegal dealings in motor vehicles following the report of the Sandura Commission. His tremendous sacrifices for the cause of freedom made his suicide, following his dismissal, all the more poignant.
31. Minister of Law and Order *Parliamentary Debates*, vol. 73, p.241. On these figures, Zimmerli states that 'It can be safely assumed that the vast majority of these were held without trial for more than three years': Zimmerli, 1971, p.265.
32. Secretary for Law and Order *Annual Report 1973*. This was the last report to make any mention of the scale of detentions.
33. *Political Prisoners in Rhodesia 1979*, Report of the International Defence and Aid Fund.
34. H. Ushewokunze in *Moto*, July 1983, vol.14, p.14.
35. Section 13. The exceptions specified in the section do not relate to security matters.
36. Reynolds J in *Allan v Minister of Home Affairs* 1985 (1) ZLR 339 at p.341.
37. *Makomberedze v Minister of State (Security)* [1987] LRC (Const) 504.
38. *Granger v Minister of State (Security)* 1985 (1) ZLR 153 at p.157. The problem of actually obtaining the damages from government is considered in Chapter 12.
39. Sections 17, 21 and 53 of the Emergency Powers (Maintenance of Law and Order) Regulations 1983.
40. An order could also be made against any person or class of persons who the Minister directed be removed from any area of the country. This power was utilised in operational areas where the security forces sought complete control of the local population.
41. The schedule and section 41 of the regulations both state that any person detained under a law providing for preventive detention and released from detention following a report of the review tribunal, shall not be re-detained for a period of one hundred and eighty days from his release on the same grounds as those on which he was originally detained. A person is deemed to be detained on the same grounds unless the review tribunal reports that in its opinion, there appear to be new and reasonable grounds for the detention.
42. *Minister of Home Affairs v Austin & Harper* 1986 (4) SA 281. See Chapter 7 for a full discussion on judicial review
43. The term 'police officer' is wide-ranging and includes any member of the Zimbabwe Republic Police, any member of the defence forces and any member of the Central Intelligence Organisation.
44. Under the Criminal Procedure and Evidence Act, any person arrested without warrant cannot be detained for more than forty-eight hours without being brought before a judge or magistrate (section 36). A person may be detained for a maximum of twelve hours for failure to furnish his full name and address if reasonably suspected of the commission of a crime (section 30). Cf section 72 of the Internal Security Act 1960 in Malaysia where in somewhat similar circumstances a person can be detained for a period of up to sixty days.
45. *R v Commissioner of Prisons ex parte Kamoji wa Wachira*, Unreported, High Court of Kenya Case 60/1984. Referred to by Mumma, 1988, at p. 454.
46. Section 44.
47. Section 49.
48. Section 60.
49. These are in the part of the regulations dealing solely with 'Detention and detained persons'.
50. A quasi-detention provision is found in section 106 of the Criminal Procedure and Evidence Act which permits the Minister of Home Affairs to prevent a court granting bail if to do so would be likely to prejudice public safety. For a full discussion see Chapter 9.
51. Amnesty International News Release AFR/46/36/85, 13 November 1985. Apparently most were subject to section 21 orders.
52. The figures were given in an interview with *Moto*, September 1989, vol.80, p.6.
53. See, for example, the statements of the Minister of Home Affairs in *Parliamentary Debates*, 5 July 1989 and 15 August 1989.
54. Minister of Home Affairs, *Parliamentary Debates*, 5 July 1989.
55. In fact there was considerable speculation that the real reason for detention was that his speeches advocating, amongst other things, diplomatic relations with Israel, earned him the displeasure of the government.
56. They were released shortly afterwards and both resumed their parliamentary seats.
57. *The Observer*, 10 March 1985
58. See Chapter 3.
59. See Chapter 12 for a full discussion of the trial.
60. 9 October 1983.
61. *Parliamentary Debates*, 19 January 1983. Also revealing is the Zambian case of *Mulwada* [1976] ZR 133 where a number of prosecution witnesses were detained by a police officer until they were prepared to give statements. The officer told the court: 'It was a most unusual case and required unusual methods of investigation. As a result I reluctantly concluded that some persons known to be involved should be detained without trial . . . I used the power . . . because if it was not used, the truth . . . would never have been ascertained' (at p.136).
62. It is arguable, applying the proximity test, that this was an instance where the situation might ultimately affect national security but at that stage the threat was too remote for the action to be legitimate.
63. Paweni was later tried but acquitted on 14 counts of fraud although in a later case involving one of Paweni's companies, the Supreme Court declared that the acquittal could not be reasonably entertained and that he should

have been convicted on all counts: *Attorney General v Paweni Trading Cooperative (Pvt) Ltd*, 1990 (1) ZLR 24 (SC).
64 *S v Haruperi*, Unreported, High Court of Zimbabwe HC-H-242-84. See also the Zambian case of *Banda (Joyce) v Attorney-General* [1969] ZR 210 where Justice Baron made a strong attack on the use of detention orders to facilitate criminal investigations. However in the later case of *Rao v Attorney-General* [1989] LRC (Const) 527 the Supreme Court of Zambia ruled that the detention of the applicant under the Preservation of Public Security Act on the grounds of suspected involvement in 'economic crimes' was *intra vires* the statute.
65 This is a point forcefully put by Vernon Mwaanga in his book *The Other Society: A Detainees Diary*, Lusaka, Fleetfoot, 1986, p. vii. Mwaanga was himself detained for some six months and his daily diary of his experiences in detention are a stark reminder of the acute problems faced by detainees and their families.
66 See, for example, Article 4 of the United Nations Basic Principles on the Independence of the Judiciary.
67 Minister of Home Affairs, *Parliamentary Debates*, 5 July 1989 and interview in *Moto* ,September 1989, vol.80, p.6.

7 Protecting the Rights of Detainees

The experiences of those held in detention without trial are often traumatic. There are frequently few legal protections available, whilst conditions in detention are nowhere pleasant and frequently atrocious. Torture, both mental and physical is common and some do not survive their indefinite ordeal. Detainees also suffer the same problems faced by convicted offenders, such as loss of employment and family breakdowns. All this without ever having been convicted of (or often even accused of) any offence.[1] If, as remains the case in many African countries, detention without trial is a fact of life, then it is vital that safeguards are provided which offer some practical protection to detainees. This chapter examines the question of the practical application of the legal rights for detainees in the Zimbabwean context.

Judicial Review

The Supreme Court has consistently reiterated that ministerial decision-making in this area remains subject to judicial review. As Chief Justice Dumbutshena stated in *PF–ZAPU v Minister of Justice*:[2]

> In my view, the arbitrary exercise by the executive of a prerogative, regardless of its effects on those who may be deprived of their rights and interests or who have legitimate expectations, is nowadays subject to judicial review. The reason for reviewing such executive action is that it would be unfair to deprive a citizen of his rights, interests or legitimate expectations without hearing what he has to say or to deny him the opportunity to find out whether the decision emanating from the exercise of an executive prerogative is legal or not, or, for that matter, irrational or unfair.

He continued:

> Once the President or the Executive exercises delegated powers embodied in a Statutory Instrument (or a Statutory Instrument, to borrow the phrase used by the learned judge *a quo*, 'made in exercise of State Executive powers') the courts, in the exercise of their judicial review powers, have a duty to test the validity of those Statutory Instruments if they have 'consequences on the private rights or legitimate expectations of other persons . . .' See *Council of Civil Service Unions v Minister for the Civil Service*.[3] Further, I am of the opinion that if the maker of the Statutory Instrument derives his power from a statute the courts can subject it to judicial review. . . The tests for condemning subordinate legislation laid down in *Kruse v Johnston*[4] by Lord Russell of Killowen LCJ have stood the test of time . . . More recently the House of

> Lords laid down the grounds upon which administrative actions are subject to judicial review. These grounds appeal to me not only because they were pronounced by an eminent Law Lord, but also [because] they make clear the wide extent of the theatre of operation in which courts can test the validity of prerogative actions.

The grounds for judicial review discussed by Lord Diplock in the *CCSU* case are 'illegality', 'irrationality' and 'procedural impropriety'.

By adopting this forthright approach, the courts in Zimbabwe have ensured that executive powers, and in particular those relating to security matters, are subject to review. For example, the Supreme Court has held that the fact that section 17 was phrased in subjective language did not give the minister unfettered discretion.[5] It agreed with the view taken in a West Indies case that:

> it impossible that a regulation could be properly construed as conferring distinct powers on the Governor; and that is what the regulations would purport to do if the words 'if the Governor is satisfied' means 'if the Governor thinks that *etc*'. No doubt Hitler thought that the measures – even the most atrocious measures – which he took were necessary and justifiable, but no reasonable man could think any such thing.[6]

Thus in the exercise of his/her discretion the Minister was required to consider objective facts when determining whether reasonable grounds justifying detention existed. This enabled a court to determine whether the detaining authority had acted fairly by considering whether the decision was illegal, irrational or procedurally incorrect. Similarly, the Supreme Court has held that the failure of the Minister to give adequate reasons for making a detention order together with his decision not to lay any further information before the court entitled it to infer that the decision was irrational.[7]

Interdict de Libero Homine Exhibendo

Another means of challenging a detention order is to apply for an *interdict de libero homine exhibendo*, which is the Roman–Dutch law equivalent of habeas corpus. This is a command by the court to the detaining authority to present the detainee in court so that it can review the legality of the arrest and continued detention. If, after examining the circumstances of the State's action the court finds the detention unlawful, it must order the release of the detainee. The Supreme Court has also ruled that the order is available if a court is concerned about the state of health and well-being of a detainee.[8] This ruling is potentially significant because, on the face of it, it greatly expands the scope of the order.[9] In practice, the order was used to secure the release of detainees and others held on security related charges. For example, in *Bull v Attorney-General*,[10] two men who were charged with contravening the Official Secrets Act, applied for what was 'in effect' an *interdict de libero homine exhibendo*. The court ruled that the detaining authority had the onus of establishing that a reasonable suspicion existed that the applicants had committed an offence. In view of the failure of the State to establish such suspicion, the court ordered the release of the men.

Constitutional Protections

Although the constitutional right to personal liberty does not apply to detainees, schedule 2(1) of the Constitution of Zimbabwe provides safeguards for persons who are detained under any law 'providing for' preventive detention. These are the rights (a) to be informed as soon as reasonably practicable after the commencement of the detention, and in any event not later than seven days thereafter, the reasons for his detention; and (b) to obtain and instruct without delay (but at his own expense) a legal representative of his choice and to hold communication with him.[11] In addition the case must be submitted to a review tribunal not more than thirty days (if this is during a period of public emergency) after the commencement of the detention. The tribunal must review the case 'forthwith' and thereafter at intervals of 180 days (if this is during a period of public emergency). The detainee or a legal representative of his choice may appear at the review.[12] Crucially, all the rights in the schedule are judicially protected from abrogation by executive action and this has enabled detainees on many occasions to enforce them in the courts.[13]

Are all detention orders subject to the second schedule safeguards? This point was raised following the detention of the York brothers under section 21 orders. Justice McNally, in the High Court, considered that there was a distinction between section 17 and 21 orders in that detention under the former was 'preventive' in the sense that the objective was to prevent the commission of offences or acts inimical to public safety or public order in the future. Preceding this came 'investigative' detention under section 21, whose object was to facilitate inquiries as to whether or not there were grounds for preventive detention. Accordingly, section 21 was a law *relating to* but not *providing for* preventive detention. The distinction was crucial because the protections in the schedule only apply to a person detained under any law *providing for* preventive detention. Thus a section 21 order was not covered by the schedule.[14] The decision was clearly intended to avoid a possible confrontation with the executive which appeared intent on keeping the men in detention[15] but even so the seemingly deliberate attempt to curtail the rights of detainees is insupportable. It is well established that where the words of a statute are clear and unambiguous, a court must give them their ordinary and natural meaning. But 'the primary meaning of a word varies with its setting or context and with the subject-matter to which it is applied, for reference to the abstract meaning of words, if there be any such thing, is of little value in interpreting statutes'.[16] Thus the meaning of a word or expression has one meaning in one context and a totally different one in another and as was said in a Zambian case 'however strongly the words themselves might suggest any particular meaning, the context might dictate another, which must prevail'.[17] It is essential that courts are alert to this point for the decision effectively meant that a person held under a section 21 order had no constitutional rights whatsoever. Already deprived of any protection in the Declaration of Rights, he was now faced with the loss of any protection under the schedule as well. It was surely not the intention of the framers of the constitution that individual rights should be subject to complete abrogation in this manner.[18] The decision also meant that a police officer could detain a person under a section 21 order, release him shortly before the expiry of the maximum thirty day period and immediately re-detain him without any need to submit the case to the review tribunal.[19]

Justice Blackie later re-considered the basis of a detention under section 21 and held that it was no less 'preventive' than a detention under section 17. He pointed out that under section 21 the police officer had the power to detain if he had reason to believe that there were grounds to justify a detention under that section. Once he had this belief, he could detain whether or not there was any need for further enquiries. The primary purpose of the detention remained the protection of public safety or public order even though further enquiries were necessary. Accordingly, section 21 was a law providing for preventive detention and the constitutional protections were thus operational. This was a result which accorded with both equity and common sense and heralded the demise of the earlier decision (although the Supreme Court never pronounced on the point). Section 53 was also a law 'providing for preventive detention' and the schedule protections thus applied.[20] The safeguards themselves are now examined.

Second Schedule Safeguards[21]

(i) Reasons for Detention

Informing a detainee of the reasons for his detention is important not least because it allows him/her to make representations to the review tribunal concerning the continued loss of liberty. The twin safeguards of obtaining reasons and making representations to such a body 'are the barest minimum which must be observed before an executive authority can be permitted to preventively detain a person and thereby drown his right of personal liberty in the name of public good and social security'.[22] What obligation does the detaining authority have? Clearly it is incumbent upon it to give sufficient information to enable a detainee to prepare his case and to make effective representations. However, what constitutes adequate reasons is contentious for the State is often anxious to disclose as little information as possible 'in the interests of security' or in order to protect its sources of information. In Zimbabwe, both the schedule and the regulations required the detaining authority to give the detainee the reasons for detention. What kind of information this entailed was considered by the High Court in 1984.[23] Sampson Paweni was served with a section 21 order alleging in general terms that he had engaged in 'acts of economic sabotage against the State and People of Zimbabwe' and further stating that 'It is considered that your activities pose a threat to the economic security of Zimbabwe.' It was argued that the reasons given were so vague as to fail to comply with the schedule. Several authorities from other jurisdictions were examined.

In an Indian case it was held that if the ground which is supplied is incapable of being understood or defined with sufficient certainty, it can be called vague.[24] Similarly in a later West Indies case, it was said that the grounds for detention 'must furnish sufficient information to enable the detained person to know what is being alleged against him and to bring his mind to bear upon it'.[25] These views were approved in the Zambian case of *Kapwepwe & Kaenga* where Justice Baron said that the 'detainee must be furnished with sufficient information to enable him to know what is being alleged against him and to make meaningful representation'.[26] Both the West Indies and Zambian legislation require that the reasons be given 'in detail'. This requirement is absent in the second schedule but even so the Zimbabwean courts adopted the Kapwepwe test. It is a pity that the second schedule is so imprecise on this point for the omission of the words 'in detail' reveals how vital it is that rights of detainees are stated as clearly and fully as possible in order to avoid any ambiguity or prejudice.

A classic example of the importance of the role of the courts in this area is the case of John Austin and Kenneth Harper. Here the reasons given for their detentions were conspicuous by their variety, ambiguity and vagueness. Justice Blackie neatly summarised the situation:

> (a) the applicants have had to make repeated approaches to the authorities and to the court for adequate reasons for their detention to be supplied to them; (b) such reasons as have been supplied have only been supplied at the last possible moment, often after the deadline set by the Court, and then, repeatedly, in inadequate form; (c) that when they were released from detention and placed on remand pending a prosecution under the Official Secrets Act, the State was unable to produce sufficient information to satisfy the Supreme Court that there was a reasonable suspicion that

> the applicants had committed the offence of which they were charged; (d) that no meaningful inquiries have ever been made of the applicants as to the matters in which it was alleged that they have participated; (e) that the State has never once produced a set of reasons for detention entirely consistent with those previously given. Some reasons overlap with the previously given reasons, but in no case are such reasons consistent; (f) that even today reasons supplied are inadequate and are not the reasons relied on at the time of their original detention.

As a result, both the High Court and Supreme Court rightly held that the reasons were not adequate.[27]

What constitutes sufficient information to make a 'meaningful representation' varies from case to case. It is suggested that the reasons must be (a) such as *prima facie* warrant detention; (b) sufficiently detailed to enable the detainees to make a meaningful representation to the tribunal; and (c) based upon information which is considered reliable.[28] This does not mean that it is never appropriate to place the evidence against the detainee before the court, for the distinction between the reasons and the evidence upon which they are based is not absolute. However, so long as the above criteria is satisfied, the court need look no further at that stage.[29] This is because the court is not concerned with the truthfulness of the reasons for the detention as this is the sole responsibility of the review tribunal. It is concerned with fairness to the detainee.[30] Thus in practice the detainee must receive the basic facts and material particulars which form the foundation or basis of the detention because together they form the grounds upon which the detention order is based.[31] For example, courts have held that adequate reasons were given when details of the date, time, place and material particulars of the alleged conduct of the detainee were provided.[32] The mere failure to give a specific date for an alleged act in the grounds for detention or to spell out the nature of the force planned against the State does not prevent a meaningful representation being made. Even so, there are cases in which a date is significant and a failure to inform the detainee of it might hinder the preparation of his defence. This is the more so when the detainee is alleged to have taken part in an illegal meeting for here the time and date is potentially of such crucial significance that it must be given to him.[33] Conversely, accusations of 'carrying on subversive propaganda' or describing a person as 'a man of desperate habits and dangerous character'[34]; alleging that a person is a 'South African espionage agent and a threat to the security of Zimbabwe'[35]; or alleging that the detainee was 'engaging in activities and utterances which are dangerous to the good Government of Kenya'[36] are too vague.

As only the grounds for detention are relevant at this stage, the detainee is not entitled to know the evidence or source of information upon which the allegations are based.[37] However, where possible the reasons must set out an assessment by the detaining body as to the reliability of the information upon which the detention is based with such particularity as is consistent with security.[38] Obviously, it is relevant to know that the reasons are not based simply upon, for example, allegations made in an anonymous letter, unsupported by any other evidence. It will fall to the judiciary to ensure adequate protection of detainees by critically examining in each case whether it is possible to make a meaningful representation in response to the allegations.

An interesting illustration of the manner in which the courts have insisted upon compliance with this safeguard in the face of pressure to uphold the validity of a detention order occurred in the case of *Austin & Harper* itself. The two men, who were senior customs officials, were arrested in February 1986 and served with section 21 orders. The High Court ordered their release because they were not given adequate reasons for their detention. They were immediately re-detained and again applied to the High Court for an order directing that they be given reasons for their detention. On 12 March the High Court was informed that the men were now under ordinary arrest with a view to charging them with a contravention of the Official Secrets Act. The following day they were remanded in custody by a magistrate, the Minister of Home Affairs having issued a certificate forbidding the granting of bail. They remained in custody until 2 April when the Supreme Court granted a habeas corpus application on the ground that the State had demonstrated no reasonable suspicion 'such as would make it lawful to deprive them of their liberty'. They were then freed but on 9 May they were served with another section 21 order which was followed by a section 17 order. Once again they were not supplied with adequate reasons for detention and on 24 July the Supreme Court ordered their release. However, later that day they were served with yet another section 21 order and on 18 July this was replaced by a section 17 order which was ruled valid. It was held that the orders set out adequate reasons in that they 'contain dates; they contain details of the information allegedly passed; they contain some particularity of the methods used; and they contain allegations which if considered reliable, could justify a decision by a reasonable Minister to order preventive detention of the appellants.' This concluded the legal moves and the men remained in detention until January 1988.[39]

(ii) Right to Review Forthwith

All cases submitted to the review tribunal must be reviewed 'forthwith'. The meaning of the word 'forthwith' varies according to its context. In cases where individual liberty is not involved it means 'within a reasonable time',[40] but in cases where the liberty of the individual is involved, some courts in other jurisdictions have interpreted it as requiring urgent action.[41] In the Rhodesian case of *R v West & Wild* a statutory provision stated that any person arrested without a warrant must be informed forthwith as to the cause of the arrest. Although no authority was cited, the word was held to mean 'as soon as possible in the circumstances'.[42] In *Hickman & McDonald v Minister of Home Affairs* Justice Pittman was content to follow the decision calling it a 'trite point of law'.[43] Here the detainees argued that a failure to review their case for thirty days constituted a breach of the second schedule. The State argued that the delay was reasonable due to the volume of cases for review coupled with the fact that members of the tribunal were part-time and the one suitable venue (the Harare magistrates' court) was only available to the tribunal once a week. The judge accepted that the non-availability of a suitable alternative venue constituted a reasonable excuse for the delay and held that as the case would be heard 'as soon as possible in the circumstances' there was no breach of the schedule. This was a disappointing decision for the convenience of the State was placed above the constitutional safeguards and no attempt was made to improve the situation. In a later case involving Dumiso Dabengwa,[44] the applicant was detained for 162 days without a review and applied for an order of release. Justice Pittman acknowledged that he himself now doubted the correctness of his previous decision. He accepted that he should have taken judicial notice of the numerous alternative venues for the tribunal such as police camps and police stations. Thus he held that the delay in hearing the case contravened the schedule and consequently the continued detention was unlawful. The Supreme Court upheld the decision with Justice Beck commenting forcefully upon the responsibility for compliance with the safeguards:

> Although different authorities are charged with the performance of the functions under the regulations and the Second Schedule . . . the reality is that it is the Executive which, acting through these authorities, is responsible for the observance of all safeguards attached to preventive detention and no matter where the

> responsibility may immediately lie for the failure to provide the means for ensuring reasonably prompt review, the duty in the final result rests on the Executive to take measures to remedy the situation.

As a result, the Minister of Home Affairs took the initiative and established a second review tribunal in Harare.[45]

The Dabengwa decision emphasises that the executive is responsible for upholding the rights of detainees. This means it has the duty to process detention cases as a matter of urgency and, in view of the importance of the review procedure, it is unfortunate that the constitution does not provide a specific time limit for review. Ideally a maximum period of perhaps thirty days is necessary, as is already the case in other jurisdictions such as Zambia and Uganda.[46]

(iii) Referral of Cases to a Review Tribunal

It is common in anglophonic Africa for detentions to be reviewed by a tribunal. In 1959 such a tribunal was established in Rhodesia to review all detention cases and to make recommendations as to the necessity or expediency of continuing such detentions. From 1965 onwards, a detainee had the right to have his case reviewed once every twelve months. Originally, the Minister issuing the order was obliged to act in accordance with any recommendation of the tribunal but this was altered in the republican constitution by the imposition of a presidential veto on any such release. In practice, the tribunal was of little practical assistance to detainees and, as one former detainee notes, 'the proceedings were a travesty of justice. I appeared before such a tribunal in 1969. The secret police submitted to the tribunal a thick file containing more than 100 allegations against me; yet all that was required of me was to say yes or no to each. The police did not produce their informers and there was no one to cross-examine.'[47]

After independence, the review tribunal continued to operate up to 1990.[48] Its function was to establish the truth of the allegations against detainees by investigating and evaluating the factual basis for the detention.[49] This represented the only 'independent' review of the necessity for the detention. It then made a recommendation to the Minister of Home Affairs as to the necessity or expediency of continuing the detention. Where the Minister, having regard to the 'paramount necessity of preserving public safety and public order in Zimbabwe' considered that the recommendation should not be followed, he referred the matter to the President. He/she then made a decision as to whether or not to follow the recommendation of the tribunal and the Minister was bound to comply with the decision. If an order was made not to act in accordance with the recommendation, a notice to this effect was to be published in the Government *Gazette*. On several occasions prior to 1990, the recommendations of the tribunal were not accepted and notices to this effect were published. The majority of such cases involved persons allegedly working for South Africa.[50] Thus, for example, Jack Lewis-Walker, a former senior civil servant, was detained on suspicion of spying for South Africa. On three separate occasions the review tribunal recommended his release but he remained in detention for more than five years.

The tribunal was made up of three persons with the chairman and one other member having legal qualifications.[51] In an attempt to give some appearance of independence, each member was appointed by the President acting on the advice of the Judicial Service Commission. In practice, the chairman was usually a practising lawyer whilst the other members were normally either legal academics or officials from the Ministry of Justice. Proceedings of the review tribunal were held in camera and were never published. All cases were required to be heard on a strictly rota basis unless the tribunal or the Minister otherwise directed. In practice it appears that the rota was adhered to and it was made clear that a court would not order a case to be given priority merely because of a delay in bringing it before the tribunal as this would be 'administering the law of the jungle – survival of the fittest'.[52] Each case was presented by a senior State counsel, normally with the aid of documentary evidence only.[53] A detainee was entitled to appear in person or be represented by a legal practitioner of his own choice and at his own expense. In practice the vast majority of detainees were unable to afford a lawyer although help was given by various lawyers on an *ad hoc* basis. A detainee could call witnesses to support his case or give evidence on his own behalf although in this case the State had the right to cross-examine him on oath. He (or his legal representative) could also address the tribunal.[54]

The tribunal was not a 'court' in that it was not bound by the rules of evidence or procedure which are applicable to other legal proceedings.[55] However it was required to consider any report submitted to it by the Minister of Home Affairs, the Director-General of the Central Intelligence Organisation or the Commissioner of Police.[56] The weight attached to any such report was entirely up to the tribunal although it probably had a strong influence on the final recommendation. The State bore the burden of proving, on a balance of probabilities, that there was a case against the detainee.[57] Being a body exercising a quasi-judicial function, the tribunal had a duty to act fairly such that, subject to one possible exception, a detainee was entitled to full disclosure of the evidence and to have an opportunity of answering any prejudicial aspects.[58] As there was no formal procedure and because membership of the tribunal varied from time to time, members were entitled to have access to the records of previous tribunal hearings or to obtain information from any other source.[59] One practical problem was that because no rules of practice were ever developed, the procedure of the tribunal varied thus causing confusion for all concerned and was potentially unfair to detainees.[60] The operations of the tribunal raised one controversial question i.e. whether a detainee was entitled to have access to all the information adduced by the State. The problem here is that disclosure to him of the means by which the information was obtained including, for example, the names of informants, or the contents of security documents, might be extremely prejudicial to the State and its informants. Section 31(3) of the regulations protected these interests by enabling the Minister to certify that by reason of the public interest the evidence of any particular witness or the contents of any report should be given to the tribunal in the absence of the detainee or his legal representative. The chairman then had a discretion as to whether or not to make such an order. The validity of the section was questioned in the Supreme Court on the grounds that although section 18(12) of the Constitution permits the holding of a case in camera, it makes no provision for withholding evidence from the accused or detained person.[61] The court rightly rejected this argument because section 18(12) only applies to cases which come before a court of law or other adjudicating body established for determining the existence of civil rights and obligations.[62] This excluded the review tribunal and accordingly, section 31(3) was held *intra vires* the Constitution. Even so, the Supreme Court recognised that although the needs of national security may well result in the denial of crucial information to a detainee 'there is a correspondingly greater duty on the Tribunal to carry out the sort of searching investigation which the detainees or their legal representatives would have done had they had access to the document'. This included being satisfied as to the genuineness of the document and on its reliability.[63] It also noted that within the confines of the need to protect national security, detainees could rely on the rules of natural justice, and in particular the right to a fair hearing free from bias. All that was required to establish bias was to leave the detainee with the impression that the tribunal was biased against him and in favour of the State.

In most anglophonic African countries the role of such tribunals is unclear for they only have the power to recommend release. As the case of Zimbabwe illustrates, this means that although they are required to investigate the truth of the allegations against detainees, in practice they can offer them little real protection and are essentially 'toothless watch-dogs'. To be a true independent 'check' on detentions a power to order release is needed. The existence of such a mandatory release system is not unknown. For example, the Namibian Constitution of 1990 provides that the Advisory Board 'shall order the release [of detainees] if it is satisfied that it is not necessary for the purposes of the emergency to continue the detention of such persons.'[64] A similar approach was adopted for the Constitution of Zambia 1991.[65] This is undoubtedly the right approach and should form the model for other African nations.

(iv) Right to Legal Representation

The right to legal representation is rightly protected in the vast majority of constitutional documents worldwide, for every accused and detained person is entitled to know their rights and be able to deal with the case against them. International human rights documents also firmly uphold the right which also has the full support of the International Commission of Jurists.[66] As the Commission rightly notes, the only known justification for suspending the right is the fear that a legal representative may smuggle contraband to his client or carry messages which could represent a danger to security. Indeed it has been argued that the legal representative of a detainee 'may unwittingly cause harm, however properly he acts, simply because people will be able to draw conclusions from what he does and who he sees after interviewing the detainees'.[67] Such arguments are only valid, if at all, in the most exceptional circumstances and cannot be used to undermine the operation of such a fundamental right. Constant vigilance by the courts is necessary to ensure that this safeguard is fully respected.[68] This is well illustrated by the case of Sampson Paweni. Whilst in detention, Paweni was denied access to his legal representatives by CIO officers and applied for an order to permit him to meet his legal representatives in private.[69] Justice Smith in the High Court strongly criticised the action of the detaining authorities pointing out that:

> CIO officers are apparently still denying detained persons one of the rights, and a most important one at that, conferred on them by the Constitution ... It is inconceivable that the existence of this right is not known to CIO officers of any standing. This court takes a very serious view of such flouting of the provisions of the Constitution by CIO officers. Counsel conceded that the CIO officers had acted improperly in denying [Paweni] the right to consult his legal representative in private. He said that if [Paweni] had applied for a mandamus to secure his right the State would not have opposed it. I fail to understand however, why it should be necessary for a detained person to apply to court . . . before he can exercise the rights which are conferred upon him by the Constitution.[70]

The court accordingly ordered that Paweni be permitted to hold private communication with his legal practitioner. It is disturbing to note the attitude of the security officials towards the rights of the detainee. Access to legal representation is a fundamental right and thus it is essential that detaining authorities fully respect it.

Consequences for Breach of Constitutional Safeguards

As it is generally accepted that the constitutional safeguards are mandatory rather than directory,[71] the main issue now concerns the consequences attaching to a breach of one of the safeguards. It is clear that where a detention order is itself unlawful, the detention is invalid and inevitably results in an order for release. This covers the situation where, for example, the maker of the detention order had no reasonable grounds for ordering the detention or the order itself was in the wrong form. In Zimbabwe, a section 21 detention order was ruled invalid where the police officer making the arrest was merely obeying orders and did not 'himself have reason to believe there were grounds for detention' as required by the section.[72]

The problem area concerns the situation where a detention order is validly made but later one of the constitutional safeguards is contravened. In Zimbabwe, the debate originated in another case involving the York brothers.[73] Here the Minister of Home Affairs failed to submit their case to the review tribunal within the required thirty-day period. The High Court ordered their release holding that the orders were void as the failure to submit went to the root of the detention. In a well reasoned judgment the court followed a West Indies decision where a detention order was held invalid as:

> [to] hold otherwise it would have to be maintained that the order of the Minister can override a provision of the Constitution with which it conflicts. That cannot be for the Constitution is the highest legal authority we know.[74]

This recognised the validity of the 'supremacy of the constitution' principle which is that the failure of the executive to comply with a constitutional safeguard renders the detention unlawful and leads inexorably to an order of release. The Supreme Court in the York case[75] merely upheld the High Court decision but crucially did not analyze the supremacy principle and so the matter was not fully considered until another decision involving Dumiso Dabengwa.[76] Here the High Court again ruled that the failure to submit his case to the review tribunal rendered the detention invalid. The prospect of releasing such an important figure as Dabengwa was unacceptable to government and the Minister appealed to the Supreme Court. The court rejected the supremacy argument because:

> the violation of a safeguard relating to continued detention subsequent to the making of an order would not *without more*, invalidate the detention, but must, initially be remedied by way of an order to ensure that the safeguard in question is afforded to the detainee.[77] [my emphasis].

The judgment was based on several authorities, the earliest being the English case of *Greene v Secretary of State for Home Affairs*[78] where the failure to give reasons for detention was held not to invalidate a detention order. The court also approved very similar decisions from the West Indies and Ireland.[79] In none of the cases was any authority cited for the proposition. An attempt to explain the basis for such an approach was made in the Ugandan case of *Matovu* where it was held, using a contractual analogy, that procedural defects amounted to a condition subsequent and were curable by the appropriate detaining authority.[80] The Supreme Court also noted that as a result of the failure of the court in the York case to hear argument or to specifically determine the point, it could not be asserted that it had specifically decided that failure to submit the case to the tribunal invalidated the detention order. Accordingly the order for release was overturned and as the case was due for review, no other order was made.

The decision failed to consider both the vital policy considerations raised and the strong authorities against the holding. The point was forcefully made in *Dale's* case[81] where Lord Justice Brett stated:

> I take it to be a general rule that the courts . . . will not allow any individual in this kingdom to procure the imprisonment of another unless he takes care to follow with

> extreme precision every form and every step in the process which is to procure that imprisonment.

It is regrettable that the Supreme Court chose not only to rely on Greene but also to make no more than a passing reference to the important Zambian case of *Chipango v Attorney-General*[82] where the supremacy of the Constitution argument was upheld. Here the failure to furnish grounds for detention within the specified period was held to invalidate a detention despite being given only two days after the required period. In the High Court, Justice Magus applied *Dale's* case and stated that there was a breach of 'constitutional conditions subsequent to arrest' which were all mandatory and fundamental rights of the individual. He rejected the approach in *Matovu* on the basis that constitutional rights are of a totally different nature to contractual rights. On appeal to the Court of Appeal, Chief Justice Doyle, having referred to the fact that the breach went to the root of the detention, held that such constitutional safeguards were:

> introduced to provide for the protection of the rights and freedoms [of the people of Zambia] and where possible [the Constitution] should be interpreted effectively to protect the right and freedoms. That the protection given is a limited protection is no reason for cutting down what is given.[83]

He maintained that the principle must be adhered to strictly and accordingly dismissed the appeal.

The supremacy argument so forcefully upheld in *Chipango* is surely correct and the failure of the Supreme Court in *Dabengwa* to consider it was a serious omission. The immense power of the executive during a state of emergency cannot be allowed to erode the already limited rights of detainees and it is the duty of the courts to protect those rights fully. This includes ensuring that those vested with executive authority 'follow with extreme precision every form and every step' of the detention process.[84] Of course a contrary argument is that the nation is put at risk if courts order the release of persons who represent a threat to national security merely because of an administrative error by the detaining authorities. It is further asserted that as no court or tribunal has considered the validity of the grounds for the detention, the question of release must remain the prerogative of the detaining authority. It is certainly true that courts do not have all the relevant information concerning the reasons for detention. Nevertheless, the rule of law requires that major procedural defects[85] must lead inexorably to an order of release, for the courts cannot condone negligence and ineptitude.[86]

Overview

In the case of Zimbabwe there are several positive features as regards the protection of detainees. Firstly, the power of the courts to review the validity of detentions meant that the rights of detainees were consistently open to judicial scrutiny. Secondly, the second schedule safeguards ensured that detainees enjoyed some basic rights. In addition, the courts generally resisted government efforts to cut these down and continued to interpret them realistically thus helping to enhance their practical value.

A United Nations study has revealed that many countries continue to utilise procedures which circumvent safeguards for detainees.[87] In this respect, Zimbabwe is no exception and the earlier discussion has highlighted some important lessons which must be learned, namely: (i) clear and unambiguous drafting of safeguards for detainees is required in order to eliminate, as far as possible, vague terminology such as 'review forthwith'. Ideally, specific time limits for compliance with the safeguards should be laid down; (ii) the exact role and operation of detainees review tribunals must be specified and a power to order release included. It is quite improper to continue a detention which the tribunal has deemed unsubstantiated; (iii) the most effective approach to ensuring compliance with the constitutional safeguards is for the courts to adopt the 'supremacy of the Constitution' approach, i.e. a failure to comply with any of the safeguards renders the detention **invalid** and leads inexorably to an order of release; (iv) all detainees must have the right of access to a lawyer of their own choice who is paid for by the State. It is quite unacceptable for the application of this right to depend wholly upon the financial resources of the detainee; (v) one of the most insidious activities by any government is the secret arrest and detention of individuals. It is in these situations that abuses of human rights most frequently occur. It is thus essential that detaining authorities are required to publish the names of all detainees within a specified period (perhaps seven days) and to disclose details of their whereabouts to their families and lawyers within a limited period (perhaps twenty-four hours); (vi) the practice of issuing a fresh detention order as soon as the previous one has expired or has been annulled by a court is improper and encourages the detaining authority to be less scrupulous over a decision to issue a detention order.

The adoption of and adherence to these principles by African States will surely lead to much greater practical protection for detainees.

Notes

1. For a graphic account of such problems in a Zambian setting see Mwaanga, 1986.
2. [1985] 1 ZLR 305 at p.326.
3. [1984] 3 All ER 935, at p.950.
4. [1898] 2 QB 91.
5. *Minister of Home Affairs v Austin & Harper*, 1986 (1) ZLR 240; 1986 (4) SA 281; [1986] LRC (Const) 567.
6. *Attorney-General of St Christopher, Nevis and Anguilla v Reynolds* [1980] AC 637 at p.656 *per* Lord Salmon. For similar views see the South African case of *Hurley v Minister of Law and Order* 1985 (4) SA 709 and the Nigerian case of *Stitch v Attorney-General of the Federation* (1986) 5 NWLR (Part 46) 1007. For a useful overview of similar developments in Nigeria, see Agbakoba and Fagbohunlu, 1991, pp.63–72.
7. *Minister of Home Affairs v Austin & Harper* above, at pp. 245 and 285. See also *Mutambara v Minister of Home Affairs*, 1989 (3) ZLR 96, where a ministerial certificate made under section 106 CPEA denying bail to the applicant was ruled invalid on the ground that there was no evidence as to why the applicant posed a threat to public safety. As there were no indicators justifying such a conclusion, the decision was held to be irrational.
8. *S v Van Wyk*, Unreported, Supreme Court of Zimbabwe SC 101/86.
9. There have been no cases on the point since the Supreme Court decision in 1989.
10. *Bull v Attorney-General* 1986 (1) ZLR 117; [1987] LRC (Const) 509. See a discussion of the case by Feltoe and Lewin, 1987, pp.29–30.
11. Schedule 2 para 2(1)(a) Constitution of Zimbabwe.
12. Schedule 2 para 2(1)(a) and (b) Constitution of Zimbabwe.
13. *Dabengwa & Masuku v Minister of Home Affairs* 1982 (1) ZLR 223; 1982 (4) SA 301 (SC).
14. *York v Minister of Home Affairs*, Unreported, High Court of Zimbabwe HC-H-264-82.
15. A confidential source closely involved in the case informed the author that the decision was taken 'in order to take the pressure off government'.
16. Edgar, 1971, pp.65–6.
17. See Justice Baron in *Sinkamba v Doyle (Chief Justice)* Unreported, Court of Appeal for Zambia Judgment No 16 of 1972. Here 'context' is used in the sense ascribed to it by Viscount Simonds in *Attorney-General v H R H Prince Augustus* [1957] 1 All ER 49. It includes 'not only other enacting provisions of the same statute, but its preamble, the existing state of the law, other statutes *in pari materia* and the mischief which I can, by those and other legitimate means, discern that the statute was intended to remedy' at p.53.
18. The proportionality principle could also be applied here so as to protect the constitutional right.
19. *Bull v Minister of State (Security)* (above). See also *Moyo v Minister of Home Affairs*, Unreported, High Court of Zimbabwe HC-H-478-83.
20. *Moyo v Minister of Home Affairs*, above.
21. See generally Hatchard, 1985, p.38.
22. Justice Bhagwati in *Khudram Das v State of West Bengal* (1975) 2 SCR 832, p.838 (Supreme Court of India).

23. *Paweni v Minister of State (Security)* [1985] LRC (Const) 612.
24. See, for example, the judgment of Chief Justice Kania in *State of Bombay v Atman Ram Vaidya* AIR [1951] SC 157.
25. Chief Justice Lewis in *Herbert v Phillips & Sealy* (1967) 19 WIR 435, at p.452.
26. [1972] ZR 248, at p.262.
27. *Austin & Harper v Minister of State (Security)*, 1986 (2) ZLR 28.
28. *Austin & Harper v Minister of State (Security)*, above.
29. *Austin & Harper v Minister of State (Security)*, above. See also *R v Secretary of State for the Home Department* [1977] 3 All ER 452; *R v Gaming Board* [1970] 2 All ER 528, at p.533 and *Bishop v Road Service Board* 1956 R & N 23.
30. See *Evans & Hartlebury v Chairman of the Review Tribunal*, Unreported, High Court of Zimbabwe HC-H-131-86. The various statutory and moral requirements directing the methods and procedures that the tribunal should adopt are all embraced by this simple term: *Barlin v Licensing Court of the Cape* 1924 AD 472; *Maxwell v Department of Trade and Industry* [1974] QB 523 at p.539 and *Crow v Detained Mental Patients Special Board* 1985 (4) SA 83.
31. *Minister of Home Affairs v Austin & Harper* above. See also the Indian case of *State of Punjab v Talwandi* [1985] LRC (Const) 600 where Chief Justice Chandrachud stated: 'His right is to receive every material particular without which a full and effective representation cannot be made. If the order of detention refers to or relies upon any document, statement or other material, copies thereof have, of course, to be supplied to the detenue as held by this court in *Ichhu Devi Choraria v Union of India* (1981) 1 SCR 640 at p.650'.
32. *State of Punjab v Talwandi*, above.
33. Example given by Chief Justice Dumbutshena in *Austin & Harper v Chairman of the Detainees Review Tribunal*, 1988 (1) ZLR 21; [1988] LRC (Const) 532. See also *Puta v Attorney-General*, Unreported, Supreme Court of Zambia 25/83 and *Musakanya v Attorney General* Unreported, Supreme Court of Zambia 35/80.
34. *State of Bombay v Atma Ram Vaidya* AIR [1951] SC 157; *Sasthi v State of WBA* [1974] SCR 525. The concept of an alibi is essentially separate and distinct from that of vagueness and is capable of succeeding even where a ground is free from vagueness. *Chisata and Lombe v Attorney-General*, Unreported, Supreme Court of Zambia 6/81.
35. *Minister of Home Affairs v Austin & Harper*, above.
36. *Republic of Kenya v Commissioner of Prisons ex parte Wachira* [1985] LRC (Const) 624.
37. *State of Punjab v Talwandi*, above. It appears that the detaining authority need not supply the detainee with the name of its informant: *Minister of Home Affairs v Austin & Harper*, above.
38. *Minister of Home Affairs v Austin & Harper*, above.
39. They were never brought to trial.
40. See, for example, *Hudson v Hill* (1874) 43 LJCP 273; *R v Ely JJ* (1855) 5 E & B 489.
41. For example, in the English case of *Lowe v Fox* 15 QBD 667 the word was held to mean 'at once'. In the Australian cases of *Drymalik v Feldman* [1966] SASR 231 and *Adams v Rogers* [1907] VLR 245 the holding of a person in custody for three hours without charge was held to breach the statutory duty to bring him before a magistrate 'forthwith'.
42. 1953 (2) SA 675.
43. *Hickman & McDonald v Minister of Home Affairs* 1983 (2) ZLR 180.
44. *Dabengwa v Minister of Home Affairs* 1984 (2) SA 345; [1985] LRC (Const) 581.
45. The two bodies held hearings alternatively on Tuesdays and Fridays at the Magistrates' Court in Harare.
46. In Zambia a case must be reviewed not more than one month after the commencement of the detention: see Preservation of Public Security Regulations, section 33(8). In Uganda written reasons must be given to a detainee within twenty eight days: see Public Order and Security Act 1967, section 23.
47. Zvogbo, 1976, p.38. Feltoe refers to the tribunal as 'little more than a rubber stamp agency for Ministerial action'. Feltoe, 1983, p.29. Niesewand, himself detained by the Smith regime, describes the work of the tribunal as one where 'no allegations are made, no evidence presented, no witnesses questioned. The tribunal is not precluded from relying on rumour or hearsay. It need not even see the detainee himself, but it usually agrees to do so as a matter of form. The Government is understandably modest about the workings of this impartial body, and there is a penalty of five years imprisonment for anyone talking about it.' Niesewand, 1973, p.181.
48. As detention without trial is currently no longer practised, the tribunal is no longer operating. However as it is possible to re-introduce preventive detention without the need for a declared state of emergency, the operation of the tribunal remains important.
49. See Chief Justice Dumbutshena in *Austin & Harper v Chairman of the Detainees Review Tribunal*, above, at p.30.
50. Section 40 Emergency Powers (Maintenance of Law and Order) Regulations 1983. Of course, there was no public disclosure of the matter until a notice appeared in the *Gazette*. It is thus impossible to know whether or not recommendations of the tribunal were queried by the Minister. There was also no sanction for failure to comply with the publication requirements so that it is possible that some recommendations were overturned without public knowledge.
51. Schedule 2 para 2(4) and section 27 of the regulations. The chairman was appointed by the President acting on the advice of the Judicial Service Commission and had to be a person who was or had been a judge of the Supreme Court or the High Court or qualified to be appointed as such. The two other persons were appointed by the President acting on the advice of the Judicial Service Commission, one of whom must have held judicial office or have been qualified to practise as a legal practitioner in Zimbabwe for not less than seven years. The Ombudsman also served as chairman, the Ombudsman Act 1982 being amended by regulation to include this provision. This was later incorporated into section 70 of the 1983 regulations.
52. See *Paweni v Chairman, Detention Review Tribunal*, Unreported, High Court of Zimbabwe HC-H-293-84.
53. Section 32 of the regulations required the Minister to appoint a person to represent him who may lead evidence, examine witnesses and address the tribunal.
54. Section 33(1) of the regulations.

55. Section 31(4) of the regulations.
56. Section 31(5) of the regulations.
57. Because detention cases involve grave issues of personal liberty, the degree of probability is higher than in other cases: see *Austin & Harper v Chairman of the Detainees Review Tribunal* above, p.31.
58. *Evans & Hartlebury v Chairman of the Review Tribunal* above, p.7. See also *Minister of the Interior v Bechler* 1948 (3) SA 409 at p.451; *Board of Education v Rice* [1911] AC 179 at p.182 and *Huyser v Louw* 1955 (2) SA 321.
59. See Rose Innes, 1963, p.163 and Baxter, 1984, p.550 *et seq*.
60. In interviews carried out by the author, two members of the tribunal complained about the lack of guidelines in their deliberations and indicated that this handicapped them in their analysis of individual cases.
61. This is based on the argument that section 18 is not subject to abrogation or derogation even during a period of public emergency.
62. Section 18(9), Constitution of Zimbabwe. This point was accepted by the Supreme Court in *Austin & Harper v Chairman of the Detainees Review Tribunal*, above, p.23.
63. Above, at p.43. The court also noted that there is an added duty on the tribunal to make it clear to the detainee that the reasons for detention were based on the contents of a secret document.
64. Article 24(2)(c). For a discussion on the detention provisions in the Namibian Constitution see Hatchard and Slinn, 1990, at p.156. Whilst the power to order release might well receive a hostile reception from governments, this could be overcome if tribunals were required to recommend release on two consecutive occasions before compelling compliance with the order.
65. Article 27(2), Constitution of Zambia 1991.
66. See the study prepared by the International Commission of Jurists, *States of Emergency*, above.
67. By the prosecution in *Dabengwa & Masuku v Minister of Home Affairs*, Unreported, High Court of Zimbabwe HC-H-160-82 at p.3.
68. A detailed examination of the constitutional right to legal representation is found in Chapter 9.
69. *Paweni v Minister of State (Security)* [1985] LRC (Const) 612.
70. At p.622.
71. See *York v Minister of Home Affairs*, Unreported, High Court of Zimbabwe HC-H-218-82 at p.16.
72. *Holland v Commissioner of the Zimbabwe Republic Police* 1982 (2) ZLR 29. A similar conclusion was reached in *Moll v Commissioner of the Zimbabwe Republic Police*, Unreported, High Court of Zimbabwe HC-B-46-83.
73. *York v Minister of Home Affairs*, Unreported, High Court of Zimbabwe HC-H-218-82.
74. *per* Malone J in *Kelshall v Munroe* (1971) 19 WIR 136 at p.146.
75. *York v Minister of Home Affairs* 1982 (4) SA 496 (ZS).
76. *Dabengwa v Minister of Home Affairs* 1984 (2) SA 345; [1985] LRC (Const) 581.
77. At p.596.
78. [1941] 3 All ER 388.
79. In *O'Laighleis* [1969] IR 93 and *R v Attorney-General & Brigadier Green, ex parte Olivia Grange & Eric Brown* (1976) 23 WIR 136. The name of the applicant and citation are incorrectly given in the judgment.
80. *Uganda v Commissioner of Prisons ex parte Matovu* [1966] EA 514. This view was also adopted by the High Court of Kenya in *Republic of Kenya v Commissioner of Prisons ex parte Wachira* [1985] LRC (Const) 624.
81. (1881) 6 QBD 376, at p.463.
82. [1970] ZR 31 (HC) and [1971] ZR 1 (SC).
83. Above, at p.7.
84. Support for this view is found in the judgment of Justice Malone in *Kelshall v Munroe* above, where he stated: '. . . in construing an emergency it is necessary to ensure that there has been strict compliance with the terms of the enactment and that the enactment conforms to the Constitution' (at p.140).
85. It may be that not all procedural defects will inexorably lead to release. See Chief Justice Doyle in *Chipango* and Chief Justice Silungwe in *Attorney General v Juma* [1985] LRC (Const) 635, at p.640.
86. See Justice Dumbutshena in *York v Minister of Home Affairs* above, and *Hdhibandhu Das v District Magistrate of Cuttack* [1969] AIR SC 63.
87. *The Administration of Justice and the Human Rights of Detainees: Report on the Practice of Administrative Detention*, United Nations Economic and Social Council document E/CN.4/Sub.2/1989/27, p.18.

8 Protection from Torture & Right to Life

Protection from Torture and Inhuman Treatment

Introduction

'Torture' means 'any act by which severe pain or suffering, whether physical or mental, is intentionally inflicted on a person for such purposes as obtaining from him or a third person information or a confession, punishing him for an act he or a third party has committed or is suspected of having committed, or intimidating or coercing him, when such pain or suffering is inflicted by or at the instigation of or with the consent of a public official or other person acting in an official capacity.'[1] International human rights documents, including the African Charter, absolutely prohibit the use of torture and inhuman punishment.[2] Nevertheless, experience shows that torture remains a common phenomenon in Africa, with governments of all political persuasions resorting to its use. Regrettably, torture and the like is often practised against those detained without trial. For example, it is reported that in Zaire detainees are often beaten, tortured or forced to live in appallingly crowded conditions, whilst in South Africa research has shown that in the 1980s, 83 per cent of detainees were tortured.[3] Similarly, an Amnesty International report on Uganda gives graphic accounts of widespread systematic torture and extra-judicial killing of detainees by soldiers of both the Obote and Okello regimes.[4] Allegations of torture against the detainees in both Kenya and Malawi have also occurred.[5] In Ghana during the Nkrumah regime, many detainees were held in conditions of severity far worse than those laid down by law for convicted prisoners. There were no minimum safeguards for detainees, the Minister was under no obligation to communicate the grounds for detention, and there was no provision for any review of the detention by any other person or body.[6] During the UDI period in Rhodesia, the use of torture against nationalists was common and many members of the present government were themselves subjected to brutal treatment at the hands of Special Branch officers and the police. As Zvogbo notes 'At Alexander Mashawira's inquest in 1965, the Salisbury magistrate confessed that the method of torture used in the prison cells was so sophisticated that it reminded him of Nazi Germany'.[7]

In Zimbabwe the use of torture, inhuman or degrading punishment or other such treatment is absolutely prohibited and is never liable to derogation or abrogation.[8] As regards the meaning of 'inhuman or degrading punishment', the emphasis is 'not upon punishment *per se* but upon punishment . . . which is either brutal, unfeeling, barbarous or which results in the lowering in rank, position, reputation or character'.[9] Thus the provision does not apply to the question of whether a particular sentence is an 'unfair' punishment.[10] The lessons which can be learned from the experience of Zimbabwe can now be examined.

The Incidence of Torture in Zimbabwe

Following independence, allegations of the use of torture and other inhuman treatment by members of the Zimbabwean security forces were frequently made by human rights organisations. In 1982–3, for instance, it was alleged that the crack Fifth Brigade, a predominantly Shona speaking force trained by North Korea, were responsible for many attacks on civilians in Matabeleland. Indeed the Roman Catholic Bishops' Conference accused the security forces of committing atrocities and of maiming 'hundreds and hundreds of people who were neither dissidents nor collaborators' during anti-insurgency operations which started in January 1983.[11] Similar allegations were made by the Catholic Commission for Justice and Peace based in Harare.[12] It was further alleged that some killings attributed to dissidents were in fact the work of the security forces.[13] Amnesty International also highlighted serious human rights abuses in the country, maintaining that in 1985 hundreds of people were arrested for political reasons in Matabeleland and that many were tortured. These allegations were consistently and categorically denied by Government.[14] The United States 'Country Reports' for 1985 further stated that torture was routine in a few government facilities, particularly during interrogation of suspected dissidents and dissident sympathisers. The report also asserted that the police, the CIO and the army were all responsible for human rights violations.[15]

Whilst the scale of such activities will never be known, individual incidents are well documented by court reports. The first area for discussion is the use of torture against detainees. Two illustrative cases are the Beit Bridge 5 and the Air Force 6. In the former, the affair started on 8 November 1984 with the gunning down of a prominent ZANU(PF) supporter, Senator Moven Ndhlovu outside his home in Beit Bridge. His murder further exacerbated an already tense political climate caused by inter-party rivalry. Following the shooting, a para-military unit and members of the ZANU(PF) Youth Wing started to round up PF–ZAPU members in the area and beat them up. Five men were detained in connection with the killing. One was Enos Tshili who was the District Secretary of PF–ZAPU and a member of the local town council. He was also a local store owner. On 9 November his store and its contents were destroyed by an angry mob and fearing for his life, he sought refuge in the local police station. He was detained there until 15 November although he was never told the reasons for this action. He was then questioned by members of the CID about the whereabouts of 'the guns', an apparent reference to the murder weapons. What happened next was graphically set out by Justice Korsah in the High Court at the trial of the five men for the murder of Senator Ndhlovu:

> [Tshili] testified that he was in leg irons and his hands were handcuffed behind him. He was made to sit on the floor. Munyengetero was the first to beat him with a sjambok, but Mike and Shoko also took turns in assaulting him with the sjambok. Other articles used in assaulting [Tshili] were a fan-belt and a donkey harness made from a conveyor belt with the rubber peeled off. The donkey harness had a metal ring at one end. After a time Musarurwa brought water in a fire bucket. [Tshili] was forced to get into a kneeling position and his head was held down in the bucket . . . After that Musarurwa took a kit bag made out of some tarpaulin material, half filled it with water and forced the head of [Tshili] into the bag and secured it around his neck to stop the water from escaping. This was repeated several times. And each time he gulped for air. After some time they removed the bag and [Tshili] vomited water through his mouth and nostrils. Musarurwa then took a white towel, immersed it in the bucket of water and blindfolded [Tshili] in such a way that every time he took a breath he breathed in droplets of water. He then felt terminals being attached

> to his toes, but he could not see who was doing this. He heard a cranking sound and simultaneously felt electric shocks pass through him.[16]

Between then and 23 November Tshili was subjected to further torture. A police officer, Inspector Mutarah, threatened to hand him back to the CID for further punishment if he did not sign a confession. Tshili signed an implicatory statement and a few days later was taken to the Beit Bridge Magistrates Court to have it confirmed. The magistrate refused to do so after having observed that the accused was in intense pain and seen the fresh injuries on his back which consisted of weals and linear cuts. He ordered that Tshili be medically examined. Strangely, this examination was not carried out timeously and 'for some odd reason a record of the confirmatory proceedings . . . disappeared from the police docket'. The other four accused also endured somewhat similar treatment. The same magistrate ordered two of them to be medically examined but this order was not complied with by the investigating officers for several months. When a prison doctor was eventually able to carry out an examination, he noted that both men had been severely assaulted. Justice Korsah noted that although the examination of one of the accused had taken place seven months after the assault, the medical findings bore 'eloquent testimony to the brutal assault to which he was subjected. And to this day, he bears these scars on his back as evidence of man's inhumanity to man'. The trial judge further noted that 'all the accused persons . . . alleged brutal torture at the hands of the police. They all said that their statements were extracted from them as a result of torture, confrontations and threats, and it has been shown that each of the accused persons was tortured as alleged.'[17] As a result, the court refused to admit the confessions and, as the State was unable to produce any other evidence against the accused, they were all acquitted.

In the Air Force 6 case, the accused all claimed they were subjected to electric shocks and physical assaults. Some also alleged that they were subjected to very long periods of interrogation, pricked by sharp objects and kept hooded for periods making it difficult to breath. The evidence of the third accused, Peter Briscoe, is illuminating. The trial judge, Justice Dumbutshena described it as follows:

> Accused Briscoe was questioned by five CIO men on September 7. He was questioned from early evening to 3 am on the following day. He was made to sit on the floor with his legs stretched straight out in front, arms spread out with fingers touching the floor . . . He was told to get up and do press-ups, first in the normal way and then with clenched fists, using knuckles. If he failed to do this, he was assaulted. He was then made to strip and ordered to do squats with arms outstretched. If he failed in this, he was assaulted. On September 8 he was taken from his cell at about 6.00 or 7.00am and questioned up to 3.00pm. The questioning was resumed at 8.30 or 9.00pm and went on until 3.30am . . . On September 9 he was told he was going to Fifth Brigade Headquarters. A hood was placed over his head . . . Later another hood was placed over the first hood. It was more difficult to breath. He was told to lie on the ground. Somebody lowered his collar and something was placed at the back of his spine. He felt burning needles on his back. If he denied questions put to him, electric current was increased . . . He was told that unless he wanted worse treatment he should make a statement . . . On September 11 he wrote his statement.

The court found that this evidence was corroborated by the opinions of two distinguished medical specialists who gave evidence on behalf of Briscoe. The trial judge then held that 'following upon various forms of inducements and undue influences' the State had failed to prove that the confessions of Briscoe and the other five accused were made freely and voluntarily.[18]

In several other cases, the courts have found that detainees were subjected to torture. For example, Robert Masikini, a CIO officer, was sentenced to death for killing a detainee during interrogation whilst in 1987 at the trial of six former ZIPRA combatants who were charged with launching an attack on the Prime Minister's house, the State did not controvert allegations that the accused were all assaulted by members of the CIO.[19] There are few reports of the torture of females but the experience of Odile Harington illustrates the particular dangers. Here the detainee, who was a suspected South African agent, was subjected to humiliating treatment by male CIO officers who beat her, subjected her to sexual humiliation and spat on her private parts. Her treatment was so severe that she attempted to commit suicide on two occasions. At her later trial, the State called no evidence to controvert her allegations.[20]

The second area for consideration is the activities of the security forces against civilians. In emergency situations where such forces have wide-ranging powers with few effective checks on their conduct, the threat to individual freedoms is considerable. Few such incidents are ever made public. In Matabeleland, the conduct of the Fifth Brigade against civilians was widely condemned by human rights agencies which alleged that members of the brigade were responsible for widespread killing and beating of civilians on the grounds that they were assisting dissidents. In 1984 it was also alleged that during a curfew in southern Matabeleland, between 100 and 150 civilians were either shot dead by soldiers in their villages or beaten to death while in detention in holding camps inside the curfew area.[21] One judicially confirmed incident of such conduct concerns the death of Elias Ndhlovu, a lieutenant in the Zimbabwe National Army, his wife and two others. Four members of the Fifth Brigade were convicted of their murder. The court found that they had forced their victims to drive into the bush, sexually abused the women and then bayonetted and shot the victims. The officer in charge of the local police station was instructed by an Assistant Commissioner of Police not to investigate the matter and accordingly a police report on the incident stated that the victims were killed 'in crossfire'. The truth only came to light when Ndhlovu's commanding officer personally investigated the affair. As the trial judge noted 'The deceased persons . . . were abducted . . . tortured and slaughtered. The State has proved beyond reasonable doubt that this was an atrocity properly so described'. The accused were all found guilty and sentenced to death.[22] In a further incident in North Matabeleland in November 1986, a lance-corporal in the Fifth Brigade who shot and killed a villager was convicted of murder, the judge noting that his deliberate 'overbearing and bullying attitude towards the local people culminated in this brutal killing'.[23]

Members of the security forces were also linked with the disappearance of civilians and with other assaults. In January 1985, the Silobela district in Matabeleland was, as the local police chief put it 'frozen from normal police patrols and the security forces were patrolling the area since it was infested by dissidents'. On 30 January a Shona speaking police officer was killed in the area by alleged dissidents. Shortly afterwards, nine local men were abducted at gun point from their farms by unidentified persons using vehicles resembling those used by the security forces in the area. The men were never seen again.[24] In 1987 relatives of the men applied to the High Court alleging that the men were abducted and murdered by members of the security forces. The State denied all knowledge of the affair and the case did not proceed any further due to lack of evidence. As regards assaults on civilians, in 1986, for example, a soldier in Matabeleland was convicted of raping a twelve-year-old girl whilst on patrol in the Lupane communal lands.[25] Another soldier was also convicted of raping three villagers at knife point in the same area. In sentencing him to nine years imprisonment, Justice Korsah stated that 'as a serving member of the army it was the task of the accused to protect the civilian population against dissident activity such as rape and murder. If the people of the communal lands cannot turn to the army who have been deployed in their areas for their protection, to whom can they turn?'[26] On another occasion, the complainant went to a police station over a domestic matter. A CIO officer and a police officer then forced him to do painful physical training drills, beat him with sticks for no apparent reason and 'made him do a merry go round on one finger (a popular torture with the CIO)'.[27] Justice Muchechetere referred to such conduct as having 'an element of sadism and brutality that is shocking'. He continued:

> assaults by members of the police on the public have always been viewed seriously. The police are in a very special position. They have been given very wide powers in this country for twenty years or so, very much wider powers than in most countries by virtue of the emergency powers. It is all too easy for them to abuse these powers and a member of the public so abused is in the unenviable position of trying to bring a charge against those whose task it is to protect him. I think it is safe to say that the courts are very concerned about police abuse of powers particularly when they assault members of the civilian population.

These words usefully encapsulate the problem of developing effective safeguards against such conduct.[28]

Reinforcing the Constitutional Prohibition

The official response to allegations of torture and the like was to reject them as being untrue. In Parliament, Mugabe himself accused Amnesty International of telling lies and labelled it 'Amnesty Lies International' whilst the Minister of Home Affairs, Enos Nkala, asserted that 'We are not in government to preside over a torture chamber'.[29] Indeed, the dreadful treatment of the Air Force 6 only produced a brief government admission that 'two of these men were assaulted and wrote confessions'.[30] In the face of the overwhelming evidence to the contrary, such assertions were quite nonsensical and politically naive but they do raise the question as to the depth of knowledge of senior ministers concerning illegal activities by the security forces. One former Minister of Home Affairs attributed such activities to lapses of discipline rather than the result of any concerted government policy.[31] This is somewhat unconvincing because during 1985, in particular, the unlawful activities of the security forces against civilians in Matabeleland were so widespread that if ministers and their senior officials did not know what was happening, they were deliberately turning a blind eye to the fact.[32]

The lack of discipline and accountability on the part of the security forces was no doubt partly attributable to the continuation of the 'no-holds barred' approach to dealing with the civilian population inherited from the Rhodesian days. But this was reinforced by apparent government acceptance (if not actual encouragement) of such conduct, a point further emphasised by the ethnic composition of the Fifth Brigade which operated in Matabeleland at the height of the dissident problem. The problem was further compounded by both a lack of training and knowledge concerning human rights issues on the part of the security forces and practical safeguards for victims. Thus in practice, the constitutional provisions were of little practical value during the period when they were most needed. The main task now is to seek ways to prevent a recurrence of the problem.

Fundamentally, any efforts at reinforcing the protections against torture require a government commitment both to respect them and to take active steps to implement them. In this regard a useful starting point is the United Nations Convention Against Torture which requires States to take effective legislative, administrative, judicial and other measures to prevent acts of torture and other inhuman treatment.[33] In response to this, several areas for improvement in Zimbabwe are suggested.

(i) Protecting Detainees During Interrogation

It is the period immediately after detention or arrest which is, in practice, the time when a person is generally most at risk from the use of torture. In Zimbabwe, persons detained under a section 21 order could be held in a prison, a police station, or any other place authorised by the Minister of Home Affairs. A 'place' included any premises, building, dwelling, flat, room, office or shop.[34] This meant that a detainee could be held virtually anywhere making it difficult, if not impossible, for his relatives or legal representative to trace his whereabouts and thus protect his interests. The Air Force 6 case also starkly illustrates the threat to the well-being of detainees when there are few, if any, restrictions on the movement of detainees.[35] Here the men were continually moved from place to place with the sole express intention of preventing them seeing their lawyers prior to making their confessions. There is also considerable evidence to suggest that the torture of detainees occurred mainly in police stations rather than prisons. Thus it was frequently asserted that Stops Camp, which forms part of the Mzilikazi police station in Bulawayo, was a major centre for such activity.[36] In addition, one of the accused in the Beit Bridge 5 case informed the magistrate that he was afraid of being killed if he was returned to police custody, such was the treatment he had previously experienced. The magistrate remanded the man to prison prior to his next court appearance, but the police failed to comply with the order and he was returned to police custody.

Another cause of concern is the manner in which the investigating authorities sought to pervert the course of justice. In the Air Force 6 case, for example, the court noted that the police had kept no records concerning the conduct and times of the interrogation of the men and found that the evidence given by one senior investigating police officer was 'more than suspect' whilst another was said to be 'a difficult witness to believe'. As the trial judge noted, 'The police deny all these nasty, cruel and degrading and sometimes inhuman acts the accused alleged they had experienced. It is easy for the police to deny such things'. In the Beit Bridge case, after having recited the incidents of torture, the trial judge noted (with apparent incredulity) that the sum total of the evidence of the senior police officer in charge of investigations was 'that he did not witness any of the accused persons being assaulted; that each of the accused freely and voluntarily recorded a confession; and that the injuries found on them could have resulted from the general situation existing in Beit Bridge at the time'. The court also found that following the refusal of the local magistrates to confirm the confessions because of the injuries to the accused, the police then took some of the accused over 200 kilometres to the magistrates' court at Gwanda in the hope that a magistrate there would confirm the confessions. Perhaps the most striking incident was in the Ndhlovu case where the local police were ordered by a senior police officer not to investigate the death of the four victims and to record that they had died in 'cross fire'.

For the practical implementation of the constitutional protection, it is necessary to develop a justiciable Code of Conduct[37] which applies to all persons involved in the interrogation of suspects. It is suggested that the Code is based on an increased role for the magistracy and greater accountability on the part of interrogators. The following are some of the necessary minimum safeguards:

(1) The detaining authority must inform a local magistrate if a person is detained for more than a period of 96 hours.[38]

(2) The detaining authority must specify in detail to a local magistrate the whereabouts of the detainee(s).

(3) The transfer of a detainee to another place is only permissible with the written permission of a senior police officer and only if this is to facilitate the investigation. In any such case a local magistrate must be informed immediately.
(4) The details of the transfer including the location of the new place of detention must be given to a local magistrate.
(5) A local magistrate must be allowed to visit the place of detention at any time and be permitted to speak with the detainee in private.
(6) A local magistrate may order a medical examination of a detainee within a fixed period. No questioning may then take place until authorised by a medical practitioner.
(7) The detaining authority must keep a full record of all interviews with a detainee, detailing the times and length of questioning, the place, and the questions and answers. A copy of the record must be made available to the detainee or his legal representative. Failure to produce such a record gives rise to a presumption that the detaining authority was in breach of the safeguards.
(8) If possible, all interviews must be recorded on tape or video and a copy made available to the detainee or his legal representative.
(9) As soon as is practicably possible, a detainee must be transferred to a prison and must be transferred immediately upon the written instructions of a local magistrate.
(10) All investigating officers must correctly identify themselves to the detainee, if necessary by their service number if their identity is confidential for security reasons.[39]
(11) A female officer must be continually present during the interrogation of all female detainees.
(12) Any failure on the part of the detaining authority to comply with these rules automatically renders the detention unlawful.
(13) Any failure on the part of the detaining authority to comply with these rules renders those responsible liable to be held in contempt of court.

Such a Code of Conduct will not unduly hamper the proper interrogation of a suspect nor delay the investigation of the case. It merely seeks to reduce the possibility of improper acts against detainees as evidenced from the reported cases in Zimbabwe. It places a considerable burden upon magistrates, but in practice they are the main source of immediate protection for detainees. By being locally based and readily available, they are in a position to liaise with the detaining authority. In order to make their role as effective as possible, it is desirable that senior magistrates in each magisterial area are designated for this task and receive additional training. It is also important that detainees are moved to prison as soon as possible because the Zimbabwe Prison Service has established an outstanding record for the protection of prisoners' rights. Indeed when Austin and Harper were released from detention in January 1988, they paid glowing tribute to the prison staff for their humane and sympathetic treatment.[40]

(ii) Training for Members of the Security Forces

It is essential that those charged with the task of interrogating detainees are made fully aware of the prohibition against torture and be subject to clear legal and administrative sanctions for any unlawful or unwarranted conduct. The example of Zimbabwe shows that the pre-independence attitude towards individual rights was retained by some members of the security forces and as a result the rights of detainees were violated on many occasions. This shows how vital it is to provide human rights training for security personnel. In 1989 a positive move was made in this direction in Zimbabwe with the establishment by the Legal Resources Foundation[41] of a legal training programme for members of the security forces. This consists of short residential courses on human rights issues held in various parts of Zimbabwe and attended by police and CIO officers. This is done in conjunction with the Commonwealth Secretariat Human Rights Unit initiative which seeks to develop human rights training opportunities for public officials throughout the Commonwealth.[42] It is hoped that such programmes will lead to the development of continual in-service training so that all persons involved in detention cases become fully appraised of their duties and responsibilities. This is an excellent approach to the problem and is a model which other African countries might well emulate.[43]

(iii) Conditions in Detention

Just as prison for convicted offenders is the punishment and not for punishment, so the loss of liberty for a detainee must not be accompanied by inhuman treatment. Surprisingly, most constitutional documents, including the Constitution of Zimbabwe, relate exclusively to the mechanics of detention. The dreadful conditions experienced by detainees in many African states makes this all the more surprising and calls for steps to remedy the omission.

In Zimbabwe most ministerial detainees were held at either Chikurubi Maximum Security Prison just outside Harare, Khami Maximum Security Prison near Bulawayo or Goromonzi Prison some 48 kilometres (30 miles) from Harare. The Prisons Act defines a prisoner as 'any person whether or not convicted under detention in any prison'.[44] Thus detainees were subject to the same treatment and conditions as ordinary convicted prisoners. It is quite unacceptable to treat detainees in this manner. Fortunately, the courts intervened in the matter.

In 1986 Justice Blackie examined the rights of detainees. He noted that it was well established that a detainee retains all the rights of an ordinary citizen except those that are expressly or by necessary implication taken away by law.[45] These include proper housing and clothing, adequate food and medical attention, protection from assault, adequate exercise in the open air and the right not to be kept in isolation. Justice Blackie also rejected the State's contention that such matters were purely administrative and held that there was a long established rule which allowed the courts to entertain applications alleging the breach of basic rights. In the case itself, an application was made on behalf of two detainees for an order preventing them from being held in Khami Maximum Security Prison and in solitary confinement at Goromonzi respectively.[46] Here Justice Blackie ordered that the men should not be held in solitary confinement but detained under conditions of diet, light, hygiene, space and exercise of the standards applying in the recognised prisons of Zimbabwe. In addition he accepted the principle that access to legal representatives and family are basic rights of detainees which are infringed if reasonable access is denied. Although the matter varied from case to case, the holding of a person 'hundreds of kilometres across the other side of the country' was held to represent a denial of basic rights. The court thus ordered the detaining authorities to hold the men within 15 kilometres of Harare, where their family and legal representatives resided.[47]

There is perhaps no absolute meaning to the term 'basic rights' in this context. However it is vital that binding rules are developed in this area in order to secure the right of a detainee to fair and humane treatment during detention.[48] This is particularly important because few detainees are able to afford legal representation. A useful starting point is the United Nations Standard Minimum Rules for the Treatment of Prisoners. These were approved by the Economic and Social Council of the United Nations in 1957 after their adoption by the First United Nations Congress on the Prevention of Crime and Treatment of Offenders. They represent the minimum conditions which are acceptable for prisoners and are intended to guard against their mistreatment. An adaptation of some of the Rules together with the United Nations Principles for the Protection of Persons under any Form of Detention could form a useful Code of Conduct for the detaining authorities.[49] Such a code should include the following:

(1) All accommodation provided for the use of detainees and in particular all sleeping accommodation shall meet all requirements of health, due regard being paid to climatic conditions and particularly to cubic content of air, minimum floor space, lighting, heating and ventilation. Provided that a detainee may receive a reasonable amount of bedding at regular intervals from family or friends.
(2) Every detainee shall be provided by the administration at the usual hours with food of nutritional value adequate for health and strength, of wholesome quality and well prepared and served. Provided that a detainee shall have the right to eat food which is supplied by family or friends.
(3) Drinking water shall be constantly available to every detainee whenever he/she needs it. Provided that a detainee shall have the right to receive regularly non-alcoholic refreshment supplied by family or friends.
(4) Every detainee shall have at least one hour of suitable exercise in the open air daily, weather permitting.
(5) Corporal punishment, punishment by placing in a dark cell, solitary confinement[50] and all cruel, inhuman or degrading punishments shall be prohibited.
(6) Detainees shall be allowed, under necessary supervision, to communicate with their family and reputable friends at regular intervals both by correspondence and by receiving visits.
(7) Detainees shall have the right to consult with a legal representative of their own choice, in private, at any time and for a reasonable period.
(8) Detainees have the right to be held in a place which is as close to their families and legal representative as is reasonably practicable and consonant with security.
(9) Detainees have the right to wear their own clothes at all times and to have regular changes of such clothing.
(10) Detainees have the right to have access to newspapers, books and magazines and to the use of writing materials.
(11) Detainees have the right to the use of a personal radio and television.
(12) Except for security reasons, detainees shall not be moved from their current place of detention without reasonable notice being given to their families and legal representatives.
(13) Detainees shall be kept entirely separate from convicted prisoners.

Such minimum safeguards are aimed at ensuring that the common law rights of detainees are complied with and that conditions in detention comply with the principle that:

> All persons under any form of detention or imprisonment shall be treated in a humane manner and with respect for the inherent dignity of the human person.[51]

(iv) Role of the Medical Profession

The medical profession has a significant role to play in the protection of detainees. The case of Steve Biko in South Africa graphically illustrates the point. In 1977, Biko, a young Black Consciousness leader, died in detention. His death was caused by brain injuries which were the result of at least three blows to the head. The post-mortem further revealed injuries to the chest wall and to the anterior abdominal wall. There were also a number of skin abrasions, and cuts on the top lip and left forehead. At the inquest, evidence was given that he was kept naked in his cell and chained in handcuffs and leg irons during interrogation. Evidence at the inquest also revealed that Biko was examined by a doctor some time before his death and that the doctor had signed a medical certificate to the effect that he 'found no evidence of any abnormality or pathology' in Biko. In reality Biko was at that time 'weak in all four limbs, in addition to suffering from a laceration on his lip, a bruise near his second rib, swollen feet, ankles and hands, slurred speech and an inability to walk properly'.[52] When his condition further deteriorated, the doctor's recommendation that Biko be moved to hospital was rejected by the officer in charge 'on the grounds of security'. The doctor then 'felt that [he] had to yield to him, there being no doubt that [his] actions were subject to the control at that stage of the police and/or prison authorities'. Without some form of duty to protect detainees imposed on medical practitioners, such occurrences will continue.[53] Additionally, there is also the danger that medical practitioners will collude with the detaining authorities. This is neatly illustrated by two Tanzanian cases where the High Court found that medical doctors had administered methadone to suspects so as to make them talk to police officers during interrogation.[54]

International concern over the responsibility of the medical profession towards the protection of detainees led to the Tokyo Declaration of 1975 which states:[55]

> It is the privilege of the medical doctor to practice medicine in the service of humanity, to preserve and restore bodily and mental health without distinction as to persons, to comfort and to ease the suffering of his or her patients. The utmost respect for human life is to be maintained even under threat.
> 1. The doctor shall not countenance, condone or participate in the practice of torture or other forms of cruel, inhuman or degrading procedures, whatever the offence of which the victim of such procedures is suspected, accused or guilty, and whatever the victim's beliefs or motives, and in all situations, including armed conflict and civil strife . . .
> 4. A doctor must have complete clinical independence in deciding upon the care of a person for whom he or she is medically responsible. The doctor's fundamental role is to alleviate the distress of his or her fellow men, and no motive whether personal, collective or political shall prevail against this higher purpose.

The Declaration is important as it provides a framework within which a medical doctor must operate in order to protect detainees. In particular the right of a doctor to override the wishes of the detaining authority in determining the appropriate treatment for an individual is a crucial practical safeguard. If members of the medical profession are prepared to adhere to the Declaration, then the conduct of the doctor in the Biko case might be avoided in future.

The Standard Minimum Rules also require the presence of at least one qualified medical officer at every institution who is to have the care of the physical and mental health of prisoners.[56] In Zimbabwe, all prisoners are medically examined on admission into prison whilst persons held in solitary confinement must be examined on every visit to the prison by the medical officer.[57] In cases of serious illness, the officer in charge of the prison, acting on the advice of the medical officer, may order the removal of the prisoner to hospital. In practice, medical care in Zimbabwean prisons is of a high standard and the requirements of the Tokyo Declaration strictly observed. However, because of the real danger of physical or mental abuse occurring when a detainee is held in custody, it is of great importance to specifically incorporate the provisions of the Tokyo Declaration into an enforceable and justiciable Code of Conduct.

(v) Redress for Victims of Torture

Victims of torture frequently encounter immense difficulties in bringing an action for damages against the State and are often forced to suffer in silence. The United Nations Convention Against Torture recognises that such victims have a right to complain and to have their cases promptly and impartially examined. The document also requires States to take steps to ensure that the complainant and witnesses are protected against all ill-treatment or intimidation as a consequence of the complaint or any evidence given. In view of this, it is vital for complainants to have access to an independent complaints procedure which is open to all and which has real investigative powers. The traditional judicial system is often unable to assist because threats of reprisals, the problem of obtaining evidence and the cost itself may prevent an action for damages succeeding. In Zimbabwe, the Office of the Ombudsman already provides an alternative complaints procedure for any person who is prejudiced by government maladministration. At present, the ombudsman's jurisdiction does not extend to complaints by the public against members of the security forces. If this were amended, there is no doubt that the ombudsman could play a key role in assisting victims of torture.[58] A further possibility is to hold an independent commission of enquiry whenever there are reasonable grounds for believing that an act of torture has occurred, although as is noted in Chapter 13, this has procedural and political difficulties.

Overview

The record of Zimbabwe as regards the use of torture and the like is unsettling for there is cogent evidence that some members of the security forces were involved in widespread brutality against sections of the civilian population. No matter how difficult to implement in practice, the lesson from Zimbabwe is that formal safeguards are needed if all members of the security forces are to attain an acceptable standard of conduct. The introduction of training courses for security personnel and the use of Codes of Conduct together with an effective role for magistrates and doctors would undoubtedly protect detainees to some extent.

But at the end of the day, it is up to government to take the lead on these issues. A clear and categorical commitment towards the recognition of the rights of detainees is imperative, backed up by the implementation of practical safeguards and the bringing to justice of those involved in such abuses.

Right to Life

During the UDI period this right was systematically undermined by the Smith regime by the use of emergency regulations. Between 1975 and 1979 it was reported that 152 executions were carried out although this figure is not entirely accurate because on 21 April 1975 the regime announced that in future all executions would be carried out in secret.[59] In 1976 emergency regulations set up 'Special Courts' to try cases connected with 'acts of terrorism' with the power to impose the death sentence. In an attempt to maintain a pretence of judicial independence, the court consisted of a legally qualified president who was appointed by the Minister of Justice together with two or three other members selected by the President. Such 'courts' were abolished at independence.

In line with the African Charter, the Constitution of Zimbabwe provides that no person may be deprived of his life intentionally unless sentenced to death by a court in respect of a criminal offence.[60] The High Court must pass a sentence of death upon any person convicted of murder.[61] It may also impose capital punishment upon an offender convicted of treason; rape; attempted murder; robbery or attempted robbery in which aggravating circumstances were present; or any offence which was potentially dangerous to life. Zimbabwe currently has more capital offences than almost any other country in Africa, thanks largely to its inheritance of the Rhodesian security legislation which remains in force. As regards specific security related offences, the Law and Order (Maintenance) Act (LOMA) provides for the death sentence in the following circumstances: (i) the unlawful recruiting or encouraging of any person to undergo training for the purpose of furthering a political object by the use of force or violence; (ii) undergoing any training for the purpose of furthering a political objective by force or violence; (iii) possession of any arms of war; (iv) carrying out, or involvement in, acts of terrorism or sabotage.[62] This is widely defined to include 'the furthering of political aims by violence or forcible means; causing or encouraging an insurrection in or forcible resistance to the government or the armed or police forces of, Zimbabwe or a neighbouring territory; interfering with essential services; causing serious bodily injury to or endangering the safety of any person within Zimbabwe; or causing substantial financial loss within Zimbabwe to any person or the State.'[63] (v) harbouring or failing to report terrorists or wilfully misleading a government official concerning the presence of terrorists (section 51, LOMA). Numerous convictions resulted from this last offence, although after 1980 no death sentence was apparently imposed. It remains a particularly controversial offence because villagers are frequently its unwilling perpetrators. This was particularly so in Matabeleland during the dissident problem for to fail to assist armed dissidents often led to death or serious injury. To assist them led to a conviction and potentially severe punishment.

In practice the higher courts took a generally realistic approach to sentencing in such cases. Thus in a case in 1985 where three women had failed to report the presence of dissidents who had attacked and raped them, Justice Korsah stated that harsh sentences on females in such cases:

> will alienate the feelings and co-operation of such persons and thus deprive the forces of law and order of the opportunity of receiving the necessary information . . .to enable them to wipe out the dissident menace for all time.

He then emphasised that it was the duty of the courts to enforce section 51 in such a way as to maximise the willingness of the people to report the presence of dissidents and that to do so 'we must first woo their confidence'. The sentences of up to 24 months imprisonment were altered to allow the immediate release of the women.[64]

In a later case, Justice Blackie propounded a similar view. Having noted that section 51 places an absolute duty to report, he considered that for the purposes of sentencing, it was important to know whether the authorities had provided proper facilities for reporting and giving adequate protection to the person, property and family of the man who gave such a report. He continued:

> The State has placed a legal duty on the accused to report, but there is a corresponding moral duty on the State to protect the accused from the consequences of making such a report. There is nothing in the record to show the accused could have made a report easily or safely. [Thus] his failure to do so is understandable, if not legally excusable.[65]

A sentence of imprisonment was replaced by an order providing for the immediate release of the accused.[66] Such an approach is both consonant with justice and equity and the approach of the courts is extremely welcome.[67]

The death sentence may also be imposed under the Railways Act[68] for the offence of 'throwing things at trains' or interfering with the railway track. Here again this was introduced during the UDI period. There have been no reported convictions for this offence since independence.[69]

The LOMA provisions are notable for their vagueness and reflect the desire of the Rhodesian government to have draconian legislation designed to deal with its political opponents. In this respect they resemble the Internal Security Act in South Africa. In 1983 the Advisory Committee on Law Reform examined the whole question of capital punishment and concluded:

> No one who responded to our consultation was opposed to our provisional proposal that none of the [offences under LOMA] should continue to carry the death penalty. Unfortunately we had no views from the Ministry of Home Affairs, but we do not think it would be right to treat the failure to comment as necessarily meaning that the Ministry was in agreement with our proposal . . . In principle we still favour the abolition of the death penalty for [offences under the Act]. We appreciate, however, that abolition in the present circumstances of unrest might mistakenly be regarded as a sign of weakness, if not of encouragement to violently minded people. We think that any decision in regard to these offences must be a political decision to be taken in the light of the situation prevailing when that decision has to be made . . . Accordingly we make no firm recommendation at this stage, but we urge the Government urgently to consider these offences with a view to abolishing the death sentence.

The Committee also considered that there was no need for the death sentence for attacks on trains and recommended its abolition.

Due to the difficult security situation prevailing at the time, government did not respond to these recommendations. The scope and ill-defined nature of the present law is a matter of considerable concern and was subject to fierce criticism from Chief Justice Enoch Dumbutshena who frequently called for its abolition. Government is apparently taking steps to shorten the list of capital offences but has no plans to abolish capital punishment entirely.[70]

Overview

It is necessary to make two points. Firstly, the Smith regime is by no means the only example of a government in Africa which has used emergency powers to set up special tribunals which both oust the jurisdiction of the ordinary courts and have the power to impose the death sentence. In every case, such action is to be utterly condemned. In this respect, the fact that Zimbabwe did not follow suit is extremely commendable. Secondly, with the ending of the state of emergency, the views of the Advisory Committee are even more valid. Wide-ranging and essentially vague security offences in themselves are inappropriate. Coupling them with a possible death sentence makes the provisions utterly reprehensible.[71] They must be repealed.

Notes

1. See United Nations Convention Against Torture and Other Cruel, Inhuman or Degrading Treatment or Punishment: Part 1, Article 1. The Tokyo Declaration of 1975, discussed later in this chapter, defines torture as 'the

deliberate, systematic or wanton infliction of physical or mental suffering by one or more persons acting alone or on the orders of any authority, to force another person to yield information, to make a confession, or for any other reason'.

2. Article 5 of the African Charter states that 'All forms of exploitation and degradation of man, particularly . . . torture, inhuman and degrading punishment and treatment shall be prohibited.'

3. See International Commission of Jurists, 1983, p.371 and Foster, 1987.

4. Memorandum to the Government of Uganda on an Amnesty International mission to Uganda in January 1982 and further exchanges between the Government and Amnesty International: AI Index AFR 59/04/83. Amnesty International has also criticised the National Resistance Army government of President Museveni for the use of torture against civilians: see Amnesty International, 1989, pp.31–34.

5. For example, the United States State Department expressed concern over the record of Kenya in 1987: see AWF 16 March 1987. See also Conboy, 1978, p. 445. In Malawi, Amnesty International has reported the frequent use of torture against detainees: see Amnesty International, 1989, and Report AFR 36/06/90 of September 1990.

6. See, in particular, the Amnesty International Report *Torture in the 1980s*; Bulletins of the International Commission of Jurists and its report *States of Emergency: Their Impact on Human Rights*, above, especially the chapters on Zaire and Ghana.

7. Zvogbo, 1976, pp.38–43.

8. Section 15, Constitution of Zimbabwe.

9. *Per* Quenet ACJ in *Gundu v Sheriff of Rhodesia* 1967 RLR 56.

10. It has also been held that the words 'punishment' and 'treatment' are entirely different concepts. As Chief Justice Beadle stated in *Dhlamini v Carter* 1968 RLR 231:

> If, during the course of his punishment, a prisoner is subjected to 'inhuman treatment', he can move the court for relief and the court will see that the 'treatment' is stopped, but that does not affect the original 'punishment' which cannot itself, become tainted with the inhumanity of the 'treatment'. For example, if, during the course of serving a sentence of imprisonment, a prisoner is subjected to inhuman or degrading treatment, the court . . . would see that the treatment was stopped, but that would not be a ground for holding that the punishment of imprisonment was inhuman, and would not entitle this court to sit as a court of appeal, as it were, on the original sentence of imprisonment and order that the sentence be reduced or altered because of the inhumanity of the treatment the prisoner had received while in gaol. Any question of reducing or altering a sentence in these circumstances is essentially a matter for the Executive acting within its prerogative powers.

Since section 12 of the Constitution expressly provides for the death sentence, section 15 must refer to something other than the imposition of the punishment itself. It seems that a court could consider the death sentence *vis à vis* the offence committed. For instance, the imposition of such a sentence for a relatively trivial act of throwing a small stone at a freight train, might well merit the intervention of the appeal court under section 15.

11. 'Reconciliation is Still Possible': Statement by the Archbishop of Harare and four bishops and other senior Roman Catholic clergy: 29 March 1983. See also Pastoral Letter dated 31 March 1983.

12. See Press Release, 30 March 1983.

13. See 'The Killing of Luke and Jean Kumalo of the Kwane School, Matabeleland, November 1985'. Amnesty International News Release AFR/46/06/86.

14. The Minister of Home Affairs invited Amnesty International to hold a joint enquiry into the veracity of the allegations. This was rejected by Amnesty on the grounds that such an exercise was not part of its functions.

15. Similar allegations were made by the Lawyers Committee, 1986, especially chapter 6 and Africa Watch, 1989, especially chapter 5.

16. See pp.3–9 of the judgment.

17. See p.45 of the judgment.

18. It is a noticeable feature worldwide that the use of torture is frequently used when there is little or no other evidence against the victim.

19. For further instances of the use of torture see the Africa Watch Report n.15 above.

20. See the judgment of Chief Justice Dumbutshena in the Supreme Court of Zimbabwe, 1988 (2) ZLR 344 (SC).

21. See Lawyers Committee, chapter 8.

22. *S v Samuel Chayama & Three Others*, Unreported, High Court of Zimbabwe. The judgment of Justice Manyarara sitting with two assessors is dated 30 July 1986. The accused were all pardoned in the presidential amnesty of April 1988.

23. Justice McNally in *S v Kamusemu*, Unreported, Supreme Court of Zimbabwe SC 34/88 at p.10.

24. *Tshuma v Government of Zimbabwe*, Unreported, High Court of Zimbabwe HC-H-87-87.

25. *S v Chaya*, Unreported, High Court of Zimbabwe HC-B-231-86.

26. *S v Mandeya*, Unreported, High Court of Zimbabwe HC-B-217-86.

27. *S v Kanyama & Zowa*, Unreported, High Court of Zimbabwe HC-H-52-87. See also the cases of *S v Kwara*, Unreported, Appellate Division AD 133/80; *S v Nyaina*, Unreported, Supreme Court of Zimbabwe SC 75/83 and *S v Chadamoyo*, Unreported, High Court of Zimbabwe HC-H-75-83.

28. In 1987 in a somewhat bizarre case, a woman was unlawfully imprisoned and threatened with detention by two government officials. On at least ten separate occasions a third official raped her, the victim submitting because of the continuing threats. The Minister of Home Affairs was ordered to pay $20,000 damages to the victim: see *Banda v Minister of Home Affairs*, Unreported, High Court of Zimbabwe HC-H-243-87. The identities of the officials were never revealed. The courts later adopted a policy of imprisoning any members of the security forces who assaulted civilians.

29. *The Herald*, 9 November 1985. According to Mubako, some of the Amnesty reports were questionable and came from a pro-ZAPU source who was not objective in his information. Interview with Simbi Mubako, May 1989.
30. See 'Zimbabwe on Trial' *The Observer*, 9 October 1983.
31. Interview with Simbi Mubako, May 1989.
32. I am grateful to Richard Carver, formerly of Africa Watch, for pointing this out. In fairness, it is not asserted that the record of Zimbabwe is in any way comparable to those in Uganda and South Africa where State terrorism was the norm.
33. Part 1, Article 2.
34. Sections 17(7) and 21(5) Emergency Powers (Maintenance of Law and Order) Regulations 1983.
35. Detainees could be moved from place to place by order of a senior police officer: Section 21(6) of the 1983 regulations.
36. See Lawyers Committee, chapter 6.
37. Codes of Conduct are becoming increasingly seen as an effective means of adding 'operational flesh' to the constitutional or legislative skeleton. See, for example, the Codes of Conduct in the English Police and Criminal Evidence Act 1984.
38. Ninety-six hours is the maximum period a person may be held under the Criminal Procedure and Evidence Act without bringing him before a court.
39. Uniformed police officers are required to wear identity numbers whilst on duty in a bid to make them more accountable to the public. This provision merely extends the duty to all investigating officers.
40. *The Herald*, 5 January 1988.
41. See Chapter 13 for details of the Foundation.
42. In 1990 a training programme was held in Harare by the Unit. The programme itself is backed up by a manual (*Human Rights Training for Public Officials*, Commonwealth Secretariat, 1990) which, *inter alia*, deals with topics such as international conventions against torture and 'standard setting' by senior police officers of conduct conducive to the promotion and protection of human rights.
43. Namibia, which like Zimbabwe went through a long struggle for independence, is also undertaking such a programme. Amnesty International is currently seeking to promote an awareness and understanding among members of the security forces of the fundamental human rights principles contained in the new Constitution.
44. Section 2 Prisons Act (Cap 21).
45. See *Goldberg v Minister of Prisons* 1979 (1) SA 14, at p.40. For example, Justice Innes stated in *Whittaker v Roos & Bateman* (1912) AD 92: 'Every person is entitled to the natural rights relating to his personal or to his civil liberties unless such rights are limited or taken away by legislative enactments or regulations, or are unnecessarily inconsistent with the purpose of the enactment under which they are held or with the circumstances of their detention.'
46. *Bull v Minister of State (Security)* 1986 (3) SA 886; [1987] LRC (Const) 547. Bull was the legal representative of Austin and Harper.
47. This is another example of the application of the core of rights principle. The right to access to a legal representative, the primary right, is backed up by the concomitant right of being held at a place which is readily accessible for that representative. In a later case, the Supreme Court held that the placement of prisoners in solitary confinement and on spare diet was a form of punishment which violated section 15(1) of the Constitution as being an inhuman and degrading punishment: see *Masitere*, Unreported, Supreme Court of Zimbabwe SC 140/90. Such a decision should also apply to detainees.
48. This is a key recommendation in the report of the Commonwealth Advisory Group, 1991, p.76.
49. United Nations Body of Principles for the Protection of All Persons under Any Form of Detention or Imprisonment (General Assembly resolution 43/173)(1988).
50. See generally, Riekert, 1985, p.245.
51. Principle 1 of the United Nations Principles (see n.49 above).
52. Despite this evidence the finding of the inquest was that 'The available evidence does not prove that the death was brought about by any act or omission involving or amounting to an offence on the part of any person'. See Maisels and de Villiers, 1981, p.4.
53. The need for some action here is evidenced by the fact that Colonel P.J. Goosen, the officer in charge of the interrogation of Biko, said that the security police did not regard themselves as bound in their work by any statutory authority: see the transcript in Woods, 1978, p.199.
54. *R v Ihuya & Four Others*, Unreported, Criminal Sessions Case No. 8/80 and *R v Kigadye & Seven Others*, Unreported, Criminal Sessions Case No. 85/80. Allegations were also made that in the Air Force 6 case doctors falsely told the court that no torture was perpetrated against the accused: see Cole, 1988, p.172.
55. Guidelines for Medical Doctors Concerning Torture and other Cruel, Inhuman or Degrading Treatment or Punishment in Relation to Detention and Imprisonment.
56. See paragraphs 22–26 of the 1984 edition of the Rules.
57. Sections 26(1) and 28(1) Prisons Act.
58. The matter is considered in depth in Chapter 13.
59. See International Defence and Aid Fund, 1980.
60. Section 12, Constitution of Zimbabwe. There is no contravention of the right if death occurs as the result of force which is reasonably justifiable for the defence of any person from violence or for the defence of property; to effect a lawful arrest or prevent the escape of a person lawfully detained; for suppressing a riot, insurrection or mutiny or of dispersing an unlawful gathering; in order to prevent the commission of a criminal offence by that person; or if death results from a lawful act of war.

61. This is unless (a) the offender was under sixteen years of age; (b) pregnant; (c) a woman convicted of the murder of her newly born child; or (d) the court is of the opinion that there are extenuating circumstances. In such cases any other sentence may be imposed. For an analysis of the meaning of 'extenuating circumstances', see Feltoe, 1986, p.42.
62. Sections 24(1), 24(2), 37 and 50 respectively of the Law and Order (Maintenance) Act.
63. Section 50(6) LOMA.
64. *Sithole & Sibanda*, Unreported, High Court of Zimbabwe HC-B-134-86.
65. *Ndlovu*, Unreported, High Court of Zimbabwe HC-B-103-87. See also *Ncube* 1983 (2) ZLR 309 and *Madigani* 1985 (1) ZLR 122.
66. The accused was not legally represented at his trial at the magistrates court and commenced his prison sentence immediately after sentence. He served six weeks before the review in the High Court.
67. Further support for this approach is given by Feltoe, 1988, pp.14–15.
68. Chapter 261.
69. In February 1987 Kephas Ncube was sentenced to death for exploding a device on a railway line. It is not clear as to whether the charge was brought under LOMA or the Railways Act.
70. Interview with Simbi Mubako, May 1989. It is understood that a Bill to shorten the list is being prepared but to date it has not been published. The decision as to whether or not to carry out the sentence is taken by Cabinet. In practice several persons sentenced to death have been released following the granting of a presidential amnesty.
71. Some twenty persons were executed between 1980 and 1990. Most were convicted murderers, with the majority being members of dissident groups. In one week in August 1985, ten men were executed. These included Ngwenya and Mpofu who were convicted of involvement in the death of six tourists in Matabeleland. The majority of those hanged were from the Matabeleland area of the country, thus raising a fear that the executions were politically motivated as part of the government's campaign against its political opponents.

9 Protection of the Law

It is widely recognised that every person is entitled to the protection of the law.[1] Thus anyone charged with a criminal offence has the right to a fair hearing within a reasonable time by an independent and impartial court established by law. Also included is the presumption of innocence, the right to be informed of the nature of the offence charged and a prohibition on the creation of retrospective offences or punishments. There is also a right to legal representation throughout the criminal process starting at the time of the arrest or detention. These basic rights are particularly liable to abrogation or curtailment by authoritarian governments, and this is especially so during times of emergency.

In Zimbabwe, the constitutional right to protection of the law is fully protected and is not subject to abrogation even during a period of public emergency. Nevertheless, State security considerations jeopardised the exercise of this right and five areas of conflict are now examined.

Legal Representation

Access to legal representation is vital to those deprived of their liberty. Without it, an individual is left unprotected and liable to suffer considerable prejudice and, as noted in an earlier chapter, this is especially so in the case of detainees. The importance of the right is recognised in many international documents. The African Charter provides that:

> Every individual shall have the right to have his case heard. This comprises . . .
> (c) the right to defence, including the right to be defended by counsel of his choice.

In Africa, south of the Sahara, virtually every current national constitution contains the right to defence in criminal cases whilst almost half of the Anglophonic African nations specifically refer to the right of a person charged with a criminal offence to representation by a lawyer of his own choice.[2]

In Zimbabwe, every accused has a statutory right of access to a lawyer.[3] Even before independence, this was seen as an inherent right available to all accused persons.[4] This is now reinforced by the Constitution which provides that throughout the criminal justice process, an accused is entitled, at his own expense, to obtain and instruct without delay a legal representative of his own choice and to hold communication with him.[5]

The Right in Practice

The Air Force 6 case neatly illustrates the approach of the courts towards the protection of the right. On 25 July 1982, three unknown saboteurs attacked the Zimbabwe Air Force (ZAF) base at Thornhill, near the Midlands city of Gweru. Aircraft and other property totalling over Zimb $7 million were destroyed.[6] Air Vice-Marshall Hugh Slatter (second in command of ZAF), Air Commodore Philip Pile (third in command of ZAF) and four other white ZAF personnel were charged with assisting the saboteurs.[7] There was effectively no evidence against the men save for their confessions in which each admitted their involvement in the sabotage. The preliminary question for the trial judge, Justice Dumbutshena (the then Judge President), was whether these statements, which had previously been confirmed by magistrates, were admissible, failing which the State had no case. The evidence which was accepted by the court revealed several disquietening aspects: (a) all the accused were denied access to their legal representatives until after their incriminating statements were recorded; (b) the accused were constantly moved from place to place as their lawyers increased pressure on the police to gain access to them. As the trial judge noted, the police action was undertaken 'in order to put off their lawyers until after statements had been obtained and confirmed'. As if to confirm this point, the State did not rely on the evidence of the police officer in charge of investigations. In fact the police action was later described in the Supreme Court as 'a calculated course of conduct that was persisted in for improper motives';[8] (c) the statements were made as a result of fear after sustained mental and physical torture perpetrated both by police officers and members of the CIO.[9]

Thus the statements were challenged not only on the grounds that they were not voluntary but also because the accused were denied access to their legal representatives at all material times. The court accepted that a breach of the constitutional right of access to a lawyer in itself rendered the statements inadmissible by reason of undue influence. The trial judge made the position of the courts in Zimbabwe very clear:

> In my judgment, if an accused person wants a legal practitioner before, or during, interrogation, the police investigators must stop their investigations and only resume after the accused has had consultations with his legal practitioner . . . If the police, in spite of the accused's request to have his lawyer present, continue with their interrogations thus denying him the protection of his constitutional rights and professional advice, it cannot be said that the police have not brought to bear upon the will of the accused by external impulses undue influence. The denial of access to a lawyer is in itself a form of psychological coercion and inducement which is brought to bear on the will of the accused.

He acknowledged that the line between proper and permissible police conduct and techniques and methods oppressive to due process is a difficult one to draw.[10] But he emphasised that criminal justice begins at the point when the police interrogate a person in their custody and that 'in their attempts to obtain confessions . . . [they] must do so within the limits laid down by the law'. Having examined the evidence, the judge preferred the evidence of the accuseds' legal representatives as to their attempts to obtain access to their clients to that of the police witnesses who he found not to be honest with the court when they said that the accused were moved from police station to police station for security reasons. Thus on this ground alone, he held the statements inadmissible. He also found that the statements were not made voluntarily. Accordingly, all six accused were acquitted.[11] An appeal to the Supreme Court by the Attorney-General was dismissed. Justice Beck, giving the judgment of the court, fully supported the decision of the trial judge and emphasised the importance of professional assistance to the proper understanding and protection of the rights of accused persons. Perhaps the words of Justice Haines in the Canadian decision of *R v O'Connor*[12] epitomise the importance of the right:

> It is the early participation of counsel both in fact development and fact presentation which lends some semblance of reality to the concept of the balance existing between the accused and the otherwise irresistible forces of the State. To waylay counsel in this crucial and vital state of fact development . . . is tantamount to waylaying the cornerstone of our concept of criminal justice . . . Proper police processing as a facet of criminal justice is no less an aspect of criminal justice; indeed it is integral because the liberty of subjects is safeguarded in the procedure as well as the substance of the law.

Choice of Legal Representative

The right of a person to choose a representative of his choice is important because an accused needs to be able to put his trust and confidence in his lawyer. In addition, in security (or other complex or technically difficult) cases the use of an expert is frequently vital to the defence and such expertise is sometimes not available locally. As a result, lawyers from other jurisdictions are 'imported' for the occasion. This occurred in Zimbabwe on several occasions, most notably in the Tekere and Air Force 6 cases. The State also instructed a British lawyer in the York brothers case.

The scope of the right depends upon the meaning of the phrase 'of his own choice' and it is on this issue that difficulties have arisen. On the face of it, the term gives any accused the unfettered freedom to choose his/her own representative. If this is so, then the trial/ interrogation can only proceed when his/her chosen lawyer is present. Such an argument is not without its practical difficulties. An unrestricted choice may lead to a deliberate attempt to delay the administration of justice. Thus an accused might choose a lawyer who he/she knows is unavailable for several months. Clearly such a scenario is unacceptable. An unrestricted right to choose is detrimental to the interests of justice for 'the right to counsel of the accused's choice does not carry with it the right to dictate the date for trial'.[13] The problem lies in determining the circumstances in which to exercise the right.

In a number of situations the courts have limited the right. Where an application is clearly vexatious or frivolous or where the accused is guilty of gross negligence in failing timeously to engage the services of his chosen lawyer, he cannot complain that his constitutional rights are infringed.[14] In addition there is no right to engage a lawyer who is 'disabled by law' from representing a client.[15] Thus the rights of the accused are not infringed if his/her legal practitioner is in custody or is not allowed to enter the country. The essence of the right is that the accused is 'able to select a lawyer who can give him effective, independent and courageous representation . . . The choice is wide open and he can select counsel who will defend him with ability, courage and independence without insisting that a lawyer disabled by law should appear for him'.[16] These are highly compelling reasons for rejecting a claim of access to a particular lawyer. But there are other situations where the choice is unfairly limited.

In Zimbabwe, the leading case involves Sampson Paweni, who was charged with defrauding the government of vast sums of money.[17] Contrary to the 'invariable and estimable practice' of discussing the proposed date of a High Court trial with defence counsel, Paweni's lawyers were given thirty-two days notice of the trial date. Both then indicated that due to other commitments, they were unable to appear for the next three months. The State refused to alter the trial date and Paweni then applied for a postponement of the trial on the basis that his constitutional rights were being infringed. Here a different situation existed compared to those above. The chosen counsel were both willing and able to appear; were not 'disabled by law' from doing so; and were timeously instructed. In addition they were not consulted as to the trial date, contrary to the long standing practice.

Even so, the application was refused. In the Supreme Court Justice Gubbay held that the inability of an accused to obtain the services of a specific legal practitioner did not in itself justify the postponement of the trial. According to him, what is protected is:

> the right of an accused to resist a legal practitioner being foisted upon him even when such services will be rendered free of charge. He is entitled to choose whom he wishes to represent him, but if his prime choice is unavailable then he is obliged to look further afield and engage someone else. In other words the right of choice is subject always to the practitioner's availability on the trial date.[18]

Only two authorities were cited for this proposition. Firstly, the South African case of *D'Anos v Heylon (Pty) Ltd*[19] which held that the test is the reasonable convenience of the parties with the requirement of getting through the court's work being the dominant consideration. The availability of counsel is merely a subsidiary question. In the second case of *Raselo & Beston*[20] the Rhodesian High Court asserted that legal practitioners should refuse to act if their availability on the trial date was in question.

The *Paweni* decision is quite unsatisfactory[21] as the principle enunciated is too broad. The term 'unavailable' is nowhere defined. What if the chosen counsel cannot appear at the trial due to sudden illness or transport problems? What if the trial date is deliberately set by the State so as to prevent an accused instructing his chosen representative? In such cases, the constitutional rights of the accused are surely infringed if the court insists on his choosing another lawyer. The test of 'availability' is surely incorrect. It has little authority to support it for the two cases relied on in *Paweni* are open to doubt. The *D'Anos* case was an application to postpone argument in a civil case but, even so, Justice Gubbay held the decision was one of 'general purport'. This is surprising as it is firmly established that civil law principles do not apply in criminal cases. The very fact that a person faces a penal sanction makes it essential that courts concentrate on applying criminal law principles only. Reliance on *Raselo & Beston* is also questionable because the case was decided at a time when there was no Declaration of Rights in Rhodesia. The introduction of the justiciable Declaration fundamentally changed the rights of the accused, a fact apparently not appreciated in *Paweni.*

It seems that the Supreme Court failed to address itself satisfactorily to the issue. There are two alternative approaches. The first is based on the decision of the Supreme Court of Mauritius in *Peroumal.*[22] Here it was held that the constitutional right to counsel 'of his own choice' is paramount and must be upheld, the more so when the accused is in no way at fault. This approach was based on the supremacy of the constitution argument.[23] Thus the right to choose must be conceded unless the State proves some reason to the contrary. This includes, the 'legal disability' of the chosen representative; the negligent delay in obtaining representation; or a deliberate act on the part of the accused or his counsel with the intention of unreasonably delaying the trial. If the State is unable to prove any such reason, the trial must be postponed until the chosen counsel is available. In this way the accused enjoys the full protection of the constitution. One criticism of this approach is that it can lead to a case not being heard within a reasonable time as required by the constitution.[24] But this provision is designed to ensure the accused does not await his trial for an excessively long period. Thus it is an additional safeguard which complements rather than clashes with the right to choose counsel.

An alternative approach is for the court to balance the prejudice caused to the accused against the public interest. Among the factors for consideration here are: whether the public interest requires a rapid determination of the case; the availability of a suitable alternative lawyer; any delay on the part of the accused in seeking his chosen lawyer; and any evidence of *mala fides* in setting down the date for trial. *Paweni* itself well illustrates the position. Here the vast sums of money involved combined with the involvement of high ranking government officials meant that 'by reason of the prevalence of the crime of corruption, particularly among state officials, and the considerable publicity which the case has attracted, it was in the public interest and the interests of justice that the appellants should be brought to trial with a minimum of delay'.[25]

On balance, the approach in *Peroumal* is preferable as it is closer to the spirit of the Constitution. It is precisely because of the seriousness of the case that an accused needs the full protection of the law.[26]

State Action Against Lawyers

Lawyers representing persons involved in security related cases or seeking to publicise human rights abuses are frequently subject to harassment and persecution by the State. An example from Kenya is typical.[27] In December 1986 Mirugi Kariuki, a lawyer who had represented political opponents of the Moi government, was detained under the Public Security Regulations. In February 1987 he sued the Kenyan government alleging that he was tortured and illegally detained. It was later alleged that his insistence on pursuing this claim was the reason for a delay in his release from detention until June 1989. The suit was filed in February 1987 by a fellow lawyer, Gibson Kuria. Shortly afterwards, Kuria himself was detained and only released in December 1987 after his passport was confiscated. Later Kuria's own legal representative was ordered to surrender his passport.[28]

In Zimbabwe, lawyers have also come into conflict with the authorities on a number of occasions. For example, two legal practitioners, Michael Hartman and Nigel Gardener, were retained by two of the accused in the Air Force 6 case. After seeing their clients for the first time i.e. after the use of torture and the making of the alleged confessions, the lawyers took the unprecedented step of calling a news conference which was attended largely by members of the international press. A statement was made detailing the history of the case and the attempts made to gain access to the accused. A question and answer session followed during which Hartman stated:

> We are in a society where law and order and by that I mean the rule of law, is honoured and adhered to and we feel as officers of the Court that if it comes to our notice that certain personnel have used torture to elicit untruthful, or what our clients say are untruthful, confessions then we are honour bound to bring that to your notice.

Gardener stated that the intention of calling the press conference was 'to prevent a further recurrence of the kind of behaviour which had been perpetrated' and to avoid the possibility of the same behaviour being meted out to other suspects. They both said their clients wanted a public affirmation of their side of the story as the local press had already published somewhat one-sided accounts of the arrest and charges. In an apparent attempt by the State to deter others, Hartman and Gardener were later charged with contempt of court. They were convicted at the magistrates' court but their appeal to the Supreme Court was allowed on the basis that there was no real risk that their words were likely to interfere with the due administration of justice.[29] The danger of government intimidation of lawyers in such circumstances is evident and needs to be firmly checked. In response, the Zimbabwe Law Society later published sensible and practical guidelines on the publicising of clients' affairs. These uphold the right of a lawyer to give an interview to the media provided that prior written instructions from the client are obtained except in circumstances when it is genuinely impossible to get such instructions.[30]

Lawyers representing clients in other security cases were also subjected to threats and criminal charges. In January 1989 David Coltart, a Bulawayo lawyer, was charged with tampering with witnesses after representing a client who was involved in the resettlement of former dissidents. It was alleged that this was the result of vindictiveness on the part of the police.[31] In 1988, Hugh Bissett, another Bulawayo lawyer, was convicted of perjury after representing a white Zimbabwean who was sentenced to seven years imprisonment for involvement in a South African inspired raid on the country. An appeal against conviction was allowed by the Supreme Court. Again allegations that government officials were hostile to his role in providing legal representation in a politically sensitive case were made.[32] Such allegations are easily made and difficult to refute. However, the cases do illustrate the potential problems faced by lawyers when taking cases involving security matters. It is absolutely improper for the State or its agents to bring pressure on the legal profession in this manner and it is crucial that both the judiciary and lawyers' organisations remain vigilant to guard against such abuses.

Overview

The right of access to a lawyer represents a fundamental protection for those deprived of their liberty. Some have argued that fears that a legal representative may smuggle contraband to or from a detained client or carry messages which might represent a danger to State security or potential witnesses justify the suspension of the right. However, the dangers attaching to a denial of the right are so great that in practice it must never be abrogated under any circumstances.

The Zimbabwean experience shows that it is vital for a lawyer to have access to his client at the earliest possible moment after detention or arrest. Any 'evidence' obtained in breach of this must be held inadmissible at the trial. It is also the duty of every practitioner to take all necessary steps to protect the rights of his client. Normally a habeas corpus application will suffice but in exceptional cases additional steps, such as recourse to the media, are justified. It is only when a lawyer is prepared and able to utilise every legitimate means to protect the interests of a client that the right is of any real practical value. The courts also have the duty to uphold the right. Pressure is often exerted on the judiciary to reach a result favourable to the State in security related cases. Often this is difficult to resist. The case of the Air Force 6 indicates that, to the lasting credit of the judiciary in Zimbabwe, there was a willingness to uphold both the terms and spirit of the Constitution.

In Camera Proceedings

It is a basic requirement that the proceedings of courts and similar adjudicating bodies are held in public and are followed by a public announcement of the judicial decision.[33] This is subject to the usual provision that permits a court to exclude persons from the proceedings where it is necessary to protect the interests of justice or the State. In times of emergency, the temptation to hold secret trials is often irresistible. For example in Rhodesia in 1975, restrictions on the reporting of judicial proceedings were introduced. A Minister was empowered to order that any civil case be heard in camera and to prohibit the publication of court records. In addition any court or board was empowered to hold any case in camera 'if it appears . . . that there exists a reasonable possibility that the economic interests of the State may be prejudiced through the disclosure of any evidence adduced or to be adduced relating to economic sanctions' against Rhodesia.

This pattern was retained in Zimbabwe where a Minister could issue a certificate prohibiting a court from disclosing any matter if this was in the public interest. An example of the improper use of this procedure was the case of Wally Stuttaford. Here a white member of Parliament was arrested in December 1982 on suspicion of involvement in a conspiracy to overthrow the government. Upon his release, he sought damages from the government. The case proceeded to the High Court but a ministerial intervention meant that not only was the case heard in camera but also that the decision itself was not made public.[34]

The use of these powers is unwarranted and encourages State agents to prevent a proper determination of cases. Fortunately, the scope of ministerial powers was later redefined in the Courts and Adjudicating Authorities (Publicity Restriction) Act 1985 which consolidated the general law and brought it into line with the Constitution. It covers criminal and civil cases before all courts and, amongst other things, it permits the Minister to seek to prevent public disclosure of court proceedings. However, the mere application for the prohibition of the publication of evidence adduced at a trial is not sufficient. Some evidence is required to support the application and to indicate that an order would be necessary or expedient in the interests of defence or public safety.[35] The Minister may also issue a certificate limiting or prohibiting the disclosure of the fact that proceedings may be or will be instituted in the future. He/she is further permitted to prohibit the disclosure of any matter relating to proceedings which do not involve the determination of civil rights or obligations. When a certificate is issued, the Minister may issue notices limiting the disclosure or transmission of particular facts, documents and records by parties to the proceedings. In cases involving national security, it is more acceptable to use this procedure rather than attempting to prevent a judicial determination of the matter. It should also be noted that, unlike many other African countries, no attempt was made to set up 'special security courts' and thus the operation of the judicial system remained intact throughout the period of the emergency.

Burden of Proof

A fundamental principle in criminal cases is that every person charged with an offence is presumed innocent until proven guilty or until he/she has pleaded guilty.[36] A law may place the burden on the accused of proving certain facts.[37] This is not necessarily controversial as it is common to require the defence to prove, on a balance of probabilities, that the accused was insane at the time of committing the criminal act, or to place the legal burden of proof on the accused in some minor statutory offences.

In security related cases the issue becomes more serious because the placing of the burden of proof often determines the outcome of the case. The Law and Order (Maintenance) Act frequently places the legal burden of proof on the accused. For example, upon a charge of committing an act of terrorism, the accused is presumed to have committed the act with intent to endanger law and order 'unless he proves **beyond a reasonable doubt** that he did not intend any such result'[38] [my emphasis]. It is most unusual to place such a heavy burden on the accused, especially in serious offences,[39] and is highly prejudicial because the failure of the accused to disprove the allegation inevitably leads to a conviction. In fact the Act contains fourteen offences which require the accused to prove some exculpatory factor, with four of them carrying the death sentence.[40] In these circumstances, the presumption of innocence is undermined and on principle such provisions are totally unacceptable and do a grave disservice to the criminal justice system.[41]

The presumption of innocence is closely related to the constitutional provision that an accused is not a compellable witness (section 18(8)). The meaning of 'compelled' is crucial. If it covers not only the threat of physical force but also moral persuasion, then the shifting of the burden of proof onto the accused conflicts with the right to silence. Justice Baron examined this point in the Botswana case of *Moagbi*.[42] Dealing with constitutional provisions identical to those of Zimbabwe, he stated:

> it does not seem to me to be tenable to attempt to prescribe types or degrees of compulsion. I can see no distinction in this context between the threat of physical assault or some other consequence, including the threat of conviction. Thus, if legislation were to purport to empower a court to commit to prison an accused who declined to give evidence at his trial, it could not be seriously argued that such a provision would not contravene section [18(8)]. Again, if legislation were to provide that if an accused person fails to give evidence at his trial the court may draw an adverse inference of guilt from such failure, this would clearly contravene both section [18(3)(a)] and section [18(8)]. I am in no doubt that 'compelled' within the meaning of section [18(8)] means the application of pressure of any kind designed to persuade an accused to give evidence.[43]

This is surely the correct approach as the right of silence cannot be swept away by a side wind. The courts in Zimbabwe have yet to determine the issue but if the approach in *Moagbi* is followed, the LOMA provisions may well be declared unconstitutional.[44]

Granting of Bail

The granting of bail is a vital aspect of every criminal justice system. Any person who is held in custody pending trial suffers the same restrictions on his liberty as one serving a sentence of imprisonment after conviction. By keeping accused persons out of custody until tried, convicted and sentenced, bail protects against the dilution of the constitutional presumption of innocence. This presumption encapsulates centuries of social learning about detaining authorities for experience has shown that people are wrongly arrested, as no one has the ability to identify offenders unerringly. Thus justice requires that an impartial court considers whether the suspicions of the detaining authority carries such a high degree of reliability that pre-trial detention should be ordered. In these proceedings, the accused is entitled to make representations for bail because the cost of pre-trial detention is high. Incarceration violently destroys the detainee's private life, effectively threatening his livelihood, his family and his domestic arrangements. Thus a judicial determination of bail mitigates against arbitrary arrest and protects the rights of the accused by ensuring an independent assessment of the question of pre-trial detention. This section focuses on the determination of bail in security related cases. Here State interests often require that an accused is held in custody pending trial. As a result, executive action to restrict the granting of bail sometimes occurs. This intervention into the judicial process raises three issues: (i) is there a constitutional right to bail? (ii) is an accused entitled to have a judicial determination of his bail application? (iii) do the rules of natural justice apply to the bail process?

Is There a Constitutional Right to Bail?

Up to 1926, the granting of bail in Zimbabwe was controlled by a Cape Town Ordinance of 1828[45] which provided that an accused was entitled to bail except in capital cases. The Criminal Procedure and Evidence Act (CPEA) which replaced it essentially repeated the principle.[46] This remained the position until 1960 when, in line with the other security related legislation aimed at combatting African nationalism, the right was destroyed. A magistrate was permitted to deny bail if he believed the accused was likely to commit an offence or 'for any other reason which seems good and sufficient'. This was justified by the Minister of Law and Order on the grounds that 'the government feels that it is farcical that a person with criminal propensities should be allowed at large to commit offences'.[47] As Seidman correctly notes, this means 'that an arrest – not a conviction after trial – demonstrates criminal propensities [and] assumes that a police accusation suffices as proof of guilt'.[48] A second blow was struck when the power to determine the question of bail was usurped by the executive. A new section was introduced into the Law and Order (Maintenance) Act 1960 and this was later inserted into the CPEA as section 106. This now permits the Minister of Home Affairs to certify that 'it is likely that public safety would be prejudiced if the applicant were admitted to bail'. Once issued, the court must refuse the bail application. Prior to the issue of the certificate, the court must adjourn the bail application for up to seven days to allow the Minister time to decide whether or not to issue the document. Thus an accused is at the mercy of the Minister, for the effect of the section is that:

> The order of refusing bail is still made in open Court by a judicial officer, but it is a pantomime of a court. The magistrate is not only compelled to accept the *ex parte* statement of fact [of the Minister of Home Affairs], not supported by any evidence, but the statute also tells him what order to give, namely a refusal of bail.[49]

This provision was condemned by the Zimbabwe High Court on the grounds that:

> it is utterly repugnant to our notions of fairness and justice, and, indeed, the entire tone of our jurisprudence that one party to a dispute should arrogate to himself so much power that he is able to deprive the other of his liberty merely by his say so and to that extent the courts are rendered powerless, once again merely by his say-so.[50]

The provision further infringes upon the principle of *audi alteram partem* in that the accused is not given the opportunity of a hearing nor a right to know the grounds for the refusal of bail.

Such a provision contravenes the fundamental and longstanding tradition that the courts and not the executive determine the question of bail. It is the judiciary which is the body best equipped to deal with the balancing act involving the need to preserve the liberty of the individual with the interests of the due administration of justice. Despite the tradition, the crucial test is whether section 106 is subject to any constitutional protection. A ministerial certificate was challenged in the High Court in 1987 in *Bull*[51] on the ground that it contravened section 13(4) of the Constitution. This states:

> Any person who is arrested or detained . . . upon reasonable suspicion of his having committed, or being about to commit, a criminal offence, and who is not released, shall be brought without undue delay before a court; and if any person arrested or detained upon reasonable suspicion of his having committed or being about to commit a criminal offence is not tried within a reasonable time, then . . . he shall be released either unconditionally or upon reasonable conditions . . .

The first question for the court was whether this section provided a right to bail. It was contended that even though the constitution contained no express provision, the section contained an implied right to bail. This contention was rejected on the ground that if a person were detained upon reasonable suspicion of having committed a criminal offence, it was permissible to hold him pending trial so long as this took place within a reasonable time. The court also held that it is only after a reasonable time had elapsed that a person enjoys a constitutional right not to be deprived of his liberty any longer. A provision which merely narrows the ambit of a law which gratuitously, in the constitutional sense, permits liberty that is constitutionally unprotected to be restored, cannot be said to be inconsistent with the Constitution. Accordingly there was no constitutional right to bail.[52] Support for this view came from the Gambian case of *Jobe*[53] where a similar constitutional provision was examined. Here Lord Diplock stated that there is:

> nothing in the Constitution which invalidates a law imposing a total prohibition on the release of a person reasonably suspected of having committed a criminal offence, provided that he is brought to trial within a reasonable time after he has been arrested and detained. Section 7(1) of the Act which prohibits release on bail, not totally, but subject to an exception if the magistrate is satisfied that there are special circumstances warranting the granting of bail, cannot in their Lordships view be said to be in conflict with any provision of the Constitution.[54]

Lord Diplock stressed that the constitutional provision which requires release does not come into operation unless a person who is arrested upon reasonable suspicion is not tried within a reasonable time. Regrettably, no reasons were advanced for this view and no authority cited.

There are undoubtedly compelling reasons to reject a constitutional right to bail in security cases. Fundamentally the protection of the public must take precedence over individual interests, no matter how serious the repercussions on that person. Further, in Roman–Dutch law and common law jurisdictions, the legislature traditionally retains the right to define bailable offences[55] and a constitutional right to bail would undermine this long established power.[56] Finally, the aim of pre-trial detention in security cases is not to 'punish' but merely to curtail reasonably predictable conduct and is thus a permissible sanction. This deals satisfactorily with the argument that pre-trial detention promotes the 'traditional aims of punishment – retribution and deterrence' and is imposed prior to the judicial determination of guilt.[57] Indeed there are seemingly no constitutional documents which enshrine the right to bail.[58] Thus there is little doubt that there is no constitutional right to bail in Zimbabwe.[59]

Is There an Entitlement to a Judicial Determination of the Matter?

The second question is whether an accused is entitled to a judicial determination of his bail application. In *Bull*, and applying the same reasoning as before, the Supreme Court denied that this was part of due process. It added that as executive intervention in the bail process went back to 1960, if the drafters of the Constitution of Zimbabwe had intended to grant the courts the right to determine bail, the document would have been worded differently.[60] Accordingly, only if a person is held for an unreasonable period is a court bound to order release notwithstanding the ministerial certificate.

The correctness of this point depends upon whether bail proceedings are part of due process. This establishes the universal principle, which goes back to Magna Carta of 1215, that individual liberty is best secured by entrusting the matter to an independent judiciary operating in public. The term 'due process' appears nowhere in the Constitution. However, the point was considered by a South African court in *Smith*.[61] Here an executive order denying bail was challenged and a constitutional provision virtually identical to section 13(4) examined. The court noted that due process does not necessarily imply court proceedings in every context, but the constitutional right to trial within a reasonable time or to release pending trial, clearly relates to a judicial process. Thus it held that an accused has the right to 'trial within a reasonable time, or if not within a reasonable time, then release pending trial subject to suitable guarantees imposed by a court of law'. This means that a statute which eliminates judicial process in matters of personal liberty, including the bail process, is 'plainly unconstitutional'.[62] It conflicts with a constitutional right and is invalid because the Constitution is the supreme law.[63] The High Court of Kenya also adopted this approach in *Ngui*.[64] Here section 123(3) of the Kenya Criminal Procedure Code, which prohibited the granting of bail in certain serious offences, was questioned. It was successfully argued that the section was inconsistent with section 72(5) of the Constitution of Kenya,[65] Chief Justice Simpson noting that section 72(5)

> is applicable to all offences. The amendments to section 123(3) have the effect of prohibiting the High Court from granting bail in cases of murder, treason and robbery, in any circumstances. Thus where, for example, a person is accused of robbery with violence bail may not be granted even though he is not tried within a reasonable time . . . We hold that section 123(3) is inconsistent with . . . section 72(5) . . . and is accordingly void to the extent that this is so.[66]

The cases of *Smith* and *Ngui* were both considered in *Bull*. The Supreme Court considered that the approach in *Smith* would result in an impermissible departure from the clear meaning of the language in the Constitution. *Ngui* was rejected because no authorities were cited and the case of *Jobe* was not brought to the attention of the court. Having followed *Jobe* and being unable to distinguish it, the court was forced to disagree with the reasoning of Chief Justice Simpson.

Fundamentally, the argument revolves around the constitutional role of the judiciary. A court must not abdicate its function as the upholder of the aims and ideals of the constitution. In cases involving personal liberty, it has a duty, as the guardian of individual liberty, to exercise its powers in an appropriate manner. In the case of Zimbabwe, it must be remembered that the Declaration was superimposed on a society which had no tradition of protecting individual freedoms. So it is not surprising perhaps that the government sought to maintain a strong authoritarian attitude towards security matters. Even so, independence and a fully entrenched and justiciable declaration brought a fundamental change in the constitutional position. Although it is unacceptable for the courts to have a constitutional policy-making function, nevertheless they must not allow the unnecessary restriction of individual liberty. Surely the drafters of the Constitution did not intend to deny an accused access to a judicial adjudication simply on the orders of the Minister. Such a serious step requires an express constitutional provision to that effect. Thus it is argued that the due process of law does import a requirement for a judicial determination of bail and that this is implied in section 13(4).

The Supreme Court also reinforced its view on grounds of national security:

> A further consideration which militates against [this] argument is that, even if it were proper to read into section 13(4) . . . a requirement that a judicial decision whether to release on bail or to remand in custody must be permitted even before a reasonable

time for bringing the suspected offender to trial has elapsed, it would nevertheless be constitutionally proper to impose a qualification such as that which is imposed by section [106] because it is a qualification that is concerned with the issue of public security. On such an issue **it is proper for those who are responsible for public security to be the sole judges of what public security requires, the judicial process being unsuitable for reaching decisions on such an issue** (*Council of Civil Service Unions v Minister for the Civil Service*[67])' [my emphasis].

The highlighted words were taken from the well-known judgment of Lord Parker in *The Zamora*.[68] In the *CSSU* case, there was an application for judicial review of a ministerial decision following the failure of the Minister to consult with the union over the banning of trade unions at a United Kingdom government communications centre. The House of Lords held that in principle, the decision-making process was unfair and the courts would have protected the reasonable expectation of consultation by judicial review. The question was whether national security considerations superseded that expectation. The court held that this was a matter of evidence. It was accepted that the decision on whether the requirements of national security outweighs the duty of fairness in any particular case is for the government alone. However this does not exclude the courts entirely. As Lord Fraser pointed out 'if the decision is successfully challenged on the ground that it has been reached by a process which is unfair, then the government is under an obligation to produce evidence that the decision was in fact based on grounds of national security'.[69] He derived authority for this from Lord Parker's words in *The Zamora* noted earlier. Lord Scarman also noted that these words were not an abdication of the judicial function but were an indication of the evidence required by the court. He continued:

> The true significance of Lord Parker's dictum is simply that the court is in no position to substitute its opinion for the opinion of those responsible for national security. But the case is a fine illustration of the court's duty to ensure that the essential facts to which the opinion or judgment of those responsible relates are proved to the satisfaction of the court.[70]

Accordingly it is argued that the Supreme Court in *Bull* erred in finding that the judicial process is excluded in matters of national security. This is reinforced by the fact that the *CSSU* case did not deal with a question of individual liberty. Further, section 13(4) is not subject to any derogation or abrogation except by the use of emergency regulations and these were not used by the Minister.

It is quite unrealistic for government to fear that the courts will disregard the national interest. The court is only interested in establishing whether the State has a reasonable suspicion that the accused has committed a security offence. As a general rule, courts do not and should not grant bail when the offence is of a security nature and it is recognised that in some cases detention may well comport with due process.[71] So due process is satisfied if a remand in custody occurs after it is judicially determined that there are reasonable grounds for suspicion. In the circumstances, it is argued that the Constitution of Zimbabwe provides for due process in bail proceedings, including security related cases.

Do the Rules of Natural Justice Apply?

The third question concerns the right of an accused to make representations to the Minister regarding the decision whether or not to issue the certificate. It will be remembered that the Minister has up to seven days to make up his mind. In common law and Roman–Dutch law jurisdictions, the right to be heard is firmly established. This right involves several components: giving notice to the person adversely affected of the intended action; furnishing him with information or facts which he may be able to controvert; and giving him the opportunity to put his side of the matter in an appropriate manner. This does not mean, however, that it is appropriate to make available in all cases the facilities which are allowed for a judicial determination of the issue.[72] In the case of executive decision making, the Minister must act fairly and listen to both sides of the question. There are numerous decisions which support the view that there is a right to be heard in cases involving individual liberty. The duty to act judicially is inferred from the nature of the decision to be taken and is not dependent upon the nature of the decision-making body.[73] The right to be heard is subject to exclusion in the face of a clear legislative intent which negates and excludes the implication. It is also subject to questions of public policy which the court must take into account in determining whether the rules apply to a particular body and what constitutes a fair hearing of any individual case.[74]

Section 106 of CPEA does not specifically place a duty on the Minister to allow representations on this issue. The point was not considered in *Bull* but a rejection of the right is implicit in the court's view of the power of the executive in security cases. The point was discussed in the South African case of *Baleka*.[75] It was argued that the right to a hearing inevitably involves a certain amount of delay in the decision-making process. If this is likely to seriously diminish the effectiveness of the measure, it is proper for the decision to be taken without full consultation. For example, the detention of a person who is considered an immediate threat to national security does not carry with it a duty to hear the detainee prior to the detention. Thus it was argued that this principle applies to bail proceedings, for a dangerous accused might be released by a court before executive attempts to comply with the duty to hear representations are completed. This view was rejected by the majority of the court which held that the statute (like section 106) provided for a two stage procedure. At the first stage, the court need only be informed that the issuing of a certificate was being considered. Thereupon it was automatically precluded from granting bail. At this stage, the legislature had specifically provided for continued detention without the right to be heard because of the security implications. The second stage cannot arise until the decision of the Minister is known or the time limit for the decision has expired. The time limit was provided to enable the Minister to obtain the necessary information in order to make a decision as to whether or not to issue the certificate. It followed that because 'the legislature did not intend the Minister to perpetrate an injustice by his decision, there is good reason to assume that the legislature intended that the [Minister] should comply with the principles of natural justice, including *audi alteram partem*, at least to such extent as may reasonably be possible in the time available.'[76] This approach is surely correct, for the stage one procedure fully protects State interests. Thus it cannot harm the State if the accused then has the right to be heard. It is generally acknowledged that the *audi alteram partem* rule is subject to some restrictions when it is contrary to national security for certain information to be disclosed. But a qualified right to be heard is still important particularly in security cases for three reasons. Firstly, there may be other relevant facts which are known only to the accused. Disclosure of these will assist the Minister in reaching a decision. For example, the accused may show that the Minister has mistaken him for someone else with the same or similar name; or that a decisive change has occurred in his personal circumstances, his health or some other factors(s) which might lead to the inference that he cannot be considered a threat to national security. Secondly, there is nothing in section 106 to indicate that the legislature intended to exclude the right completely. The fact that a right is restricted does not lead to the inference that the legislature intended to abolish it entirely. *Audi alteram partem* is not an all or nothing rule.[77] State security considerations will prevent the Minister from furnishing the accused with security information but this does not affect the duty of the Minister to hear the accused. Thirdly, the implication that the legislature did not intend to abrogate the right entirely is strengthened in that there is no alternative means for the accused to make any representations concerning his detention. For example, even those detained without trial under a ministerial detention order are entitled to receive reasons for their detention and to make representations to a review tribunal.

In 1987 the point was briefly considered by the High Court in Zimbabwe in *Carvalho*.[78] Justice Sandura approved the dissenting judgment of Justice Eloff in *Baleka* who stated: 'I think it unlikely that the Legislature contemplated that [the Minister] should conduct his own hearing, and that he should afford the persons concerned the right to be heard'.[79] In the case itself, the applicant was facing serious charges involving the unlawful exportation of foreign exchange. However, he had no travel documents, held substantial property in Zimbabwe and all his family lived there. Such factors might well have influenced the Minister if he was under a duty to hear the applicant's representation. Thus a limited right to be heard cannot conceivably adversely affect national security and it is argued that the section 106 procedure does import a requirement that the Minister consider any representations made by the accused person. The correctness of this approach was accepted in the later case of *Mutambara*[80] where the High Court set aside a ministerial order holding that the Minister was obliged to give an applicant for bail a chance to state his/her side of the story and must take account of what that person has said when arriving at a decision. This accords with common sense and justice and the decision in *Carvalho* must now be considered wrongly decided.[81]

The intervention of the executive into the judicial process is always a matter of great concern. Section 106 was introduced by a white racist government at the height of the enactment of extremely repressive security legislation aimed at curtailing African nationalism. It followed the lead taken in South Africa in this regard. Such a provision has no place in independent Zimbabwe. It is unknown in neighbouring States such as Zambia, Botswana and Kenya and its continued use does the criminal justice system a grave disservice. Government secrecy in such matters is misplaced, especially because the evidence and its sources will probably be revealed if the case comes to trial. Whilst security considerations make the granting of bail unlikely, the judiciary must be allowed to fulfil its traditional function of balancing the interests of the State with those of the individual.[82]

Ousting the Legal Process

Every person is entitled to have his civil rights and obligations determined by an independent and impartial court.[83] This right is threatened by the use of indemnity provisions. In times of or following a period of armed conflict or civil unrest, access to the courts is sometimes denied. This is often the result of an indemnity granted to the security forces. The position in Rhodesia well illustrates the point. As the success of the freedom fighters increased during the 1970s, the Rhodesian security forces became increasingly harsh in their treatment of the black civilian population. Reports of such conduct was both damaging and dangerous to the authorities and the view was taken that the forces required a 'free hand' in the matter and, if possible, the concealment of the atrocities. In April 1975 the Catholic Commission For Justice and Peace published a booklet entitled *The Man in the Middle*. This alleged that the Rhodesian security forces had tortured and assaulted innocent civilians and destroyed property in certain tribal areas of the country. It was alleged that the acts were committed with the intention of extracting information about the movement of guerillas and of intimidating the African populace into co-operating with the security forces. These allegations, and others of a similar nature, were refuted by the government although it rejected a call for an independent enquiry on the grounds that any aggrieved person had a perfectly adequate remedy through the ordinary courts. Categorical assurances were given that the courts would remain open for individuals to air their grievances. Accordingly, a number of civil claims were brought in the High Court. In response to this, the Indemnity and Compensation Act 1975 was passed, apparently because government felt that the pending court actions were being brought purely for political reasons. The Act banned the bringing of civil and criminal proceedings in any court of law against the State in respect of acts done in good faith while acting for the purpose of, or in connection with, the suppression of terrorism or maintenance of public order. A written certificate by the Minister that the act was done for this purpose was deemed conclusive proof that the act was so done. No court could question the certificate even if it could be proved that the act in question had nothing whatsoever to do with the suppression of terrorism.[84] The statute was heavily criticised by the former Rhodesian Federal Chief Justice Sir Robert Tredgold on the ground that in effect the Cabinet was made the sole judge in its own cause.[85] The Bill was referred to the Senate Legal Committee which reported that it was inconsistent with the Declaration of Rights. The Senate agreed with the report but when it came to a vote unanimously approved it. The Act was repealed after independence.[86]

By 1982 considerable disquiet over the activities of the security forces in Matabeleland led to the making of emergency regulations based on the 1975 Act.[87] The Minister of Defence was empowered to prevent the bringing of legal proceedings against any member of the security forces in respect of anything done 'for the purpose of or in connection with preservation of the security of Zimbabwe' if of the view that (i) the act was committed in good faith; (ii) the act was for the purpose of or in connection with the preservation of the security of Zimbabwe; and (iii) it was in the national interest that such proceedings or claims be restricted to the remedies specified in the regulations.

A number of critical comments are necessary. First, the meaning of 'in good faith' was entirely vague and ambiguous. Second, the regulations provided for a subjective test in that the Minister's decision on the merits of the case was final and purported to oust the jurisdiction of the court. Third, the regulations indemnified members of the security forces in advance as well as retrospectively. This effectively placed the security forces above the law. Finally, the regulations enabled the government to maintain what amounted to a state of martial law without any resort to parliament. In this respect, the 1975 statute at least provided for some parliamentary debate on the issue. The regulations were considered by the Senate Legal Committee (SLC) which found that they conflicted with the constitutional right to trial by an independent and impartial court. On 1 October 1982, an adverse report was made to the Senate and following consultations between the committee and government law officers, the regulations were repealed and replaced.[88] The constitutional problem was tackled by providing that no liability would attach to 'any member of the security forces . . . in respect of anything done in good faith by such member . . . for the purposes or in connection with the preservation of the security of Zimbabwe' (section 4(1)). A certificate in writing from the Minister of Defence confirming that the action complied with the section was 'prima facie proof in any court of law of the fact that such matter or thing was so done'.[89] The SLC found that this cured the defect and withdrew its adverse report.[90] This was surprising as the new section now purported to abrogate the right of payment of compensation in a case where a certificate was issued, contrary to the constitutional right to compensation for unlawful arrest or detention. In 1984 the matter was finally considered by the Supreme Court in *Granger*[91] which accepted the plaintiff's submission that section

4(1) was not in accordance with schedule 2(1) of the Constitution. This permits derogation from the right to compensation where the action is taken 'to deal with any situation arising during a period of public emergency', provided the action does not exceed anything which 'could reasonably be thought to be required for the purpose of dealing with the situation'. The Supreme Court held that section 4(1) was not a law providing for the taking of action for the purpose of dealing with a particular situation which had arisen as envisaged in paragraph 1(1) of the schedule.[92] In addition, the court found that the indemnity in the regulations differed materially from that contained in the schedule. The former constituted a subjective test as regards the question of good faith whilst the latter provided for an objective test.

The decision is clearly correct. A law which provides that there is no liability for damages **for action taken** cannot be included in an indemnity provision covering a law which provides **for the taking of action** as required in the schedule. Similarly, a subjective test seeks to oust the jurisdiction of the courts whereas the schedule provides that the courts are the sole arbiters as to whether the action was reasonably required in the circumstances. Accordingly, the Supreme Court held that section 4(1) was inconsistent with the Constitution and thus void.[93]

The granting of an indemnity during a period of public emergency is quite unacceptable as it gives the security forces a licence to operate outside the law.[94] In support of such legislation, it is argued that cases might otherwise be brought with the sole intention of embarrassing the security forces.[95] Alternatively, it is said that even if a court is informed of the facts, it is seldom in a position to determine the necessity of the acts.[96] These are hardly credible arguments. The right of the citizen to have free access to the courts is undeniable whilst State interests are protected if the case is heard in camera. In addition, the courts are perfectly able to take a pragmatic approach in such cases.

The constitutional safeguards have proved capable of maintaining a balance between the State and the individual by ensuring that rights and liabilities are determined by judicial means. The fundamental problem of the use of security powers to create a virtual state of martial law remains. In peacetime it is quite improper to resort to such powers and it is hoped that they are not used again in the country.

In 1981 there was an attempt to oust the legal process, albeit in less serious circumstances. A dispute developed between the Minister of Health and the Family Planning Association over the use of a contraceptive. The association, which was headed by a European, considered the contraceptive device was unsafe but the Minister did not agree and made emergency regulations which permitted him to take possession of the assets of the association.[97] These provided that the return of the property was a matter entirely for the Minister. The SLC found the regulations unconstitutional and they were replaced by fresh ones which provided for a judicial determination of the matter. The desire to protect family planning services is certainly commendable. What is questionable is the manner in which this was attempted, for the regulations were clearly used for administrative convenience and were in no way connected with the reasons for the state of emergency.[98]

Overview

The use of indemnities to oust the jurisdiction of the courts is a most undesirable practice. This is especially so when the indemnity relates to future conduct, for this is tantamount to an acceptance by the government that the security forces will, or at least are liable to, contravene individual freedoms. Such action is only undertaken by repressive regimes.[99] In view of the serious consequences attaching to indemnities, it is hoped that if any future action in this regard is contemplated, it is undertaken by statute. This procedure is well illustrated by passing of the Protection of Wildlife (Indemnity) Act in May 1989 which indemnifies persons acting in good faith against criminal liability arising out of actions taken against poachers.

Notes

1. See, for example, Article 7 of the African Charter.
2. See, for example, the constitutions of The Gambia, Kenya and Zambia. See generally, van Maarseveen, 1978.
3. Sections 101 and 183 Criminal Procedure and Evidence Act.
4. *R v Kuraza* 1967 RLR 225. Chief Justice Beadle stated that: 'The right . . . in no way depends upon the difficulty or the complexity of the case; it is an inherent right which every accused person possesses.'
5. Sections 13(3) and 18(3).
6. About £5.5m/US$9.5m. Seven Hunter fighter jets and one Cessna F.337 were destroyed. One British Aerospace Hawk Mk 60 jet fighter, which had arrived from Britain just ten days earlier and which had flown less than 25 hours, was also destroyed. For an account of the attack see Cole, 1988, pp.1–10.
7. *S v Slatter* [1986] LRC (Crim) 66.
8. *S v Slatter*, Unreported, Supreme Court of Zimbabwe SC-49-84.
9. For details on this point see Chapter 8.
10. Approving *Haynes v Washington* 373 US 514. The trial judge also approved the approach of Chief Justice Warren in *Miranda v Arizona* 384 US 478; 86 SC 1602, where he said that statements given freely and voluntarily without any compelling influence are admissible in evidence.
11. An appeal by the Attorney-General to the Supreme Court was dismissed, the court fully supporting the views of the trial judge.
12. (1964) 48 DLR 110 at p.115. Justice Gubbay in Slatter specifically approved these words. See also *Smith v Illinois* 105 S Ct 490 (1984).
13. Justice Eberle in *Taylor* 1983 CLB 597 (Canada). Cf *S v Nhidza*, Unreported, Supreme Court of Zimbabwe SC 147/89 where the Supreme Court held that negligence on the part of the appellant in timeously seeking a legal representative of his choice was a problem of his own making.
14. *R v Second* 1969 (2) RLR 285 (RA).
15. *Awolowo v Federal Minister of Internal Affairs* 1962 Lag LR 177 (Nigeria) and *Public Prosecutor v Venkata* 1961 AP 104 (India).
16. Chief Justice Skinner in *Patel v Attorney-General* [1969] ZR 97.
17. *Paweni v Acting Attorney-General* 1985 (3) SA 720 (SC).
18. Above at p.723.
19. 1950 (1) SA 324.
20. 1960 R & N 803 (High Court of Rhodesia and Nyasaland).
21. With the vast majority of accused persons unable to obtain legal representation, the possibility of a lawyer being 'foisted' upon an unwilling accused is difficult to envisage.
22. Supreme Court Judgment No 228 of 1983. See also *Muyimba v Uganda* [1969] EA 433.
23. See Chapter 5 for a full discussion.
24. Section 13(4), Constitution of Zimbabwe.
25. In *Govere & Others*, Unreported, Supreme Court of Zimbabwe SC 125/85 four government officers were convicted of accepting bribes from Paweni. Sentences of up to five years imprisonment were imposed.
26. The core of rights principle should also apply here as the primary right of access to a legal representative must include a concomitant right to a lawyer of the person's choice.
27. This information is derived from the Centre for the Independence of Judges and Lawyers, 1989, pp.20–22. The report also alleges that lawyers in Burkina Faso, Zaire, Nigeria, Liberia, South Africa, Zimbabwe and Ghana were also subject to harassment and persecution during this period.
28. This was after he had gone to the United States to receive a human rights award on behalf of Kuria.
29. See *S v Hartman* 1983(2) ZLR 186.
30. *Legal Practitioners: Guidelines on Publicity*, Law Society of Zimbabwe, 20 April 1988. The Guidelines refer with approval to the note of caution referred to by Chief Justice Georges in *S v Hartman* above, where he stated that 'Nothing in this judgment should therefore be taken as casting doubt on the wisdom of the well established custom of lawyers not to discuss in public outside the courts matters concerning cases in which they are involved' (at p.196).
31. See Africa Watch, p.41.
32. See previous note at p.39. In both the Coltart and Bisset cases the allegations were never substantiated.
33. This is reflected in section 18, Constitution of Zimbabwe.
34. To date, the High Court judgment has not been released.
35. See the Zimbabwe High Court decision of *S v Mutambara* 1989 ([illegible]) ZLR 96.
36. Section 18(3)(a), Constitution of Zimbabwe.
37. Section 18(13)(b).
38. Section 50, LOMA.

39. See Williams, 1982, p.290 *et seq* and Cross and Tapper, 1990, p.146 *et seq*.
40. Seven others carry a maximum prison sentence of between five and ten years.
41. The Emergency Powers (Maintenance of Essential Services) Regulations 1989 SI 160A/89 provided for the summary dismissal of any employee if 'without lawful excuse, the proof of which lies on him' he engaged in industrial action.
42. *Attorney-General of Botswana v Moagbi*, Unreported, Criminal Appeal Case 28 of 1979.
43. Since this decision, the National Security Act 1986 was passed. This provides that it is an offence punishable with up to thirty years imprisonment for any person to 'carry out acts which are considered prejudicial to the safety or interests of Botswana'. It also provides that an accused is presumed guilty until he proves his innocence. It will be interesting to see whether this section is held constitutional in view of the Moagbi decision. In Zambia, the compulsory furnishing of a sworn statement regarding assets as required by the Corrupt Practices Act 1980 was held unconstitutional as being contrary to the presumption of innocence: see *Simataa v Attorney-General*, Unreported, High Court of Zambia, 1986.
44. Evidential matters were also affected by the Emergency Powers (Evidence in Criminal Proceedings) Regulations 1978 SI 668/78. These rendered certain documents, either copies or originals, admissible in spite of the hearsay rule. The regulations remained in force after independence. See also Emergency Powers (Evidence in Criminal Proceedings) (Amendment) Regulations No 1 1984 SI 153/84.
45. Ordinance No. 40, 1828, sections 27–44.
46. For an account of the historical development of bail in Zimbabwe see Seidman, n.d., pp.1–4. See also Hatchard, 1988, pp.952–4.
47. 51 *Hansard* col 1633.
48. Above, p.7.
49. *Smith v Attorney-General, Bophuthatswana* 1984 (1) SA 196, at p.200.
50. Justice Sansole in *Bull v Minister of Home Affairs* [1987] LRC (Const) 547 at p.550.
51. *Bull v Minister of Home Affairs* [1987] LRC (Const) 555.
52. See the judgment of Beck JA at p.562.
53. *Attorney-General of The Gambia v Momdou Jobe* [1984] AC 689 (PC).
54. At p.697.
55. For example, in Zimbabwe bail cannot be granted in capital offences.
56. Of course this remains subject to any constitutional provision to the contrary: see *Ngui v Republic of Kenya* discussed below.
57. See the discussion in *United States v Edwards* 430 A 2d 1321.
58. In fact, even the Eighth Amendment to the United States Constitution merely provides that 'excessive bail shall not be required'. This is due, at least in part, to the fact that federal statutes have always provided for the right to bail in non-capital cases.
59. Of course, section 106(2) ceases to be valid if the constitution is violated, for example, by a failure to bring the suspect to trial within a reasonable time: see *Fikilini v Attorney General* 1990 (1) ZLR 105.
60. Above, p.564.
61. *Smith v Attorney-General, Bophuthatswana* 1984 (1) SA 196.
62. At p.201.
63. This corresponds to section 3 of the Constitution of Zimbabwe which declares the supremacy of the Constitution.
64. *Ngui* [1986] LRC (Const) 308.
65. This is essentially in identical terms to section 13(4) of the Constitution of Zimbabwe.
66. At p.311.
67. [1985] AC 374.
68. [1916] 2 AC 277 (PC).
69. At p.402.
70. At p.405.
71. For example, in *United States v Melendez-Carrion* 790 F 2d 984, the court concluded that pre-trial detention under the Bail Reform Act 1984 was analogous to the detention of adults of Japanese ancestry during World War Two. The court reasoned that the concern regarding the possibility that Japanese–Americans were engaging in espionage represented the 'rare circumstance' in which detention comports with due process (at p.1004).
72. See *Buthelezi v Attorney-General, Natal* 1986 (4) SA 377, at p.379 and *Heatherdale Farms v Deputy Minister of Agriculture* 1980 (3) SA 476, at p.486.
73. *Ridge v Baldwin* [1964] AC 40.
74. See *Smith* above at p.201 and *R v Hull Prison Board of Visitors ex parte St Germain* [1978] QB 678 (CA).
75. 1986 (1) SA 361.
76. Stegmann J at p.387.
77. See the discussion in *Buthelezi* above at p.380.
78. HC-H-627-87.
79. 1986 (1) SA at p.406.
80. *S v Mutambara* 1989 (3) ZLR 96.
81. In South Africa the Appellate Division also reached the same conclusion in *Attorney General, Eastern Cape v Blom* 1988 (4) SA 645 (A).
82. For a recent example of an enlightened judicial attitude to bail see the Tanzanian case of *Director of Public Prosecutions v Daudi Pete* (Criminal Appeal No. 28 of 1990) where the Court of Appeal held that a provision which enabled bail to be denied was so widely drawn as to contravene the constitutional right to liberty of the person. See also the comment on the case by Coldham, 1991, p.178.

83. Section 18(9) Constitution of Zimbabwe.
84. For a detailed examination of the Act see Feltoe, 1975, p.121.
85. See his comments in *Rhodesia Herald*, 6 September 1975.
86. It was retained long enough for Edgar Tekere, then a senior government Minister, to rely on it in order to obtain an acquittal on a charge of murder. See Chapter 11 for details of the case.
87. Emergency Powers (Security Forces Indemnity) Regulations SI 487/82.
88. Emergency Powers (Security Forces Indemnity)(Amendment) Regulations No. 2 SI 159/83.
89. At that time the Prime Minister was also Minister of Defence. In the circumstances this was undesirable for if the ministerial certificate was challenged as being made in bad faith, the Prime Minister himself would have been required to file affidavits and even appear in court. With the establishment of the executive presidency, the post of Minister of Defence is now held separately.
90. Minutes of Meeting, 12 May 1983.
91. *Granger v Minister of State Security* 1984 (2) ZLR 92.
92. See above for a discussion on this provision.
93. The regulations were later repealed: Emergency Powers (Sundry Regulations)(Repeal) Regulations 1985 SI 359/85.
94. The fact that indemnity laws should be used only after the conclusion of 'hostilities' (if at all) is illustrated in Uganda. The Indemnity Proclamation (Legal Notice 6 of 1986) was made following the assumption of power by the Museveni regime. It stated that all civil actions against the government for any tortious action or breach of statutory duty committed by security forces or intelligence agencies between 1 November 1978 and 26 January 1986 was barred.
95. This argument was advanced by the Minister of Law and Order in the debate on the 1975 Act: see *Hansard* 28 August 1975.
96. See the comments of the Minister of Law and Order, *Hansard*, above.
97. Emergency Powers (Family Planning) Regulations 1981 SI 643/81. The Minister stated: 'This racist running the association threatened to dismantle the whole outfit . . . In our desire to preserve human freedom in planning our families we requested emergency powers to take over the association and put it at the service of our people.' *Parliamentary Debates*, 13 July 1983.
98. One wonders whether there can ever be any connection between contraception and emergency powers!
99. For example the South African Defence Act places what amounts to a complete ouster on judicial scrutiny of the actions of the defence forces. See *Kaluma v Minister of Defence* 1984 (4) SA 59 (SWA).

10 Freedom of Movement & of Conscience

Freedom of Movement

Restrictions on the freedom of movement are felt more than the infringement of many other freedoms because they affect almost everyone. The right to move freely throughout Zimbabwe, the right to reside in any part of Zimbabwe, the right to enter and to leave Zimbabwe, and immunity from expulsion are all constitutionally protected.[1] They are subject to restrictions including those required in the interests of defence, public safety and public order although no law may permit citizens of Zimbabwe from leaving or being excluded or expelled from the country.[2] In practice, security laws affected both the right to move within Zimbabwe and the right to leave and re-enter the country.

Right of Movement within Zimbabwe

Emergency regulations worldwide frequently impose restrictions on internal movement. Such limitations were a feature of the UDI period in Rhodesia. A senior police officer had complete discretion to control the movement of persons into and out of a particular area, whilst the Minister of Internal Affairs could direct the police to move 'the public or any section of the public out of or to any particular portion [of an area] in the interests of public safety or public order'. He could also direct the imposition of a curfew. These powers were used to create 'protected villages' which were designed to prevent the rural peasant population assisting the guerillas. In July 1974 the first protected village was established with nearly 50,000 rural inhabitants being forcibly moved into 21 villages. By 1978 the numbers in the villages had grown to about 750,000.[3] The imposition of curfews also became widespread in many rural areas. Although ostensibly carrying a penalty of up to two years imprisonment, in practice many civilians were shot for breaching an order. Perhaps the following notice epitomises the situation:

> As from dawn on January 20 1978 the following restrictions will be imposed upon all of you . . .
> 1. Human curfew from last light to 12 o'clock daily.
> 2. Cattle, yolked oxen, goats and sheep curfew from last light to 12 o'clock daily.
> 3. No vehicles, including bicycles or buses, to run in the area.
> 4. No person will either go on or near any high ground or they will be shot.
> 5. All dogs to be tied up 24 hours each day or they will be shot.
> 6. Cattle, sheep and goats, after 12 o'clock are only to be herded by adults.
> 7. No juveniles (to the age of 16 years) will be allowed out of the kraal area at any time either day or night, or they will be shot.

8. No schools will be open.
9. All stores and grinding mills will be closed.[4]

The security problems after independence again led to the imposition of restrictions upon internal movement. A senior police officer was permitted to order a curfew whenever public disorder occurred or was apprehended.[5] Emergency regulations also permitted the Minister of Home Affairs to order the imposition of a curfew in order to ensure that people in the designated area did not become involved in security operations against terrorists.[6] Regulations also permitted a senior police officer to restrict the movement of persons in a curfew area to no more than fifty metres from a dwelling; to control all traffic in the curfew area; and to close down all shops and offices in the area or control their opening hours.[7]

The imposition of curfews became a common feature of life in many parts of the country during the dissident problem. The most highly publicised incident occurred in 1982 when, following the abduction of the six foreign tourists in Matabeleland, a night curfew was immediately imposed covering more than 90,000 square kilometres (35,000 square miles). Another major curfew led to the cordoning off of a large part of Bulawayo and the imposition of a 9pm to 4am curfew following the 1981 attacks on the homes of the Prime Minister and Enos Nkala. In addition, in February 1984, a curfew covering 13,000 square kilometres (5,000 square miles) was imposed in southern Matabeleland following an upsurge in dissident activity. Originally lasting from dusk to dawn, it was later extended to around the clock. Stores were closed and traffic prevented from entering or leaving the area. During the three-month operation it was alleged that members of the security forces tortured, raped and occasionally killed villagers during operations against dissidents.[8] In addition, the curfew regulations were used to close stores and to prevent the transportation of food into the region. This was at a time of severe drought and the action undoubtedly inflicted great suffering on the people in the area.

Although denied by government, there is little doubt that the restrictions were designed to coerce the local population into co-operating with the security forces. The use of curfews also enabled the security forces to operate with little control and 'brought about the maiming and death of hundreds and hundreds of innocent people who [were] neither dissidents nor collaborators'.[9]

Both the regulations and the Law and Order (Maintenance) Act provided that anyone found out of doors contrary to an order was guilty of an offence.[10] As a result there were many convictions. For example, in one case[11] two men were found within a curfew area in circumstances in which they did not and could not have known that they were committing an offence. Nevertheless, they were both convicted and sentenced to three months imprisonment, suspended for three years. In another case,[12] a man was fined Zimb $50 for breaking a curfew although he was too drunk to know what he was doing. In rural areas it is not always possible for news of a curfew to spread rapidly and the imposition of strict liability offences greatly exacerbates the plight of the local population.[13]

Other controls on the movement of traffic were also invoked, including restrictions on the navigation of vessels on Lake Kariba which dated from 1976.[14] In addition, in 1987 when the Sandawana area of Matabeleland/Midlands was declared a protected area. An order provided that 'no person who is normally resident beyond a radius of fifty kilometres from any point on the perimeter of the protected area shall enter or remain in the protected area except with the written permission of the officer in charge of the police station at Mberengwa or West Nicholson . . .' In addition, restrictions were placed on the movement of cars.[15] Significantly, the use of these regulations was not related to any security problems but were introduced to combat an increase in unauthorised mining of precious stones.

The right of free movement within a country is recognised in many human rights documents. The African Charter states that 'Every individual shall have the right to freedom of movement and residence within the borders of a State provided he abides by the law.'[16] This is not an absolute right as restrictions on movement on the grounds of public safety or national security are well established in both international and domestic law.[17] Few would argue that a State should not have the power to restrict internal movement during periods of serious civil unrest which threatens national security. But it is the abuse of these powers which is worrying, for entrusting the security forces with uncontrolled and wide-ranging powers over the civilian population is a potent threat to individual freedoms. The use of curfews and other restrictions on movement means that in practice it is difficult to differentiate between the actions of the Rhodesian forces during the freedom struggle and those of the Zimbabwean security forces in Matabeleland. The basis for the action in both cases was the security legislation of the former white regime, with the only changes being the later reinforcement of those powers.

There was no obligation on the part of the authorities to give any information or explanation regarding the use of these powers and the secrecy and the manner in which the security forces operated greatly undermined the justification for such action. This problem was exacerbated by the placing of restrictions upon the reporting of the measures being taken by security forces.[18] For example, on 5 November 1983 the Minister declared a large area of Matabeleland and part of the Midlands province subject to reporting restrictions for a period of two months.[19] Of course, any information concerning operational details of the security forces which is capable of assisting its opponents is clearly secret. However in this case the restrictions were imposed with the intention of permitting the security forces unlimited freedom of action, to the detriment of the local populace.

The result of this was that the restrictions placed on the right to free movement rendered the constitutional protection essentially ineffective at precisely the moment when it was most needed. The danger of abuse of power means that it is necessary to ensure that the nation is fully informed of the scope and reasons for restricting internal movement and the use that is made of the powers.[20] This could be done by requiring the Minister to report to Parliament whenever such restrictions are imposed and to permit a parliamentary and/or judicial delegation to visit the restricted area to observe the situation at first hand.[21]

Right to Move Into and Out of Zimbabwe

During the colonial period, the movement of African workers across colonial borders in southern Africa was common. In particular, many men from Mozambique and the then Federation of Rhodesia and Nyasaland went to work in the mines in South Africa. There was also a considerable movement of people within the Federation itself. The colonial powers throughout Africa did little to deal with the issue of citizenship for Africans and it was left to the newly independent states to tackle the question. No common procedure was adopted so that the right to citizenship varies from country to country. Deteriorating economic and social conditions have led to the expulsion of 'non-citizens' from several states. For example, between 1983 and 1985, Nigeria expelled up to three million people on security and economic grounds. In 1983 as many as 200,000 ethnic Rwandans fled from Uganda following the decision of Milton Obote to expel them as 'alien' migrants, despite the fact that many were born in Uganda and had lived there for decades. Perhaps the most publicised incident involved Idi Amin in Uganda in 1972 when he declared that all Asian residents must leave the country within three months. This was in spite of the fact that many were Ugandan citizens. About 15,000 Asians who presented proof of citizenship to the authorities had it arbitrarily revoked.

Any forced expulsion from a country is traumatic, especially for those claiming citizenship. Not surprisingly, many human rights documents and national constitutions seek to protect rights of entry and residence. In Zimbabwe the Constitution recognises citizenship acquired either by birth, descent or registration, ensuring that considerably more people acquired citizenship than was the case in most other African states. For citizens of Zimbabwe, the Constitution specifically restricts the making of any law which 'prevents any person from leaving Zimbabwe or excluding or expelling from Zimbabwe any person who is a citizen of Zimbabwe' (section 22(4)). However, following the Peter Walls affair, this protection was later made subject to emergency regulations. On 15 April 1980 it was announced that Walls, a Zimbabwean citizen and the former Supreme Commander of the Rhodesian Forces, would preside over the new Joint Command of the armed forces with overall responsibility for the amalgamation of the Zimbabwe Army.[22] In July 1980 he left the country and it was announced that he was taking extended leave pending retirement at the end of the year. In a television interview in Britain he then intimated that he had been within hours of staging a coup following the election victory of Robert Mugabe. This revelation provoked a swift response from government. In Parliament the Minister of Information told Members that the remarks had totally undermined African confidence in whites holding senior positions in the new government and had seriously damaged race relations. The Prime Minister himself denounced Walls accusing him of disloyalty and saying that he would not be permitted to continue living in the country. This announcement was followed by the making of emergency regulations which provided that:

> If it appears to the President that it is necessary in the interests of public safety or public order that any person, **whether or not he is a citizen of Zimbabwe** should not remain in or enter Zimbabwe, he may . . . declare such person to be an undesirable resident.[23] [my emphasis].

The provision was defended by government on the grounds that an alternative remedy to preventive detention was needed. The regulations were 'aimed at citizens whose loyalty is questionable or suspect, and persons who, because of their rank or past experience, might be in a very good position to act in a manner which could be prejudicial to Zimbabwe's security situation.'[24] The regulations were perfectly valid because, as the Senate Legal Committee acknowledged, the right of a citizen to enter and leave Zimbabwe remains subject to derogation during a period of public emergency.[25] The regulations were also intra vires the Emergency Powers Act. Although that statute provides for the making of regulations relating to 'the deportation and exclusion from Zimbabwe of any person who is not a citizen of Zimbabwe', the President is also empowered to make regulations whether or not they are inconsistent with the specified powers.[26]

The major concern over the regulations is that they gave the Minister the power to deport any Zimbabwean citizen on the vague and undefined ground that he/she was an 'undesirable resident'. For example, would the regulations have covered the deportation of a citizen suffering from AIDS on the grounds of public safety? There was also no duty to give reasons for the decision to deport, no right to make any representations nor a right of appeal. In addition, any person was liable to detention for up to fourteen days pending enquiries as to whether he/she was an undesirable resident.[27] This compared unfavourably with the position of non-citizens who retained an automatic right of appeal against deportation.[28] It is strange that citizens were denied such basic rights. Although the provision was supposedly only to apply to Walls, it was re-enacted into the 1983 regulations and remained in force until the end of the state of emergency. The whole process was also objectionable on the ground that no announcement of any deportation was necessary and thus the Minister was able to expel a citizen secretly, thus undermining the effectiveness of habeas corpus proceedings.[29] It is not known how often it was utilised, although certainly two men involved in the Air Force 6 case were released from detention on condition that they agreed to leave Zimbabwe forthwith and steps were taken to declare both 'undesirable residents'.[30]

The regulations meant that Zimbabwean citizens remained liable to deportation at any time. Thus they seriously eroded an important right which is recognised unreservedly in Article 13 of the Universal Declaration of Human Rights. Other human rights documents also provide that the freedom to enter and remain in the country of one's citizenship is absolute. The African Charter is unique in curtailing this right. Article 12.2 provides that it is subject to restrictions provided for by law 'for the protection of national security, law and order, public health or morality'. In view of the record of many African nations, this proviso is both regrettable and unnecessary.[31] In the case of Zimbabwe, the principle and procedure for the deportation of citizens illustrates the unacceptable manner in which emergency powers were utilised and the weakness of the constitutional protection which once again was rendered meaningless at the moment when it is most needed. Thus it is asserted that the fundamental right of nationals to move freely into and out of their own country is one which is never liable to abrogation, and that this principle should be incorporated into the Constitution.

Freedom of Conscience

The constitutional right to freedom of conscience is subject to any law which is made in the interests of defence, public safety or public order so long as it is reasonably justifiable in a democratic society.[32] The only incident affecting the exercise of the right arose in 1985 when a leadership dispute between two factions of the Apostolic Church threatened to lead to violent confrontation. Emergency regulations were made ordering the closure of all churches and missions belonging to the sect and prohibiting entry until the Minister was satisfied that the conflict was resolved.[33] Despite the fact that there was a likelihood of a judicial determination of the affair, the regulations were stated to apply 'notwithstanding any order or judgment of a court whether given before or after the commencement of the regulations'. They were repealed in 1986 after the Minister was satisfied that 'peace, order and tranquillity prevailed' within the Church.[34] The validity of the regulations were never tested in the courts although, presumably, they were based on the perceived need to protect public order or safety. Whether such an argument would have appealed to the courts is certainly highly debatable.

The underlying importance of the regulations is that they illustrate the potentially powerful weapon available to the government if it wished to curtail the activities of religious bodies. In a country where some churches are outspoken critics of alleged human rights abuses, a future government might be tempted to make regulations designed to silence such criticism.

Notes

1. Section 22, Constitution of Zimbabwe.
2. Section 22(4), Constitution of Zimbabwe.

3. For a full account of security forces activities during this period see Cilliers, 1985.
4. Noted in Fredericksе, 1984, p.39.
5. Section 53, Law and Order (Maintenance) Act.
6. Section 13, Emergency Powers (Maintenance of Law and Order) Regulations 1983.
7. Sections 13(1), 12 and 14 respectively of the 1983 regulations.
8. For a detailed analysis of the 1984 curfew see the Lawyers Committee, chapter 8. The report estimates that between 100 and 150 civilians were either shot dead by soldiers in their villages or beaten to death whilst in detention in holding camps inside the curfew area.
9. Quoted in 'Reconciliation is still possible': statement signed by the Archbishop of Harare, four bishops and other senior Roman Catholic clergy, 29 March 1983.
10. Section 13 Emergency Powers (Maintenance of Law and Order) Regulations, 1983. The offence is one of strict liability and punishable by up to two years imprisonment. See also section 53 Law and Order (Maintenance) Act where the maximum sentence is six months imprisonment.
11. *Mungofa & Jeri v S*, Unreported, General Division G-S-48-80.
12. *S v Tasore*, Unreported, General Division G-S-79-80.
13. Emergency powers regulations also enabled the security forces to move any section of the public out of an area or exclude persons from any area to 'ensure that they [did] not become involved in security operations against terrorists'. Section 4, Emergency Powers (Maintenance of Law and Order) Regulations 1983.
14. Government Notices made under the Emergency Powers (Maintenance of Law and Order) Regulations 1976 were: Securing of Vessels on Lake Kariba and the Zambezi River Notice GN 658/76; Restrictions on Navigation and Securing of Vessels on Lake Kariba and the Zambezi River Notice GN 725/76; Restrictions on Navigation on Lake Kariba (East) Notice GN 726/76.
15. Any person contravening the order faced up to twelve months imprisonment: Emergency Powers (Sandawana Protected Area) Order 1987 SI 137/87.
16. Article 12(1).
17. See, for example, Article 12, International Covenant on Civil and Political Rights. Surprisingly, the African Charter is silent on this point.
18. Section 44 of the Emergency Powers (Maintenance of Law and Order) Regulations 1983 empowered the Minister of Home Affairs to restrict the reporting of activities of the security forces for the purpose of combating or suppressing terrorism.
19. Emergency Powers (Control of Information) (Declaration of Designated Area) Notice SI 574/83.
20. Disputes as to ownership of land have also been dealt with by regulations: see Emergency Powers (Resolution of Disputes Over Occupation of Rural Land) Regulations SI 234A/84 and Emergency Powers (Resolution of Disputes Over Occupation of Rural Land)(Amendment) Regulations SI 250/84.
21. Parliamentary delegations already make nationwide tours when acting as Committees dealing with such matters as the District Development Fund and Public Accounts. To extend this role to investigate the use of curfew etc is entirely practicable. The presence of members of the judiciary might also enhance the status and objectivity of such a delegation.
22. The appointment itself was quite remarkable for he was now in command of many of the officers and men he had fought against just a few months previously.
23. Emergency Powers (Maintenance of Law and Order)(Amendment) Regulations (No. 1) 1980 SI 572/80. These were later incorporated into the 1983 regulations (section 68).
24. Notes on evidence given to the Senate Legal Committee by government law officer: Minutes of 12th Meeting, 6–9 October 1980.
25. A motion that the regulations were contrary to the Declaration of Rights was negatived by a vote of 3 to 1: Minutes of the 12th Meeting, October 6-9 1980. See also the Senate debate of October 16 1980 where the report of the committee was accepted.
26. See the Emergency Powers Act, discussed in Chapter 4.
27. The regulations incorporate section 8(1) Immigration Act 1979 for this purpose.
28. See section 21 Immigration Act which provides for an appeal to the nearest magistrate.
29. Cf the case of ***Mandirwhe*** which is discussed in Chapter 5.
30. See Ministry of Home Affairs Press Release of 13 September 1983.
31. Some countries have recognised the problem. Thus in both Sierra Leone and Zambia, emergency regulations which provided for the expulsion of persons involved in certain economic activities specifically stated that this did not apply to citizens. See section 22 Public Economic Emergency Regulations 1987 (Sierra Leone) and section 3 Emergency (Essential Supplies and Services) Regulations 1988 (Zambia).
32. Section 19, Constitution of Zimbabwe.
33. Emergency Powers (Apostolic Church) Regulations 1985 SI 352A/85.
34. Emergency Powers (Apostolic Church Regulations)(Repeal) Notice 1986 SI 98A/86.

11 Economic & Political Rights

As was noted in Chapter 1, one striking feature of the use of emergency powers in Africa is their impact on a wide range of economic and political rights. Zimbabwe provides an excellent case study in this regard.

Economic Policy and Emergency Powers

At independence the Zimbabwean economy was extremely weak and imbalanced. Mandatory sanctions had effectively prevented any new international investment after 1965 and thus the industrial and agricultural sectors, in particular, desperately needed modernisation. The imposition of martial law and curfews together with the displacement of millions of villagers during the war also meant that the economy in the rural areas was almost completely disrupted. In addition, improvements to living standards were urgently required to enable the majority of the population to enjoy the fruits of independence. During the pre-independence period, opportunities for Africans in the employment field were extremely limited, being characterised by considerable discriminatory practices. Wages for African workers in the private sector were scandalously low and opportunities for advancement negligible. In the public service, the more senior positions were invariably the sole preserve of whites as few Africans had any opportunity to acquire an adequate standard of education in order to challenge for them. In addition, entry levels for Europeans were always at a far higher level than Africans. Thus the new government made the re-structuring of the economy a priority and it entailed the expenditure of large sums of money on development projects throughout the country and in the rural areas in particular. This was financed partly through high levels of taxation which resulted in large budget deficits and increased inflation. With serious drought problems also threatening the entire region, implementation of the policy was extremely difficult. The need for economic development and re-structuring was given as a further reason for the retention of the state of emergency. As the then Minister of Home Affairs put it:

> the processes of radical transformation do not always come about in an orderly coherent way. Social change does not move in a polite minuet; revolution is not a tea party with silver teapots and waiters. To meet emergent economic threats, we need emergency powers.[1]

A keystone of the new government economic strategy was the introduction of a prices and incomes policy. This was partly done through the use of emergency powers. For example, orders made under emergency regulations prohibited the sale of any goods at a price exceeding that on a fixed date.[2] Penalties of up to five years imprisonment were imposed for any breach thereof.[3] The then Minister of Home Affairs explained that the original order was made in response to the fear that people 'of a certain colour skin' had acquired credit facilities and trading licences with the aim of making super profits by increasing prices. He added that government intended to use the regulations to enable it to improve living standards for the majority.[4] Other emergency regulations restricted the raising of incomes above prescribed maxima and laid down minimum wages.[5]

It is somewhat puzzling that emergency regulations were resorted to in these circumstances for other aspects of the policy were implemented using the normal legislative process. For example, the Minimum Wages Act 1980 (now the Labour Relations Act 1985) sought to diminish the gross imbalance between the incomes of Europeans and Africans by prohibiting discrimination in pay on the grounds of race and gave the Minister power to direct the payment of minimum wages. As no constitutional rights were affected by the regulations, it appears they were used merely as a matter of government convenience.[6]

Another aspect of the matter was the use of emergency regulations to implement economic and monetary policy. Thus, amongst other things, regulations permitted the Minister to alter the rates of interest charged by moneylenders,[7] and to increase interest rates on mortgage bonds.[8] Two sets of regulations are particularly interesting. Firstly, in November 1980 emergency regulations amended the Electricity Act[9] and permitted the Minister to impose a development levy designed to assist the financing of a new power station in the country.[10] These regulations were replaced in April 1981 by the Electricity Amendment Act. During the parliamentary debate on the Act, the Minister of Industry commented that the use of the regulations was 'in order to impose the levy with effect from 1 January 1981'.[11] However, no explanation was forthcoming as to why legislation was not introduced in November 1980. This was a startling abuse of power as not only were the regulations used in circumstances which were, at best, only very loosely connected with the reasons for the state of emergency but also they purported to circumvent the legislative process by amending a statute. Secondly, emergency regulations empowered the government to raise finance prior to parliamentary approval in the annual budget.[12] The Minister of Finance, Economic Planning and Development defended this action claiming that it was 'the sacred duty of government to govern and avoid disorderly conduct in national monetary affairs'.[13] Again, this was a quite improper use of emergency powers for although the regulation of the economy is a duty of government, the raising of finance is a matter for Parliament and it was quite wrong to usurp the legislative process in this manner.[14]

A further reason which government gave for the retention of the state of emergency was the chronic shortage of foreign exchange and deteriorating economic conditions which were considered a potential threat to law and order and thus required the use of emergency powers. It is difficult to follow this reasoning. The shortage of foreign exchange was (and is) a constant cause for concern for the government for it meant that new equipment, spare parts and the like were either difficult to obtain or simply unobtainable. In an effort to overcome the problem, barter arrangements were entered into with some Eastern European countries and alternative methods of payment with neighbouring countries devised. Even so the need to pay for many vital imports in hard currency remained. Zimbabwean exports earned the country considerable quantities of foreign currency but this was often more than offset by the cost of foreign debt repayments and the need to modernise the economy. The security situation also dictated the need for considerable expenditure on defence, including the acquisition of highly sophisticated weapons.[15] In addition, the periodic shortages of basic commodities was often due to a lack of foreign exchange and led to the creation of a black market which affected the poorer members of society in particular. There were also several reported instances of individuals and companies attempting to enter into illegal foreign exchange transactions.

In Africa the use of emergency powers to deal with economic problems is not unknown. In Zambia in 1988, and at a time of acute shortages of basic commodities, regulations provided for the revocation of trading licences from traders suspected of supplying essential commodities to the black market.[16] Emergency regulations then provided for the acquisition of businesses belonging to those whose licences were revoked and the confiscation and disposal of the goods confiscated from such persons.[17] The regulations were made when the economy was under siege with essential commodities being unavailable except on the black market, where they fetched exorbitant prices.[18] In Sierra Leone in 1987, President Momoh declared a state of economic emergency on the grounds of widespread financial malpractices and the grave economic crisis. Emergency regulations prohibited the hoarding of currency, rice or other essential commodities and provided for a penalty of up to seven years imprisonment for any contravention. The smuggling of foreign exchange, precious metals or any essential commodity was similarly banned.[19] In both cases, the regulations were made in response to an immediate threat to national economic survival and were acceptable so long as they remained a temporary expedient. In Zimbabwe the economy never reached such a crisis level and in reality emergency powers were utilised to reinforce the criminal law. Thus of the two provisions directly related to economic crimes, one enabled police officers to detain without trial any person reasonably suspected of committing an offence relating to exchange control.[20] The other concerned the prevention of the illegal mining and exporting of precious stones, especially emeralds. Zimbabwe earned vital foreign exchange from the sale of its gems and the relative ease with which they were mined meant that many unauthorised persons were involved in the racket. In 1981 the problem was so acute that according to the Minister of Home Affairs 'to combat this evil . . . we have had to resort to emergency powers'.[21] This led to restrictions on the movement of persons and traffic in the affected areas.[22] How such a provision has any relation to emergency powers is hard to imagine.

The economic related regulations were essentially aimed at a radical restructuring of the economy. The twin objectives of economic development and economic equality were entirely laudable but it is difficult to see how this re-structuring process justified the continuation of the state of emergency. At no time was there any situation which threatened the organised life of the community nor was there any imminent threat of political instability.[23] As regards economic crimes, there was no evidence to show that such activity was ever a threat to economic security. Indeed the existing criminal laws were already capable of dealing with the problem and the real need was for increased police vigilance and expertise to combat criminal activity.[24] The conclusion is inevitably that there was no justification for the continuation of the state of emergency on economic grounds and that the use of emergency regulations was purely a matter of executive convenience.

Protecting Transportation Links

Being landlocked, Rhodesia was totally dependent upon South Africa for its imports and exports during most of the UDI period. After independence the Zimbabwean government made strenuous efforts to utilise alternative trade-routes, because further reliance on the southern route was politically unacceptable and economically unwise being both expensive and subject to disruption or closure by the South African authorities.[25] In 1980, the nine majority ruled States in the region formed the South African Development Coordination Conference (SADCC) to promote a more balanced and self-reliant regional development strategy based on cooperation and mutual self-respect. The economies of the SADCC States were highly dependent upon foreign trade. Thus Zimbabwe had a ratio of total trade to GDP of around 45 per cent whilst other countries had ratios significantly in excess of 50 per cent. The formation of SADCC was viewed with hostility by South Africa as it ran counter to its strategy of establishing a Constellation of Southern African States (CONSAS) which were so economically dependent and vulnerable to reprisals that they would never pose a threat to Pretoria. A key part of the SADCC programme was the rehabilitation of the road and rail links between Zimbabwe and the Mozambican ports of Beira and Maputo and the maintenance of the vital 290 kilometre (180 mile) oil pipeline between Beira and Mutare in eastern Zimbabwe which supplied the bulk of Zimbabwe's oil needs. The pipeline was closed throughout the UDI period and it was not made operational until June 1982. RENAMO then made this a prime target for attack. As a result in November 1982 Zimbabwe dispatched an army battalion to Mozambique to defend the line and continued to keep many thousands of troops there to guard it.[26] The advantages of using the alternative trade-routes were overwhelming for not only was the movement of goods less susceptible to South African pressure, but also the cost of transportation was significantly reduced. The need to maintain secure routes in order to promote SADCC's transportation policy was seen in Zimbabwe as a justification for the use of emergency powers.

In reality, few emergency regulations had any connection with transportation problems. The main ones, which dated back to the UDI period, enabled a Minister to control or regulate the production, transport, distribution, sale or purchase of any goods 'when it appears to him necessary or expedient'.[27] The first set of regulations were made following the original declaration of a state of emergency in 1965 with the intention of overcoming the international trade sanctions imposed after UDI. The Zimbabwean government used them for a variety of very different purposes: (i) In 1981 there was a fuel shortage caused by acute supply difficulties. The regulations were used to make orders introducing fuel rationing and providing for the provision of criminal sanctions for any contravention of them;[28] (ii) On four occasions the regulations enabled the Electricity Supply Commission to increase tariffs or to surcharge electricity consumers by up to a fixed percentage. The last surcharge was a staggering 325 per cent of the charge payable;[29] (iii) In 1982 bus fares and charges for bus operators were raised;[30] (iv) On several occasions statutory provisions regarding the carriage of goods were amended.[31] The policy behind this was never elucidated but was seemingly an attempt to enhance the economic viability of the ailing transportation sector.

These regulations only lapsed with the ending of the state of emergency. Clearly, the use of the powers was not in line with the declared reasons for the need for such powers and, as such, they represented an abuse of power by the government.

Economic Sanctions Against South Africa

Linked with the policy of economic independence was the question of economic sanctions against South Africa. Zimbabwe consistently called upon the international community to sever economic links with Pretoria and ministers frequently expressed a willingness to impose economic sanctions despite the grave economic repercussions to Zimbabwe. The possible future implementation of such sanctions was seen as another reason for continuing the state of emergency.[32] This was quite wrong. Whilst the actual imposition of sanctions may well have justified a state of emergency, it was quite improper to retain it merely in anticipation of the event. Quite properly, international law clearly emphasises that the threat must be actual and imminent and this was never the case in Zimbabwe.

Workers rights and Emergency Powers

Security of Employment

In 1982 emergency regulations introduced, for the first time, security of employment for all workers.[33] These provided that no employer could terminate any contract of employment by notice unless there was mutual agreement between the employer and the employee or the employer had obtained the prior written approval of the Minister of Labour. These provisions were justified as ensuring that 'large number of workers were not suddenly and arbitrarily thrown out of their jobs and made to walk the streets looking for employment without the Government having been made aware of the situation and been satisfied that the steps taken by the employer concerned were totally justified.'[34] In 1987 these regulations were replaced by statute. The protection of workers rights is fundamental to every society and the aim of the policy itself was laudable. However, the method of achieving this was indefensible. The regulations did not seek to deal with an exceptional situation and, as was later shown, could and should have been introduced by statute in the first place.

Remarkably, in 1989 and in response to a series of damaging strikes over pay and other conditions by junior doctors and teachers, emergency regulations were made which removed security of employment for workers.[35] These provided that 'a general manager or an officer designated by him' in an 'essential service' could alter the terms and conditions of employees, including the suspending of any working rule (including those relating to health and safety) and the directing of workers to perform their duties after normal working hours. Any failure to comply with such orders rendered an employee liable to either suspension from duty for up to three months without pay or summary dismissal. Such power was not apparently restricted in any way nor was it qualified by any objective test. The effect of the regulations was that management in essential services had sweeping powers to vary unilaterally contracts of employment, which were not subject to any review or control.[36] When it is remembered that the term 'essential services' encompassed the financial, commercial and industrial sectors of the economy as well as hospital, transport and electricity services etc, it meant that the regulations applied to virtually any type of employment.[37] Accordingly, the right to security of employment and the like enshrined by statute was totally undermined. The regulations posed a major threat to workers' rights and were indefensible.

Restricting Freedom of Choice of Employment

There was a considerable exodus of whites from Zimbabwe immediately after independence. This particularly affected the public service where some 4,400 civil servants, representing 60 per cent of the total establishment, left twelve days after independence taking advantage of a premature retirement scheme with enhanced benefits negotiated at the Lancaster House conference. The result was the loss of much expertise and experience. Unlike many other newly independent African nations,[38] a large number of well qualified Zimbabweans did return from abroad at or after independence but, even so, personnel shortages in several key areas such as medicine, engineering and veterinary science remained. The need to train and retain local manpower in the country was viewed as being of such importance that this justified the use of emergency powers. These seriously eroded some workers' freedom of employment. For example, following completion of an apprenticeship, apprentices were required to work in Zimbabwe for a period equal to that of their training within the country.[39] Similarly, medical students at the University of Zimbabwe were required to complete at least a two-year housemanship in the country before conferral of their degrees even though all university requirements for the award were satisfied.[40] In a letter to the Senate Legal Committee, three medical students complained that the relevant regulations were outside the scope of the Emergency Powers Act and commented: 'How medical employment can be said to relate to national security is beyond comprehension'.[41] In fact, the regulations were undoubtedly *intra vires* the Act as an 'essential service' specifically covered any hospital service.[42] But the concern expressed is understandable and illustrates the lack of public awareness as to the scope and nature of emergency powers. Because of the loss of skilled manpower after independence, the desire to retain locally trained personnel was quite understandable. However, it is difficult to see how these powers related to the reasons for the state of emergency. In reality the emergency regulations were clearly made for executive convenience and again illustrate the manner in which government was able to utilise it powers to govern by decree.

Restricting the Right to Take Industrial Action

In Africa, trade union activity has been seen as a serious threat to governmental stability. For example, the trade unions played an important role in the overthrow of Emperor Haile Selasse I in Ethiopia and the removal of General Gowon in Nigeria. Often such fears have resulted in the curtailing of trade union activity. For example, in The Sudan in November 1989, striking doctors were detained by the new Revolutionary Command Council and charged with 'waging war against the State'.[43] It was also alleged that some political detainees, including some trade union leaders, were held as hostages against the good behaviour of government opponents. Similarly in Ghana in 1978, a state of emergency was declared in response to a series of strikes in protest at a stringent budget. Decrees providing for detention without trial and restrictions on movement were made aimed at 'ridding the country of anti-social elements'. Many striking workers were detained, the Supreme Military Council justifying the action on the grounds that workers were being exploited by aspiring politicians, foreign agents and aggrieved businessmen. In Zambia in 1985, a series of strikes by hospital workers who were demanding a pay rise for all public sector employees resulted in a presidential decree banning such strikes and stoppages. Later strikes by bank, railway and postal workers over the automatic deduction of union dues resulted in President Kaunda invoking his powers under the Preservation of Public Security regulations to ban strikes in essential industries. The detention of students and trade union leaders critical of government economic policy was also common for some years.[44] Similarly, in Kenya in the 1970s, any threat posed by a trade union was dealt with by bringing it under direct governmental control. This enabled the government to put the movement in a straitjacket which culminated in a presidential ban on strike action in 1974 following a series of successful strikes started by bank workers in Nairobi.[45]

Zimbabwe has followed the lead of other African governments and restricted the right to take industrial action. This was in response to strikes which threatened to disrupt key industries. For example, an unofficial strike of rail men in 1982 crippled the network for nearly one week at the cost of Zimb $2 million per day. Regulations were then made which contained a no-strike clause:

> Any employee, trade union or other person declaring or taking part in a strike is guilty of an offence and liable to a fine of $1000 and/or five years imprisonment.[46]

In addition, any employee who failed to report to work without leave of absence was deemed, unless he proved to the contrary, to have taken part in a strike. This led to the arrest of 240 striking rail workers who were all convicted of being involved in the strike. They received suspended prison sentences after agreeing to return to work. In May 1989 junior hospital doctors went on nationwide strike over pay and conditions. Seventy-seven were charged under the Law and Order (Maintenance) Act with involvement in hindering the carrying out of an essential service.[47] Later, emergency regulations again outlawed strikes in essential services.[48] Thus an employee was liable to be suspended or summarily dismissed for engaging in unlawful industrial action. In September 1989 this led to 119 telephone workers in Harare who were on strike over a pay claim being charged with contravening the regulations.[49]

Such restrictions not only deny workers the right to defend their economic interests by legitimate trade union activity but also deprive society of a vital mechanism for resolving industrial disputes and promoting development. They are also a hallmark of those countries ruled by repressive regimes. In Zimbabwe the threat of a breakdown of medical, transport or communications services probably justified the taking of drastic steps to maintain essential services, but even here, the scope of the powers amounted to a virtual abrogation of the rights of workers. In these circumstances it is important to distinguish between measures which seek to protect vital services, such as the use of members of the security forces to take them over and to run them, and the use of regulations which are aimed at undermining the legitimate rights of workers.

Political Rights and Emergency Powers

The regulation of political freedom during a state of emergency is a frequent occurrence. Often this takes the form of restrictions on political opponents by detention or banning orders.[50] During the state of emergency in Zimbabwe, political freedom was generally respected although restrictions were placed on the exercise of these rights on some occasions.

In 1983 regulations were made which empowered the President to suspend a local council or councillor from exercising any duties where he was satisfied that it was 'necessary or desirable in the interests of the public or any section thereof'.[51] Any councillor so affected was then disqualified from seeking re-election. There was no provision for a right to a hearing nor any requirement for the giving of reasons. The regulations were made with the intention of suspending the Mayor of Gweru, Patrick Kombayi, who was under investigation for alleged abuse of office. A parliamentary enquiry later upheld his suspension and the majority of councillors then resigned in protest. New elections were ordered but Kombayi's nomination papers were rejected. His application to the High Court disputing this action was unsuccessful.[52] Justice Korsah noted that an important right was affected but stated:

> The petitioner argues that it would be unjusticiable to take away the citizen's rights permanently through the use of emergency powers without giving the citizen the opportunity to answer allegations made against him. That may be so, but it does not follow that a court of justice must do violence to the provisions of this statute in order to secure for him the right he claims.

Of course the right was not taken away permanently and action against the former mayor was necessary given the catalogue of malpractices noted by the court. However, an important right was removed unilaterally and a dangerous precedent set. The regulations were not used again but indicate the potential threat to political rights by emergency powers.

Another instance of political restrictions concerned the prohibition on the use of certain symbols which were used to identify political parties.[53] The use of a well-known symbol, such as a bird or animal, at an election is important as many the electorate are illiterate and thus the favoured Party is identifiable only by its symbol on the ballot paper. Shortly before the 1985 General Election regulations prohibited the use of thirteen symbols on the ground that they were similar to other devices used by the armed forces. This did not affect the ruling party, but PF–ZAPU was forced to change its well-known party symbol. Of course it is impossible to judge whether this had any effect on voting patterns but it certainly represented a subtle attack on a then political rival.[54] A further, apparently isolated, incident occurred in 1982 when emergency regulations were used to prohibit the displaying of a PF–ZAPU flag in Zihute Village in the Mangwende Communal Lands.

Although clearly connected with action against dissidents, the precise reason for the order is unknown.[55]

One somewhat bizarre interference with political rights concerned the re-naming of urban areas. At independence, many place names reflected the white presence in the country. Some towns and cities bore names in honour of leading personalities at the time of the occupation e.g. Fort Victoria and Salisbury. Others were local names either misspelt by whites or revised to make them more amenable to the European tongue. Most city streets bore the names of early explorers, politicians, pioneers or place names from the former imperial power. In 1980 two major thoroughfares in the capital were renamed after Presidents Samora Machel and Julius Nyerere, reflecting their assistance in the freedom struggle.[56] The presence of colonial names was unacceptable to the majority of Zimbabweans and government set up a committee to review name changes. The most important task was the re-naming of the major urban areas. It came as a considerable surprise when, without any public debate or consultation, these changes were effected by emergency regulations.[57] The names of six cities (including the capital city which was altered from Salisbury to Harare), eight municipalities, fifteen rural councils and twenty-five urban councils were changed. The announcement of the new names resulted in a 'stunning anti-climax to the elation evoked among millions of Zimbabweans'.[58] Some names were hotly contested. In particular, Fort Victoria was re-named Nyanga in the regulations only for the government to later change it to Masvingo as a result of considerable local pressure. Why emergency powers were invoked in this instance is not clear and once again their use was quite improper. Whilst the parliamentary process would inevitably have led to some disagreement, the matter would at least have been fully debated.[59]

Overview

Marks has argued that underdevelopment itself constitutes an emergency situation. He reasons that for third world countries:

> until a new international economic order is achieved, the economic and social conditions of underdevelopment will constitute an emergency situation making the implementation of at least some human rights difficult, if not impossible.[60]

Such a view may have some validity when chronic underdevelopment has led to severe shortages of basic food commodities and the like. But as the International Law Association has rightly noted, very often such underdevelopment is used as a pretext for the perpetration of authoritarian regimes, involving severe repression of civil and political rights.[61] Another serious danger recognised by the distinguished Nigerian jurist T.O. Elias is the tendency of an authoritarian regime to perpetuate a state of emergency on the pretext of under-development.[62] This being the case, it is argued that there is no reason to depart from the approach of section 4 of the ICCPR towards the question of the justification of a state of emergency on economic grounds.

Based on the reasons propounded by government, the situations considered in this chapter did not justify a continuous state of emergency in Zimbabwe. The need to radically re-structure the economy was something faced by all African countries at independence, most of which were in a far worse economic state than Zimbabwe. Quite properly, few resorted to emergency powers. In Zimbabwe there was no 'economic emergency' such as that later faced by Sierra Leone, for instance. There were no constitutional restraints on the economic reforms sought by government and, based on Article 4 of the ICCPR, no justification for the state of emergency. The possibility of economic sanctions against South Africa was ever present but this constituted a future threat which might have justified a state of emergency if, and only if, they were actually imposed. Here the government lost sight of the need for an **imminent** threat to the community as the basis of a state of emergency. Perhaps the one area where swift government action was necessary was in order to maintain the operation of essential services during the periods of industrial unrest. Even here, there was a failure to distinguish between the need to maintain such services by, for example, the use of army personnel and the need to negotiate with the strikers in order to reach a fair and equitable settlement. Here, as on other occasions, the reasons and justification for the use of emergency powers was completely ignored by government.

The need to protect vital transportation links from severance and resultant economic strangulation requires wide governmental powers. In Zimbabwe, the threat to the supply routes through Mozambique was very real but the fact that an alternative (if more expensive and politically irritating) route through South Africa was available meant that there was no threat of an economic collapse. Indeed except for a temporary fuel shortage, there was generally a constant supply of essential commodities. It follows that restrictions on workers rights were also not justified. It is also difficult to see the justification for the use of emergency powers in the area of political rights.

An additional point raised concerns the need to maintain a link between the reasons for the emergency and the resulting regulations.[63] In several instances, regulations were made which had no connection with the reasons for the emergency, for instance, the hiking of bus fares and operators charges and the imposition of a levy to finance the construction of a power station. This constituted a complete abuse of executive power and showed a total lack of discipline on the part of government coupled with a disregard for the normal legislative process.

Finally, this chapter highlights the manner in which emergency regulations can affect virtually every area of life, often without the knowledge of the general public. The spectre of rule by the executive becomes very real indeed in such circumstances.

Notes

1. *Parliamentary Debates*, 13 July 1983.
2. See Emergency Powers (Price Stabilization) Order 1981 SI 925/81. The Emergency Powers (Control of Prices, Service Charges and Rents) Regulations 1987 SI 252A/87 prohibited price increases in many sectors of the economy. These included medical, dental, legal, educational and transportation charges. Rents for all commercial and domestic premises were also frozen. Similar regulations made in 1988 limited price increases in services such as hairdressing, entertainment, dry-cleaning, laundering and shoe-repairing: Emergency Powers (Control of Prices, Service Charges and Rents) Regulations 1988 SI 72A/88. See also Emergency Powers (Control of Prices, Service Charges and Rents)(Amendment) Regulations 1988 (No. 1) SI 138/88 and (No. 2) SI 175/88. These remained in force until July 1989: see Emergency Powers (Control of Prices, Service Charges and Rents)(Repeal) Regulations SI 153A/89.
3. In 1988 eight persons were convicted of breaching the regulations and fined. See *Siyawamaya v S*, Unreported, High Court of Zimbabwe HC-H-76-88.
4. See *Parliamentary Debates*, 13 July 1983. This assertion was never elaborated upon and it is thus difficult to gauge the extent and seriousness of the problem.
5. Increases of up to 18% were imposed: Emergency Powers (Control of Salary and Wages Increases) Regulations 1981 SI 925A/81 (amended by SI 714A/82); Emergency Powers (Lower Paid Employees)(Compensation) Regulations 1981 SI 455C/81; Emergency Powers (Lower Paid Employees)(Compensation) Regulations 1984 SI 238A/84; Emergency Powers (Control of Income Increases) Regulations 1985 SI 185/85 (amended SI 219B/85). For a judicial application of these powers see *NRZ v NRZ Contributory Pension Fund* 1985 (1) ZLR 161. Later increases were promulgated in Emergency Powers (Control of Income Increases) Regulations 1988 SI 26A/88. The Emergency Powers (Control of Income Increases) (Repeal) Regulations 1989 SI 139A ended the operation of an incomes policy through the use of emergency regulations and thus for the first time since 1981, the ordinary law came into force. It should be noted that this policy was inherited from the former Rhodesian days: see Emergency Powers (Control of Incomes) Regulations 1978 SI 508/78; Emergency Powers (Control of Incomes)(Amendment) Regulations 1978 SI 754/78; and Emergency Powers (Control of Incomes)(Amendment) Regulations 1979 SI 387/79, all of which remained in force after independence.

6. There was also perhaps a desire to avoid adverse criticism of the policy in the legislature, especially from the white roll members.
7. Emergency Powers (Usury Act) Regulations 1982 SI 39/82. The Usury Act itself was amended by the regulations.
8. Emergency Powers (Building Society) Regulations 1982 SI 39/82.
9. Emergency Powers (Electricity Act) Regulations 1980 SI 779/80.
10. See also the Emergency Powers (Tariff Surcharge)(City Councils) Order 1985 SI 275/85; Emergency Powers (Tariff Surcharge)(Electricity Supply Commission) Order 1985 SI 274/85.
11. *Parliamentary Debates*, 29 April 1981.
12. Emergency Powers (Finance)(Special Advances) Regulations 1984 SI 207/84.
13. *Parliamentary Debates*, 13 July 1984.
14. Another example of this policy were the Emergency Powers (Income Tax Surcharge) Regulations 1982 SI 169/82 which amended the Finance Act in order to authorise the imposition of a surcharge of 15 per cent.
15. This was in response to the security threat posed by South Africa to Zimbabwe and other frontline States. This is highlighted by the fact that Pretoria, which already had the most powerful armed forces in the region, was spending on average 2.5 times more on military expenditure than the frontline States combined: See SIPRI, 1987, p.148.
16. Trade Licensing (Revocation) Order 1988 SI 39/88.
17. Emergency Powers (Essential Supplies and Services) Regulations 1988 SI 38/88.
18. As Mbao rightly points out, the need to proceed with caution with such regulations is underlined by the fact that they are dealing with fundamental human rights and basic freedoms: see the statute note by Mbao, 1989b, at p.128.
19. Public Economic Emergency Regulations 1987 Public Notice 25/87.
20. See Chapter 10 for a full discussion on this power.
21. *Parliamentary Debates*, 17 July 1981.
22. See Chapter 9 for a full discussion.
23. See *Denmark et al v Greece* discussed in Chapter 1.
24. For example, the Minister of Home Affairs could prevent the granting of bail under the Criminal Procedure and Evidence Act (see Chapter 9) whilst the Exchange Control Act provided heavy penalties for illegal foreign exchange dealings. Preventive detention was used against some individuals suspected of illegal foreign exchange dealings but arguably this was merely to by-pass normal criminal investigations of the matter (see Chapter 6).
25. For example, from Zimbabwe it is about three times more expensive to ship goods via Cape Town compared to Beira in Mozambique.
26. The commitment was once again reiterated by President Mugabe in his Presidential speech to Parliament see *Parliamentary Debates*, 27 June 1989. See also *Africa Confidential*, 1 December 1982. In December 1988 President Mugabe indicated that Zimbabwean troops were operating 'far beyond those corridors to include adjacent districts in order to destroy the bandit bases which had acted as springboards for sabotage operations upon our pipe and railway lines and upon our service roads'. *Parliamentary Debates*, 7 December 1988. For a fuller discussion see Hatchard, 1991b, p.219.
27. Emergency Powers (Control of Goods and Services) Regulations 1979 SI 880/79.
28. A number of convictions resulted. Thus in S v *Makaranga*, Unreported, High Court of Zimbabwe HC-H-91-83 a person who was found in possession of 40 litres of petrol without authority was fined Zimb $200.
29. See Emergency Powers Orders SI 432/82; SI 362A/83; SI 362B/83.
30. Emergency Powers (Road Service Permits)(Fare Increases) Order 1982 SI 660/82. See also Emergency Powers (Omnibus Terminus Charges) Order 1985 SI 109/85.
31. See the Emergency Powers (Road Motor Transportation) (Carriage of Agricultural Produce) Order 1988 SI 175A/88, Emergency Powers (Road Motor Transportation)(Carriage of Agricultural Produce) Order 1989 SI 182/89 and the Emergency Powers (Road Motor Transportation) (Carriage of Coal) Order 1989 SI 245/89 which all amended the Road Motor Transportation Act.
32. See Minister of Home Affairs, *Parliamentary Debates*, 20 January 1987.
33. Emergency Powers (Termination of Employment) Regulations 1982 SI 714B/82. These remained in force until March 1987 when they were repealed by the Emergency Powers (Termination of Employment)(Repeal) Regulations 1987 SI 77/87. This was due to the government using its existing statutory power with the enactment of the Labour Relations (General Conditions of Employment)(Termination of Employment) Regulations 1985 SI 371/85. Why the emergency regulations remained in force for a further two years is quite inexplicable.
34. Justice Smith in *Tavengwa v Marine Centre (Pvt) Ltd*, Unreported, High Court of Zimbabwe HC-H-46-84 at pp.4–5.
35. Emergency Powers (Maintenance of Essential Services) Regulations 1989 SI 160A/89.
36. Only public servants and employees of parastatals were provided with a guaranteed avenue of appeal: Regulation 5(1).
37. See the discussion on the meaning of 'essential services' in Chapter 3. In an interview shortly after the making of the regulations, the Minister of Labour appeared unaware of the scope of his powers – another indication perhaps of the complexity of the law caused by the constant making and re-making of emergency regulations. See *Financial Gazette* (Harare), 10 August 1989.
38. For example, in Zambia there were three Zambian graduates and less than 1,000 holders of a Secondary School (High School) certificate in the entire country at independence in 1964.
39. Emergency Powers (Apprenticeship) Regulations 1982 SI 345A/82 and Emergency Powers (Apprenticeship) (Amendment) Regulations 1982 (No. 1) SI 460/82 which amended the Apprenticeship Act.
40. Emergency Powers (Medical Students) Regulations 1983 SI 637/83 and Emergency Powers (Medical Students)(Amendment) Regulations (No. 2) 1987 SI 281/87.

41. Letter dated 7 February 1984 contained in the Minutes of the Senate Legal Committee.
42. See section 2, Emergency Powers Act. The Senate Legal Committee also noted that the regulations did not provide for forced labour within the meaning of section 14 of the Constitution in that they did not specify any penalty or injurious consequences.
43. This was under section 96K of the State of Emergency Decree and carried the death sentence.
44. For a detailed analysis see Michelson Institute, 1987, p.45.
45. See Swainson, 1978, p.365. For a similar view in Liberia see Kieh, 1980, p.203.
46. Emergency Powers (Maintenance of Railway Services) 1982 SI 8A/82.
47. Sections 32 and 34.
48. Emergency Powers (Maintenance of Essential Services) Regulations 1989 SI 160A/89. These were reinforced by the Emergency Powers (Declaration of Essential Services) Notice 1990 SI 109A/90 which was designed to render the anti-strike provisions applicable to all public servants.
49. They later returned to work in the face of threats to dismiss them.
50. See, for example, the studies of Ghana and Zaire in International Commission of Jurists, 1983. See also the discussion on detention without trial in Africa in Chapter 6 above.
51. Emergency Powers (Local Authorities) Regulations 1983 SI 134/83. They also amended the Urban Councils Act.
52. *Kombayi v Mawere*, Unreported, High Court of Zimbabwe HC-B-93-83.
53. Emergency Powers (Political Symbols) Order 1985 SI 138B/85.
54. Other regulations have (a) amended the Rural Councils Act to reduce the voting age in rural council elections from 21 to 18 years; and (b) modified the Electoral Act in connection with the registration of voters.
55. Emergency Powers (Prohibition of Flag) Order GN 768/82 made under section 57 of the Emergency Powers (Maintenance of Law and Order) Regulations 1980. This empowered the Minister of Home Affairs to prohibit, *inter alia* the possession, use or distribution of any article if he was of the opinion that it would otherwise prejudice the maintenance of public safety.
56. An adjoining road (formerly Railway Avenue) was renamed Kenneth Kaunda Avenue in honour of the Zambian president. This is a far less prestigious road than the other two and probably reflected the fact that Zambia supported Joshua Nkomo and ZAPU during the freedom struggle.
57. Emergency Powers (Alteration of Names) Regulations 1982 SI 427/82.
58. *The Herald* (Harare), 7 May 1982.
59. The government obviously learned its lesson as the changing of place names was later put on a proper statutory basis with the regulations being re-enacted into the Names Alteration Acts 1983 and 1985.
60. Marks, 1982, p.182.
61. ILA, Belgrade report, 1980, paras 67–71.
62. Noted in Chowdhury, 1989, p.21–22.
63. See the discussion in Chapter 1.

12 Protecting Individual Freedoms: The Traditional Safeguards

Introduction

One of the legacies of the colonial period in Africa was the tradition of authoritarian rule backed up by wide-ranging emergency and security laws and a non-recognition of individual freedoms. Many independent African nations have followed this pattern with leaders, who bitterly criticised the abuse of human rights by the colonial power, being guilty of much the same conduct. Indeed Zimba argues that such criticism was no more than propaganda to discredit colonialism as being incompatible with human rights and democracy in order to win international sympathy for their cause.[1] The examples given earlier in the book tend to reinforce this analysis. Of course, the use of emergency powers is not necessarily improper or an unjustifiable abrogation of some individual freedoms if they are implemented within an acceptable constitutional framework. No one would seriously wish to deprive a State of the necessary legal weapons with which to tackle a genuine emergency situation. However, it is the basic assumption of this book that individual freedoms need constant protection as they are the cornerstone of every society. Indeed some freedoms are so fundamental that they are never liable to abrogation nor derogation for this would otherwise undermine the rule of law. Thus whilst it is not appropriate to place rigid controls on government action in times of emergency it is absolutely necessary to retain genuine safeguards against unwarranted abuses of individual freedoms. This means that a balance is required between the interests of the State and the rights of individual. The African experience shows that to date, the scales have been generally heavily weighted in favour of the State.

The next two chapters are concerned with examining techniques of safeguarding individual freedoms during a state of emergency. In this chapter the operation of the legislative, judicial and constitutional safeguards are discussed. The following chapter considers other potential safeguards. The discussion is of special relevance in that it seeks to devise a model for other African States to emulate and is particularly timely given the new and healthy respect for individual freedoms being expressed throughout Africa.[2]

Legislative Safeguards[3]

The emergence of the one-party state in many African nations and the general ineffectiveness of 'opposition' parties elsewhere has undermined much of the traditional role of the legislature as a check on the power of the executive. It is rightly said that during a period of crisis, a legislature can do little more than identify difficulties, allocate resources and give officials a wide discretion,[4] a process described as 'departicipation'.[5] A typical example is that of Malawi where membership of the legislature is dependent upon presidential approval and a member automatically loses both his/her parliamentary seat and membership of the ruling Party if he/she votes against the government in a parliamentary vote of no confidence.[6] The creation of one-party states has further eroded the position of the legislature for all parliamentary candidates are subject to vetting by the Party.[7] Of course the new 'winds of change' throughout Africa now hold out the promise of more effective parliamentary government, although the role and influence of the legislature remains to be seen. Whatever changes transpire, it is inevitable that the role of the legislature will be diminished during a state of emergency. But this must not result in the 'departicipation' of the legislature because it must retain a safeguarding function. It is against this background that the situation in Zimbabwe is examined and assessed.

ZANU(PF) always had a commanding majority in parliament. Indeed the first ten years of independence saw the virtual disappearance of all other political parties. With the unity agreement, PF–ZAPU members joined the ruling party whilst the seats of the 20 white members were abolished in 1987. As from April 1990, the Parliament of Zimbabwe became a unicameral body consisting of 150 members[8] made up of 120 popularly elected members on a constituency basis, eight Provincial Governors and ten chiefs. The remaining twelve members are appointed by the President from a representative cross-section of the community as he considers desirable in the national interest or in order to enhance the representative character of Parliament.[9] Following the 1990 general elections, there remained just three members from other parties.

Parliament has the general power to make laws for the peace, order and good government of Zimbabwe. However its role is not to govern nor to determine or direct policies but rather to scrutinise, influence and legitimise executive actions; to provide a means of critical oversight; to ensure, as far as possible, that executive powers are used properly and effectively; and, in exceptional circumstances, to call the executive to account for its actions, failing which the executive is liable to be brought down.[10] Its powers of overseeing executive action in times of public emergency are effected both by 'ordinary' parliamentary methods and others which are unique to emergency situations.

The ordinary methods include questions to Ministers; motions for an Address in reply to the presidential speech; motions for the adjournment of the House of Assembly; private members motions; and supply debates. In the context of the state of emergency, these were all used to elicit information, criticise executive action and make suggestions on future policy. Up to 1987, questions on security and related matters were frequently asked at the regular session of Prime Minister's Question Time. For example, in the session 1986–87, Mugabe answered questions on dissident activity in Matabeleland; the actions of RENAMO rebels in the east of the country; the imposition of sanctions against South Africa; and the progress (or otherwise) of the unity talks. With the establishment of the Executive President, this session was replaced by the somewhat clumsily named 'Vice-President and Senior Ministers' Question Time' but security related questions were still regularly asked.[11] From time to time, other Ministers involved in State security also responded to questions. The annual debate on the presidential speech also provided a platform for debate. As Edgar Tekere once poetically asserted: 'I like this debate because it has a latitude of freedom. I can speak as I please and I can touch upon anything I please, anything I dream and I am going to dream'.[12] This freedom of debate gave backbenchers the chance to discuss security related matters, particularly those which affected their individual constituencies. In their own contributions, Ministers were expected to reply to issues raised by other speakers and sometimes took the opportunity to state government policy. For example, in August 1988, a Minister of State reiterated the adherence of government to its policy of reconciliation despite evidence that some white Zimbabweans were assisting South African efforts to destabilise the country.[13] Motions for the adjournment of the House and private members motions were also used periodically to highlight current security problems. For instance, in the 1987–88 parliamentary session, there were motions concerning security and economic problems; operational difficulties at Mozambican ports; and the use of the Vagrancy Act. Finally in the 'supply' debates, where matters of administration and policy relating to the various ministries are considered, backbenchers were able to question individual Ministers over proposed expenditure particularly over defence spending. However, no debate was allowed on the 'Special Service' grant to the President's Office which related to expenditure on security matters.

The other ordinary parliamentary safeguards are the power of the legislature to seek the removal of either the government or the President. Given the make-up of Parliament, these safeguards had no practical importance during the period in question.

As regards the additional legislative safeguards during a state of emergency, the most important was the requirement for parliamentary approval of the emergency proclamation and its renewal. Members used the six-monthly renewal debates to comment on government activity with a regular criticism being the use of emergency regulations for purely 'administrative' purposes. This action even resulted in the repeal of a handful of such regulations. The powers surrendered by Parliament during a period of public emergency should not deprive it of the right to review emergency regulations. The Public Order Act, the predecessor of the Emergency Powers Act required the Minister to lay emergency regulations before the House **for approval.** If this was not forthcoming within seven days, the regulations ceased to have effect. This procedure had the distinct advantage of ensuring legislative scrutiny of all regulations. Unfortunately, the Emergency Powers Act reversed the procedure so that emergency regulations remained valid until **disapproved** by the House. This had extremely important implications, for the general constitutional convention is that rule by the executive lapses so that its power is limited in both duration and effect.[14] The change meant that the onus was on Parliament to initiate an enquiry into regulations, failing which they remained operative until revoked by executive order or lapsed upon the ending of the state of emergency. In practice, members made little effort to scrutinise emergency regulations. Over one hundred were made after 1980, with the necessity of most being questionable, but on only one occasion did Parliament debate the possible invalidity of a regulation. Of course, the legislature only sits for between 80 and 100 days per year, but even so, the importance of the regulations surely required a return to the pre-Emergency Powers Act position.[15]

Perhaps part of the reason for limited scrutiny of regulations by members was the work of the Senate Legal Committee.[16] Originally established under the Constitution of Rhodesia 1969, its function was to give an opinion as to whether any provision contained in certain Bills and statutory instruments, including emergency regulations, 'would be or are in contravention of the Declaration of Rights'.[17] The committee customarily consisted of four senators, including two lawyers. If the committee considered that the emergency regulations contravened the Declaration of Rights, an adverse report was made to the Senate. If accepted and 'the House of Assembly has not resolved that the provision shall not be revoked' or the offending provision(s) were not repealed or amended so as to remove the contravention, the President was bound to repeal the regulations.[18] Between 1980 and 1990 the committee examined some sixteen provisions in detail of which seven were considered to be in breach of the Declaration. As a result of consultations with government law officers, changes in the wording meant that only two adverse reports were made, resulting in the revocation of the offending provisions.[19] Following the parliamentary changes in 1990, the committee was replaced by the Parliamentary Legal Committee which has an expanded power to scrutinise statutory instruments and to declare whether or not they are in conflict with the enabling statute. Robert Mugabe himself recognised that the Senate

Legal Committee had 'proved useful as an early warning system on the constitutionality of statutory instruments'[20] and its continued operation is welcome. If manned by able members, the new committee can continue as a useful safeguard by advising the legislature of the potential problems posed by delegated legislation.

Overview

Given the overwhelming parliamentary majority of the ruling party, it was never likely that the legislature would be in a position to play a major safeguarding role. Even so, the mere fact that debate, and on occasions quite heated debate, took place on matters involving the state of emergency was important as it at least focused attention on government policy. Similarly, despite the fact that the government always obtained overwhelming parliamentary support for the renewal of the state of emergency, the procedure itself was useful. It enabled regular debate to take place on the reasons for the continuation of state of emergency and gave an opportunity for backbenchers to question Ministers. The independence of mind of a few members ensured that the such occasions were often lively and stimulating. Whilst it was not practicable to expect the legislature to make a detailed assessment of the reasons for the renewal, a critical analysis of government activity was helpful. The procedure was also useful to government as it served to emphasise the openness of the political system and thus enhanced its legitimacy and democratic nature. Without this constant review, the state of emergency was not subject to any form of critical scrutiny, and this is a classic recipe for rule by the executive. Perhaps to emphasise the importance of the occasion, approval by a two thirds (or higher) majority of the total membership of Parliament should be required, as is the case in, for example, Tanzania.[21]

As was seen in earlier chapters, one particularly disturbing characteristic of the Zimbabwean emergency was the use of emergency regulations to by-pass the ordinary legislative process. This practice threatened to undermine the whole parliamentary process and posed a real threat to individual freedoms. The Zimbabwean situation reveals that a number of basic principles are needed to limit this practice:

(1) The normal legislative process must be adhered to whenever possible. Even if there was an urgent need to change place names or to impose a development levy, it was still possible for Parliament to deal with the matter swiftly. Indeed, in 1982 the Ministers Salaries Act passed all its stages in one day.[22]

(2) Regulations must not be used where there are already adequate powers under the existing law. For example, the Criminal Procedure and Evidence Act provided for the ordering of a recognisance to keep the peace.[23] For those involved in the Apostolic Church dispute this surely would have sufficed in order to quell the violence.[24]

(3) In circumstances where the use of emergency regulations is essential, they should be replaced as soon as possible by statute. Only when this is not possible, due to constitutional restrictions, should regulations remain in force. In practice, in only a few cases did government make any effort to replace the regulations.[25]

(4) The use of regulations to amend legislation must be used sparingly. Once again the case of Zimbabwe well illustrates the point for on at least fifteen separate occasions statutes were amended by regulation. For example, the Vocational Education and Training Act was amended to permit the Minister to provide for the survey of manpower resources, training facilities, the earnings of staff 'and any other particulars or information which the Minister deems fit'. Similarly the Precious Stones Act was amended by the imposition of a

minimum sentence of three years imprisonment for the theft or unlawful export of precious stones and emeralds.[26] Once again it must be emphasised that the legislative process was not only by-passed but to a great extent usurped because any law (bar certain constitutional provisions) could be amended at the sole behest of the executive. Subordinate legislation was truly subordinate no longer so long as the state of emergency remained in force. There is little, if any, justification for this kind of power and in principle it must be condemned.

Judicial Safeguards

The Charter of the United Nations affirms the determination of the world community to establish conditions under which justice can be maintained so as to achieve the promotion of and to encourage respect for human rights and fundamental freedoms. In 1985 this aim was furthered by the adoption of the United Nations Basic Principles on the Independence of the Judiciary at the Seventh United Nations Congress on the Prevention of Crime and Treatment of Offenders. This recognises that the organisation and administration of justice should be inspired by those principles and that efforts should be taken to translate them fully into reality. In this respect, the Basic Principles state that the independence of the judiciary shall be guaranteed by the State and enshrined in the Constitution or the law of every country. Further, it is the duty of all governmental and other institutions to respect and observe the independence of the judiciary.[27]

In practice, and particularly in times of emergency, such independence is threatened by, for example, the loss of jurisdiction to special courts or tribunals; laws which indemnify members of the security forces against legal liability for their actions; the suspension of habeas corpus; ousting of judicial review; and the creation of a climate of fear or the appointment of executive-minded judges leading to judicial timidity and ineffectiveness. The manner in which the judicial safeguards have operated in Zimbabwe can now be examined.

The Independence of the Judiciary in Zimbabwe

Judicial independence is constitutionally protected in that judges of the Supreme Court and High Court hold office until the age of 65 years (or 70 years if so desired);[28] the office of a judge of either court cannot be abolished during his tenure of office without his consent;[29] and the remuneration of judges is paid out of the Consolidated Revenue Fund[30] and cannot be reduced whilst a judge remains in office.[31] Judges of the Supreme Court and High Court are only removable for inability to discharge the functions of their office, whether arising from infirmity of body or mind or any other cause, or for misbehaviour.[32] In the case of the Chief Justice, if the President considers that the question of his removal should be investigated, he must appoint a tribunal of inquiry made up of three experienced lawyers. If the tribunal so recommends, the President must then refer the matter to the Judicial Service Commission which then makes a binding recommendation on the matter. The Commission consists of the Chief Justice;[33] the chairman of the Public Service Commission;[34] the Attorney-General; and two or three other members appointed by the President.[35] Under the Lancaster House document, the President, acting on the advice of the Chief Justice, was entitled to set up a similar investigation into the possible removal of a judge of the Supreme Court or High Court. In 1984 a constitutional amendment provided that either the Prime Minister or the Chief Justice could so advise the President. This followed considerable concern over the decision of the Chief Justice to take no action when a recently appointed Supreme Court judge, Justice Waddington, resigned to take up a similar post in a South African bantustan. It appeared that his acceptance of the

Zimbabwean post was merely a vehicle to enable him to obtain the other appointment. The amendment was never used and with the establishment of the Executive President, the Constitution has reverted back to the pre-1984 position. This is encouraging as it reduces possible excessive executive involvement in the removal process.

One unfortunate omission from the Constitution is any mention of judicial immunity from prosecution. The importance of this protection is that 'it enables judges to act fearlessly and impartially in the discharge of their judicial duties as it will be difficult for the judges to function if their actions in court are made subject to legal proceedings either civil or criminal'.[36] The President himself enjoys such immunity and the position of the judges will be strengthened if such a protection is extended to them.

Judicial Independence in Practice

In times of crisis the government must discharge its duty of protecting the State and its citizens. For the judiciary the response to executive actions is always something of a balancing act. To take a legalistic approach and determine a case strictly on its merits is procedurally correct but may lead to a threat to national security and a possible confrontation between the two bodies. Accordingly the judiciary may be inclined to take a 'pragmatic' approach to the problem by seeking to engineer a compromise between the wishes of the executive and the rights of the individual. The relationship is further complicated by the attitude of the executive to the judiciary. Pressure, both overt and covert, may be exerted in order to gain judicial 'compliance' to executive wishes, which is a fate suffered by the courts in many countries. This strategy is reinforced by appeals to the 'People' containing accusations of judicial intransigence and its betrayal of the 'Government and the People'. Thus protections of individual freedoms are only of any practical value if judicial independence is in fact a reality. This is particularly so when matters of security are involved.

The importance of the judicial role was noted by former Chief Justice Fieldsend:

> Where inroads [into the exercise of individual freedoms] are made by emergency regulations and orders made under them, it is of the greatest importance that the courts should be vigilant to ensure the wishes of the executive are acceded to only when there has been compliance with every formality required by the legislation.[37]

The practical application of this approach in Zimbabwe is now considered.

Absence of Purely Political Appointees

The appointment of judges is open to considerable abuse. By seeking to retain and appoint known supporters of the government, the appearance of judicial independence is retained whilst in practice the judges become the mouthpiece of the executive. The activities of the members of the Rhodesian judiciary during the UDI period is a startling reminder of this danger. The appointment of judges on purely political grounds is quite wrong but, as a former Chief Justice of Zimbabwe has correctly pointed out:

> What is important at that level is not necessarily the complete absence of any 'political' consideration, but a positive commitment to the choice of professionally competent persons of proven integrity. No one should be appointed a judge for purely political reasons when he is not otherwise fitted for office.[38]

In Zimbabwe, although there was an acute shortage of judges after independence, no purely political appointments to the superior courts were made. For example, the appointments in 1980 of Chief Justice Fieldsend and of Justice Baron to the Supreme Court were well deserved as both were outstanding lawyers as well as staunch opponents of the Smith regime.[39] The first black Zimbabwean judge, Justice Dumbutshena, was an experienced lawyer having practised for many years in Zambia. In fact he was associated with the internal settlement having returned in 1979 to become member of Parliament.[40] Justice Manyarara was also an MP during the Muzorewa regime. An interesting illustration of this even-handed approach is the case of Fergus Blackie. He was a supporter of Ian Smith, a Rhodesian Front MP during the UDI period and was closely associated with the activities of the former regime. Nevertheless, in 1986 as the most senior member of the *de facto* Bar, he was appointed a Judge of the High Court. This is surely an outstanding example of the appointment for 'non' political motives.[41] In fact, even after ten years of independence, only two High Court judges were members of the ruling Party and no judge was appointed merely because of the support of ZANU(PF).[42] Indeed in 1990, a white judge, Justice Gubbay, who was originally appointed to the Rhodesian bench in 1977, was appointed Chief Justice.

A related issue is the application of indirect pressure by government on judges. Fear of reprisals for determining a security related case contrary to the wishes of government, such as the loss or reduction of promotion prospects, can lead to political influence in decision-making. It is a measure of executive respect for the judges that no overt pressure was exerted[43] although criticism of the activities of some judges was forthcoming from both Party and government. Nevertheless, judges who were the subject of such attacks were not 'punished'.[44] The most notable example of this was the promotion of Justice Dumbutshena to the post of Chief Justice in March 1984 despite his having handed down a number of judgments against the government in security-related cases, including that in the Air Force 6 case.

Appointment of Judges to Hear Particular Cases

Another tactic used to undermine judicial independence in some countries is to pressurise the Chief Justice into assigning certain cases to specific judges who are known to have pro-government sympathies. The possibility of this occurring in Zimbabwe was first tested in 1980 at the trial for murder of Edgar Tekere, the then Minister of Manpower Planning. The government made it clear that it would not interfere in the matter and was prepared to let the judicial process take its course. The trial in the High Court was heard by a white judge, Justice Pittman and two non-white assessors. The defence objected to the appointment of the trial judge, who had strong links with the Smith regime, and asked for the appointment of a foreign judge to hear the case. This was refused. Justice Pittman was certainly closely associated with the former regime having been a former Rhodesia Front MP and having served as Minister of Justice and Minister of Combined Operations during the late seventies when the bush war was at its height. He also had the 'distinction' of being the last judge to be sworn in by the President of Rhodesia prior to the implementation of the internal settlement. Whilst not disputing that he and his bodyguards were responsible for the killing of the victims, a white farmer, Tekere sought the protection of the Indemnity and Compensation Act 1975 – the very statute which the nationalists had so roundly condemned prior to independence.[45] In December 1980 the High Court, by a majority, found all accused not guilty of murder on the ground that the acts which led to the shooting were covered by the indemnity provisions.

The appointment of a trial judge with such a background in this type of case illustrates the manner in which government refrained from interfering with the allocation of cases. Indeed between 1980 and 1990, all cases, including those involving security related matters, were assigned without any outside influence.[46]

Decisions Against the State

On several occasions the State lost cases of major importance on both constitutional and security related matters. This might easily have led to an open confrontation with the judges. The Zambian case of *Silva & Freitas*[47] highlights the potential problem. In 1969 two Portuguese soldiers strayed into Zambia from Angola (the latter then being a colony of Portugal). With the strained relations existing between the two countries on account of the independence struggle being waged by the people of Angola, there was considerable hostility towards the two men in Zambia. Although there were clear extenuating circumstances, magistrates convicted the men of illegally entering the country and imposed a heavy fine or two years imprisonment. On review in the High Court, a white judge, Justice Evans quashed the sentence on the grounds that in view of the trivial and technical nature of the offence, it was excessive and unlawful. This led to a wave of hostility throughout the country against the judiciary with President Kaunda denouncing the decision as being politically motivated and demanding an explanation from the Chief Justice, James Skinner, who was a white with Zambian citizenship. A demonstration led by members of the Zambia Youth Service took place outside the High Court in Lusaka with banners accusing the judges of being racists and imperialists. Chief Justice Skinner and Justice Evans were both attacked and forced to barricade themselves in their offices whilst considerable damage was done to the High Court building itself. Later President Kaunda launched another attack stating:

> Judges are human and have got to live in the society in which they work. And living in the society means identification with that society . . . I think Justice Evans should have known that taking up the case like that in a sensitive situation he was playing with fire.[48]

As a result, Justice Evans brought forward his date of retirement and left the country almost immediately. Although asked to stay on, Chief Justice Skinner later resigned and took up a similar appointment in Malawi after most judges had resigned there owing to the increased powers of the traditional courts. Two other white judges also felt unable to continue in office. Their departure left a considerable gap and the affair undoubtedly undermined the independence of the judiciary in the country.

With several white judges on the Bench in Zimbabwe the possibility of a similar confrontation was very real unless the independence of the judiciary was clearly recognised and its decisions respected, whatever the outcome. A real threat of such a confrontation arose following the arrest of the York brothers in January 1982. This followed the discovery of a considerable quantity of arms and ammunition buried (but contained and protected in a drum) on one of the family farms in Matabeleland and was at a time of considerable civil unrest in the area. The existence of this cache was revealed to the police by one Winston Rudman. After his arrest Alan York made a statement to the police, but he alleged in court that he had only made this apparently inculpatory statement because of threats that the police would arrest his entire family including his ailing father if he did not co-operate. At the trial in the Magistrates Court the prosecution faced two insurmountable problems. In the first place Rudman had, apparently without their knowledge, gone to South Africa. So the one witness who could speak as to whether or not the Yorks were involved in the arms cache, was missing. Secondly, the prosecution failed to prove that the statement by Alan York was made freely and voluntarily and without undue influence so it was not admitted in evidence. Without this, the State case collapsed and the brothers were acquitted. The suspicions of the State were not allayed by this and on about 6 May 1982 the brothers were re-detained. These detention orders were ruled invalid by the High Court and so on 1 July fresh orders were served. On 8 July a High Court judge again ruled that the brothers were unlawfully detained.[49] Within an hour the brothers were released only to be detained again on the same day in terms of yet another pair of ministerial orders. Once again, these were ruled unlawful. At this stage the then Minister of Home Affairs, Herbert Ushewokunze, advised the court that in his view the security of the country required the continued detention of the brothers and he declined to release them. He then launched a furious attack on the judiciary in Parliament:-

> The manner in which our law courts dispense justice is gravely frustrating and undermining the work of law enforcement agencies like the police. The security of the State is sacrificed at the altar of individual liberties.[50]

After condemning the judiciary during the UDI period, the Minister continued:

> But even after this, recalcitrant and reactionary members of the so-called Benches still remain masquerading under our hard-won independence as dispensers of justice or, shall I say, injustice by handing down perverted pieces of judgement which smack of subverting the people's government. We inherited *in toto* the Rhodesian statute which these self-same magistrates and judges used to avidly and viciously interpret against the guerrillas. What is so different now apart from it being majority rule? Our posture during constitutional negotiations with the British . . . that the judiciary must be disbanded, can now be understood with a lot of hindsight. We are aware that certain private legal practitioners are in receipt of moneys as paid hirelings, from governments hostile to our own order, in the process of seeking to destabilise us, to create a state of anarchy through the inherited legal apparatus. We promise to handle such lawyers using the appropriate technology that exists in our law and order section. This should succeed in breaking up the unholy alliance between the negative Bench, the reactionary legal practitioners and governments hostile to us, some of whose representatives are in this country.[51]

Not unexpectedly, critical reaction was swift. On 15 July the President of the Law Society of Zimbabwe issued the following press statement:

> Representatives of the Law Society Council met the Minister of Justice to express their concern at the recent statement made in Parliament by the Minister of Home Affairs about the legal profession and the judiciary. The Minister of Justice confirmed that it remained the view of the Government that it is the duty of legal practitioners to act fearlessly in the interests of their clients and in the interests of the administration of justice; and that a legal practitioner should not decline to act for a client for fear of the consequences of acting in support of what may be an unpopular cause. It is considered that the attack on certain unnamed legal practitioners and the judiciary could have the effect of deterring legal practitioners from acting as they are duty bound to act and the Minister of Justice confirmed that Government does not wish the remarks of the Minister of Home Affairs to intimidate legal practitioners in this way. He has given his personal assurance to the President of the Law Society that Government does not wish the remarks of the Minister to intimidate legal practitioners in this way and that they should feel free to continue to act in the best interests of the administration of justice and without fear of arbitrary arrest and detention when they have lawfully and properly so acted. He also indicated that what the Minister of Home Affairs had said were his own personal views and not the official view of

> Government which should be expressed by the Ministry of Justice in such matters. Finally, the Council of the Law Society regrets that the Minister of Home Affairs saw fit to make what it considers to be an unwarranted attack upon the judiciary thereby undermining the confidence of the people in the courts of our country.

The following day, the Chief Justice took the unprecedented step of issuing his own press statement:

> Being deeply concerned at the attack on the judiciary, the magistracy and the legal profession in Parliament on Tuesday July 13, 1982, I considered it right to consult with both the Prime Minister and the Minister of Justice before making any statement. I can now say that I have been assured by the Prime Minister and the Minister of Justice:
> (1) that this unjustified and intemperate attack in no way represents the views of the Government;
> (2) that the Government has trust and confidence in the judges and magistrates and gives them full support in the administration of justice; and
> (3) that it recognises that the legal profession forms an integral part of the administration of justice and gives assurance that its members will not be subject to any reprisals or pressure in fulfilling their lawful duties to their clients.

The controversy was re-opened on 29 July 1982 when the Prime Minister told parliament:

> I must say that, much as I appreciate the difficult task that our judges are faced with, and the difficult task should invoke more sympathy from this House than condemnation, the Government cannot allow the technicalities of the law to fetter its hands in what is a very clear task before it, to preserve law and order in the country – (Hon. Members: Hear Hear) – maintain peace in the country and forge ahead to build a non-racial society. We shall, therefore, proceed as Government in a manner we feel is fitting, in a manner which will enable us to be in control of the situation **and some of the measures we shall take are measures which will be extra-legal.**[52] [my emphasis].

Fortunately a confrontation was averted as on 3 August the disputed detention orders were revoked and replaced by fresh orders which were ruled valid by the High Court. This decision was critically examined in an earlier chapter but it must be said that the judge went to great lengths to ensure these orders were ruled valid.[53] A valiant attempt to defuse the situation was then made by the Minister of Justice in a press statement:

> My Government, pledged as it is to the protection of the rights of individuals, the preservation of peace and the maintenance of law and order, fully recognises the role which an independent judiciary should play in the sustenance of our democratic order. It is Government's belief that the executive and judiciary should work as partners and thus complement each other in the fulfilment of their functions. The recent decisions of our courts, especially the series of judgments concerning the York brothers and the action Government took in relation to them, have given rise to a completely mistaken view that conflict exists between the executive and the judiciary. The re-detention of the York brothers on July 29 and the subsequent court ruling that their re-detention was illegal, tended to strengthen this view, more especially that the York brothers were not released immediately following the court order. There has never been any real conflict between the executive and the judiciary. What has been at issue is a misunderstanding as to the

> procedure to be adopted in effecting arrests and detentions. Indeed, each time the court invalidated any detention order, Government acceded to the ruling by rectifying the order. Admittedly, the adoption of wrong procedures has resulted in some detention orders being declared invalid and the detention unlawful by the courts. But this irregularity has now been corrected and the law on the subject thoroughly studied. Valid procedures will in future certainly be followed. Accordingly, the order re-detaining the York brothers has now been varied so as to make it accord with the law.

Following a meeting between members of the family and the Prime Minister, on 28 August the brothers were finally set free, the Prime Minister arranging for them to be driven from prison in his car. Thus ended a protracted crisis which at one stage threatened to undermine relations between the executive and judiciary.

The York affair brought a critical response from one commentator who considered that the words of the Prime Minister conveyed

> the disturbingly clear message that, whatever the Minister of Justice might say, it is government policy to disobey the law whenever the government considers such disobedience necessary for the preservation of law and order. This is why, whenever I am asked (as I frequently am) whether the rule of law prevails in Zimbabwe, I regretfully answer that it does not.[54]

Given the overall record of government, this was most unfair. In retrospect, the affair was the result of administrative blunders rather than a deliberate attempt to undermine the judicial process, although this of course does not provide any excuse for disobeying a judicial order. The statement made by Mugabe is the only time he has explicitly supported the use of extra-legal measures and his choice of words was undoubtedly unfortunate, although no doubt the tense political and security situation then existing in Matabeleland contributed to the outburst. Mugabe himself sought to repair the damage by asserting in an international journal that:

> Whilst as an executive we by no means always agree with the decisions of our judges, our constitution requires and has ensured an independent judiciary. Experience shows that we indeed have an independent judiciary . . . The government has not, *qua* the government, by word or deed interfered with the independence of the judiciary.[55]

After this episode, the government had mixed fortunes in several security cases but acceptance of the decisions in all but one case indicated that the policy set out by the Minister of Justice generally prevailed. The one blemish on this record occurred in October 1989 following the detention of Morgan Tsvangirai, the secretary-general of the Zimbabwe Congress of Trade Unions. He was detained by the CIO shortly after he had issued a statement criticising the closure of the University of Zimbabwe and the arrest of student leaders. On two occasions the High Court ruled that his detention was unlawful and ordered his release. The detaining authorities simply ignored the rulings and Tsvangirai remained in detention until his release the following month, a tacit admission in itself that there was no basis for his detention in the first place. It is quite inexplicable why the government undertook such an unnecessary and clumsy attempt to silence one of its critics, particularly as it was certain to lead to considerable adverse international publicity. Such action must be condemned for disregard for the rule of law is a dangerous path indeed. As former Chief Justice Dumbutshena has noted:

> When the executive ignores the orders and judgments of the courts, there is an inevitable breakdown of law and order, resulting in uncivil chaos because the courts cannot enforce their orders.[56]

Overall, these isolated instances should not detract from the excellent record of the government. In practice, the judges remained the guardians of individual freedoms and gave full scope to those freedoms when required. The overall commitment to judicial independence was reiterated in 1989 by the Minister of Justice when commenting on the refusal of the Speaker of the House of Assembly to comply with a decision of the Supreme Court in favour of Ian Smith.[57] The court had held that a breach of the Declaration of Rights had occurred when Parliament had purported to withhold the parliamentary salary of Smith during his suspension from the House of Assembly.[58] The Minister stated that government 'respects the right of the Supreme Court to make pronouncements on all matters of law and respects and recognises that the Supreme Court had jurisdiction to interpret the law as it saw fit'. He added:

> Inevitably, a decision or judgment of the Court on a matter involving a personality as notorious as Mr Smith of the UDI track record is bound to draw considerable criticism from members of the public. That is a healthy development in a democratic society such as ours.[59]

Given the political will to retain an independent judiciary,[60] the future can be viewed with cautious optimism. However the judges must recognise that they have a responsibility to identify with the society in which they operate and to be responsive to its needs.[61] Decisions such as that in the Bickle case[62] demonstrate the importance of this approach. When dealing with security legislation, they must continually heed the words of former Chief Justice Fieldsend for it is very easy to rapidly 'retreat from enlightened judicial activism to a conservative judicial positivism'.[63] How quickly this can occur is well illustrated in South Africa where in 1986 several enlightened decisions of the Appellate Division[64] appeared to show that the judges considered that it was 'their duty to approach legislation providing for detention without trial in the spirit not of compliance, but of independent scrutiny'.[65] Barely two years later came an almost complete withdrawal by the higher courts from exercising jurisdiction over emergency powers.[66]

Protection of Individual Freedoms Against Unlawful Action by the Security Forces

Cases such as the Air Force 6, Denis Granger and John Makomberedze, discussed earlier, illustrate that the judiciary was able to safeguard some individuals against the unlawful actions of members of the security forces. The importance of magistrates in the protection of individual freedoms must not be overlooked. They are the 'grass-roots' protectors of individual freedoms and must exercise this role diligently. The importance that this occurs at all levels is highlighted by the actions of the magistrates in confirming the 'confessions' of the Air Force 6 despite clear evidence that these were obtained illegally. Some claimed that they were unaware of the efforts being made by the lawyers to obtain access to their clients, despite the fact that the national press was prominently reporting these efforts at the time. Justice Dumbutshena found it was 'a most unlikely thing' that the magistrates were unaware of this fact and noted that the magistrates should have asked the accused whether they had been able to see their lawyers. In the Supreme Court, Justice Beck emphasised that it was not reasonable for a magistrate to proceed with confirmation proceedings 'without first making proper enquiry and investigation into whether the accused is being denied access to his legal representative if he has any reason . . . to suspect that the accused's desire for access . . . is being improperly frustrated'. The burden on magistrates and judges of the higher courts is a heavy one. If they are not prepared to ensure that accused persons are fully protected against illegal actions by government agents, then grave injustices may occur. The startling difference between the approach of the trial judge and magistrates in the Air Force 6 case neatly illustrates the need for a constantly vigilant judiciary coupled with sufficient training and supervision for magistrates to enable them to fulfil their vital function.

The Zimbabwe experience highlights a number of important aspects concerning the protection of individual freedoms. Firstly, the courts must remain the protectors of those freedoms even in the most sensitive political/security related cases. Secondly, constitutional rights and governmental powers must be interpreted in favour of individual freedoms. Thirdly, all government agents must be legally accountable for their actions. Finally, detention without trial is a potent weapon in the hands of the executive and can circumvent the efforts of the judiciary to protect individual freedoms. Even here, the judges still have a vital role to play by ensuring that the State and its agents follow the correct procedures involved in the detention process.

Role of the Law Society

Another organisation capable of playing a crucial role during a state of emergency in enforcing judicial safeguards is the governing body of the legal profession. The usefulness of this role was well illustrated in Lesotho, where the Law Society was held entitled to bring an action in connection with the detention of three of its members under emergency regulations. As a result of the case, the High Court of Lesotho held that the declaration of a state of emergency and emergency regulations made thereunder were null and void.[67] Indeed, the equivalent body in Ghana was banned by the government because of its outspoken criticism of human rights violations. In Zimbabwe, the Law Society also performed a useful function. By responding swiftly and firmly to any perceived unwarranted governmental interference in the operation of the legal system (such as the York brothers case) it acted as an influential and informed pressure group. Further, it acted as a guardian of the rights of legal practitioners, as evidenced by the case of Hartmann and Gardner.

Lawyers and their professional bodies also play a key part in assisting the judiciary to play a safeguarding role for no court can long remain ahead of the legal profession which serves it. Redress of violations of individual freedoms require counsel to master a large array of facts to support their arguments and to help formulate effective remedies. Effective redress for violations of individual freedoms can only take place if members of the legal profession are ready not only to act as guardians of the independence of the judiciary but also prepared to transcend the narrow confines of their legal training with experiments in procedures and doctrines which will further the goal of social justice. In this respect, the need for comparative research is a prerequisite.[68] The active support of the governing body of the legal profession in this regard is of inestimable value.

Payment of Damages and Costs

There are two other problems which reduced the effectiveness of the judicial safeguards. One concerns the enforcement of court orders against the State. In several cases, the government refused to pay damages to individuals following a judicial determination that their rights were infringed by the action of government agents. Such a response is not unique. For example in Zambia in 1974, there were a series of cases in which heavy damages were awarded against the government for unlawful detention and ill-treatment. The President then moved to prevent payment of damages where the claim was based on a 'technical error'.[69] In Zimbabwe the problem lies in enforcement of the judgment. The

State Liabilities Act states that no execution, attachment or process against State property is permitted if the amount awarded by the court is not paid. Instead, at the State's discretion, the sum awarded **may** be paid out of the consolidated revenue fund. The result is that if the State refuses to comply with an order of damages, the individual has no remedy. In several cases the Government of Zimbabwe refused to pay damages involving security matters. In 1986 Robert Mugabe told the House of Assembly that the payment of damages in some cases was a wrongful use of taxpayers money. He added:

> where people take advantage of our liberal situation to go to court and win on technicalities, they should not expect that government is going to use the peoples' resources to enrich them when we believe in some cases that they are wrongdoers . . . I do not think, in that case, we would be doing justice to the nation and so we would have to look at these cases ourselves . . . [If] this person says he was wrongfully arrested when, in fact, to our knowledge, he was consorting with dissidents, we cannot grant him damages at all . . . However, if an ordinary civilian is arrested and he appeals . . . and we feel it is a genuine case, we will pay those damages . . . We will discriminate [*sic*] security cases and other cases that we feel merit our compliance but there are certain others where I think we shall introduce a law to this parliament to nullify those damages.[70]

No such law was ever introduced but on several occasions individuals did not receive their award of damages.[71] The attitude of government on this issue is quite indefensible. Anyone unlawfully arrested or detained has a constitutional right to compensation and it is not for government to usurp the jurisdiction of the courts. The 'liberal' situation referred to by Mugabe is merely the normal and democratic operation of the law. The result being that the functions of the judge were usurped by the executive and that an important safeguard on the abuse of power by government agents eliminated.[72]

The second issue concerns legal aid. It is quite unsatisfactory that this is not available as of right to impecunious litigants who seek to enforce their constitutional rights. This should be provided for in the Constitution itself.

The final issue concerns the payment of costs in constitutional and security cases. In view of the present absence of legal aid, inevitably some individuals cannot commence what might result in expensive litigation against the State because they enjoy little prospect of recovering their costs. This means that judicial safeguards on individual freedoms often remain the preserve of a fortunate few who can afford it. It is suggested that this problem is speedily remedied. The awarding of costs against the State in appropriate cases would be a useful addition to the judicial safeguards because it might encourage State officials to act more responsibly.

The judicial safeguard depends upon the legal representatives of those involved in security cases, acting fearlessly in the protection of their client's interests. Pressure on such lawyers is a cause of concern, as epitomised by the attack launched by the Minister of Home Affairs in the York case and the charging of Hartmann, Coltart and Bissett.[73] Such cases, however isolated, means it is important to protect lawyers against the vindictiveness of government agents. It is thus suggested that the leave of the Attorney-General be required prior to instigating proceedings against a lawyer.

Overview

Perhaps the most compelling reasons for the protection of judicial independence were given by the then President of Tanzania, Julius Nyerere. After army mutineers had received light prison sentences, he announced that government would not vary them for:

> To interfere with the Court's decision would be to do exactly that thing for which the nation condemns the soldiers: it would be to abrogate the rule of law . . . The rule of law is the basis on which rests the freedom and equality of our citizens. It must remain the foundation of our state. We must not allow even our disgust with the mutineers to overcome our principles.[74]

The Basic Principles on the Independence of the Judiciary provide that 'the judiciary shall decide matters before them impartially on the basis of facts and in accordance with the law, without any restrictions, improper influences, inducements, pressures, threats or interferences, direct or indirect, from any quarter or for any reason'.[75] Further, 'there shall not be any inappropriate or unwarranted interference with the judicial process, nor shall judicial decisions by the courts be subject to revision'.[76] In many African countries such principles are ignored and this has resulted in the undermining of judicial independence.

In spite of the state of emergency, the Government of Zimbabwe has generally adhered to the Basic Principles. It refrained from exerting overt political pressure on the judiciary and accepted, with few exceptions, adverse decisions. Thus even though operating during a state of emergency, judicial independence in the post-1980 period was very much a reality.

The effectiveness of the judicial safeguard can be analysed on two levels. At the practical level, the use of judicial review and habeas corpus undoubtedly provided an avenue through which to challenge the validity of executive actions. For example, the decision that the making of a ministerial detention order incorporated an element of objectivity. At the psychological level the public affirmation of the rights of detainees and criticism of members of the security forces helped to bring pressure to bear on government to abide by the rule of law. Indeed cases such as the Air Force 6 forced government to justify its actions to the international community. It is true that there are limits to this safeguard and that the cases discussed in the book are the visible tip of a large iceberg. Indeed it is not realistic to expect the courts to prevent and redress all abuses of power. The lack of awareness of legal rights; lack of access to a lawyer; cost; procedural and evidential limitations and the like all contributed to the problem of access to the courts. This was exacerbated by a reluctance on the part of the prosecuting authorities to bring criminal proceedings against members of the security forces and by the use of indemnity regulations. Even so, the presence of an independent judiciary coupled with a vibrant magistracy showed that the judicial safeguard can play a vital part in the process of protecting individual freedoms during a state of emergency.

Constitutional Safeguards

This study has shown that, if respected by government, a justiciable and entrenched Declaration of Rights is invaluable as a safeguard of individual freedoms during a period of emergency. However, the study has also drawn attention to a series of defects in the present constitutional safeguards which need to be addressed. If this is done, then the structure can form an excellent model for other African countries to follow:

(i) Linking Emergency Regulations with the Reasons for the State of Emergency

After independence over one hundred emergency regulations were made on a wide range of topics whilst several pre-independence regulations were retained. As previously noted, many had no connection with the reasons for the state of emergency and were promulgated merely for executive convenience. Thus it is asserted that to avoid such abuses of power, the constitution must require the executive to give detailed reasons for the declaration/ renewal of the state of emergency, following which only those regulations directly connected with those reasons will remain valid. For example, the only grounds given by the Minister of Home Affairs in July 1989 for seeking the renewal of the state of emergency were related to RENAMO activities and the 'ever present threats' from South Africa.[77] If such reasons validated the continuation of the state of emergency (as is debatable in any case), then only those regulations specifically relating to these issues would have remained valid. In practice, this would have led to the repeal of virtually every emergency regulation.

(ii) Limiting the Location of the Emergency

A state of emergency may apply to the whole or any part(s) of the country although in practice it always applied nationwide. In order to limit the use of emergency powers as far as possible, it is desirable that as restricted a geographical area as possible is included in the emergency declaration. Normally the type of crisis will be decisive. Thus a true economic emergency may well apply nationwide, whilst a security threat, such as that posed by RENAMO in limited parts of the country, could be dealt with at a localised level. This is something which might be implemented by the use of the parliamentary power under the Emergency Powers Amendment Act 1986.[78]

(iii) Publicity of Regulations

Throughout the duration of state of emergency, there was a failure on the part of government to publicise emergency regulations. These were only published in the Government Gazette and was quite insufficient given its very restricted availability and readership. This meant (perhaps deliberately) that most citizens remained in ignorance as to the scope of governmental powers. To remedy this it is imperative that the constitution imposes a duty upon government to publish full details of all emergency regulations in both national and local newspapers, including those in the vernacular.[79]

(iv) The Creation of Criminal Offences

Post-independence emergency regulations created over twenty criminal offences, each carrying a possible prison sentence. It is not known how many convictions resulted as most cases were heard by magistrates. However on several occasions stiff sentences were imposed for a breach of regulations. The creation of criminal offences in this manner is worrying, particularly because of the potentially severe consequences for individuals and the limited parliamentary scrutiny. For example, a spate of road traffic accidents in 1984 involving buses led to the making of regulations which imposed harsh penalties on drivers of buses and heavy vehicles ranging from not less than six months imprisonment for speeding to not less than two years imprisonment for reckless driving. These sentences were far in excess of those available under the applicable road traffic statute.[80] The desire to reduce accidents is laudable but the use of regulations to introduce such draconian powers is a gross abuse of power.

A further problem is that offences often impose strict liability in that it is unnecessary to prove that the offender intended his/her action or even knew that such conduct was criminal. With the low level of parliamentary control and no effective publicity of such offences, the danger of the unwitting breach of regulations is very real. For example, in one case, a man was found on a bus carrying a camouflage jacket. He was convicted of possessing an item contrary to emergency regulations and was sentenced to six months imprisonment with hard labour 'to show how seriously the law views the offence'. On review his explanation that the jacket was left behind by a soldier who had attended a funeral at his house was accepted. It was noted that 'it is highly likely that the unfortunate young man did not even know he was committing an offence'.[81]

Criminal sanctions are an inevitable part of an emergency situation and their imposition *per se* is understandable. But they pose a considerable threat to individual freedoms and thus require strict constitutional safeguards on their use:

(1) criminal sanctions should only be imposed in circumstances directly connected with the emergency;
(2) the creation of criminal offences must be widely publicised;
(3) minimum sentences should never be imposed in any circumstances;
(4) criminal sanctions should never have retrospective effect;[82]
(5) the creation of strict liability offences should occur only when security matters are involved e.g. breach of a curfew order.

Several additional constitutional safeguards are required if an adequate model is to be developed. These were discussed in previous chapters but encapsulate the following principles:

(1) improved rights for those detained without trial and, in particular, the right to release for breach of any constitutional safeguard;[83]
(2) the incorporation of enforceable Codes of Conduct for those dealing with detainees;[84]
(3) improved safeguards regarding the declaration of the state of emergency and the use of emergency regulations;
(4) the right to have all bail applications determined solely by the courts;[85]
(5) absolute protection for Zimbabwean citizens against restrictions on the right to enter and leave the country.

Overview

This study has shown that in the case of Zimbabwe the Constitution played a crucial role in the protection of individual freedoms. Indeed the effectiveness of the entrenched and justiciable Declaration of Rights provided a stark contrast with its counterparts in the preceding constitutional documents. None of the proposed additional safeguards affect the right of government to take adequate steps to protect the nation in times of crisis. But they are designed to reduce the chances of an abuse of emergency powers. If reinforced by the above, the document will form an excellent precedent for the development of constitutionalism in Africa. In view of the 'gales of change' sweeping across the continent, it is hoped that other countries will take heed of the Zimbabwe experience.

Notes

1. Zimba, 1984, p.200.
2. For a useful analysis of these moves see the special constitutional issue of the *Journal of African Law*, vol. 35, 1991.
3. See generally, Hatchard, 1989a, p.116.
4. Seidman, 1987, p.86.
5. See Klieman, 1978, p.190. Cf Tordoff, 1977, p.235.
6. See Hatchard, 1989b, pp.21–2.
7. See, for example, sections 68 and 75, Constitution of Zambia 1973, and sections 23–24, Constitution of Malawi.
8. Constitution of Zimbabwe Amendment (No. 9) Act.
9. He may also appoint any person who, by reason of his or her special qualifications or attributes, would be of value to Parliament.
10. See Bonner, 1985, p.37.

11. Mugabe appointed three Senior Ministers. As well as Nkomo, Bernard Chidzero was appointed Senior Minister of Finance, Economic Planning and Development whilst Maurice Nyagumbo was appointed Senior Minister of Political Affairs.
12. *Parliamentary Debates*, 18 August 1987.
13. Minister of State for National Security in the President's Office, *Parliamentary Debates*, 16 August 1988. This was in connection with the Bulawayo bombing cases discussed in Chapter 2.
14. See Allen, 1965, p.169 *et seq*.
15. Parliament also has the power to resolve that a situation existed which if allowed to continue 'may lead to a state of public emergency' and which 'may require the preventive detention of persons in the interests of defence, public safety or public order'. Such a resolution is effective for one year: see the Emergency Powers (Amendment) Act 1986.
16. I would like to thank the then Parliamentary Counsel, Dr J.C. Nkala, for allowing me access to the Minutes of the Senate Legal Committee.
17. Section 37, Constitution of Zimbabwe.
18. Schedule 4(8) Constitution of Zimbabwe.
19. These were Emergency Powers (Control of Residential Rents) Regulations 1982 SI 713/82 and Order GN 360A/83 made under the Emergency Powers (Control of Goods and Services) Regulations 1979 SI 880/79. In December 1988, for the first time, a report of the Senate Legal Committee that a statutory instrument (Public Service (Officers)(Misconduct and Discharge) (Amendment) Regulations 1988 (No. 1) SI 111/88) contravened the Declaration was not accepted by the House of Assembly. See *Parliamentary Debates*, 1 December 1988.
20. Mugabe, 1984, p.5.
21. Here two-thirds of the members of both the National Assembly and the National Executive Committee of the ruling party CCM must give their approval to the declaration. As Peter notes, 'Such an elaborate system, though long and tiresome, is healthy because it checks [an] arbitrary declaration of a state of emergency' (at p.41).
22. It is curious that parliamentarians worldwide are able to deal swiftly with legislation which is of benefit to themselves.
23. Section 334.
24. See Chapter 10. Similarly, an application for the grant of a liquor licence is a more acceptable manner of dealing with the situation than amending the Liquor Act itself. The Act was amended by regulations to enable the grant of a permit to be made to the government sponsored Youth Council of Zimbabwe for the supply of liquor.
25. The Emergency Powers (Investigation of State Claims) Regulations 1984 SI 154A/84 gave the Minister power to deal with the property of those persons suspected of having defrauded the government. Over thirty companies and individuals were affected. The regulations were later incorporated into the Prevention of Corruption Act 1985. Similarly, section 66, Emergency Powers (Maintenance of Law and Order) Regulations 1983 modified the Firearms Act by greatly increasing the penalties for the illegal possession of firearms. This was later re-enacted into the Firearms (Amendment) Act 1983. The same regulations prohibited the unauthorised possession of a camouflage uniform. This was later incorporated into the General Laws (Amendment) Act 1985.
26. Amendments were also made to the Vocational Education and Training Act by the Emergency Powers (Vocational Training etc) Regulations 1981 SI 465/81 and the Medical Dental and Allied Professions Act by regulations in 1983 (SI 257/83). Other examples are found throughout this book.
27. See also the similar views of the International Commission of Jurists, 1983, pp.434–7 and Nyerere, 1968, pp.109–14. For an interesting non-African view see Steinberg, 1987, p.359.
28. Section 86(1) Constitution of Zimbabwe.
29. Section 86(3) Constitution of Zimbabwe.
30. This is the central fund for government income and expenditure: see section 111, Constitution of Zimbabwe.
31. Section 88, Constitution of Zimbabwe.
32. Section 87(1) Constitution of Zimbabwe.
33. Or if this is not possible, the most senior Supreme Court judge available.
34. He/she must be a former senior civil servant (section 74, Constitution of Zimbabwe).
35. At least one of these persons must be an experienced lawyer: section 90, Constitution of Zimbabwe.
36. Statement of Objects and Reasons in the Judges (Protection) Act 1985 (India).
37. In *Hayes v Baldachin* 1981 (1) SA 749, p.755.
38. Telford Georges, 1967, p.38.
39. John Fieldsend resigned from the Rhodesian bench in 1968 following the Madzimbamuto case (discussed in Chapter 1). He was Secretary to the British Law Commission prior to his return in 1980. Leo Baron was a former legal practitioner who was actively involved in the nationalist struggle. He was detained without trial by the Smith regime and his action against this was heard jointly with that of Madzimbamuto. He was a highly respected Supreme Court justice in Zambia before returning to Zimbabwe.
40. Other notable appointments were those of Professor Telford Georges, a highly respected judge and academic from the West Indies, as the first black Chief Justice, and Wilson Sandura who was formerly Secretary for Justice and who is currently Judge President of the High Court. A number of judges who were sent from Tanzania were also of a high calibre.
41. Justice Smith was a legal draftsman for Ian Smith during UDI and also acted as legal adviser to the RF.
42. Interview with Simbi Mubako, May 1989.
43. This was the unanimous view of all High Court and Supreme Court judges interviewed.
44. An example of harassment of the judiciary in Tanzania is the case of *Kassella Bantu* (1969) HCD 170. Here a District Magistrate released the accused, who was then a member of parliament, on bail pending his trial along with sixteen others for the alleged murder of cattle thieves. As a result of the decision, the magistrate was himself detained.
45. See Chapter 8 for a discussion of the Act and related emergency regulations.

46. Chief Justice Dumbutshena has confirmed this point. He added that in 1983 the then Chief Justice asked him to take the case of the Air Force 6 because of its importance. Interview by the author with the Chief Justice, Harare, April 1989.
47. [1969] ZR 121
48. Interview with *Times of Zambia*, 29 September 1969.
49. The decision was later upheld by the Supreme Court.
50. *Parliamentary Debates*, 13 July 1982.
51. *Parliamentary Debates*, 13 July 1982.
52. *Parliamentary Debates*, 29 July 1982.
53. The decision was an attempt to 'relieve the pressure on the government' at that time: confidential source.
54. Comment by R. Christie, a former Rhodesian law professor: see Christie, 1983, at p.301.
55. See note 20 above, p.6. In November 1989 the Minister of Justice again emphasised the fact that whilst government did not always agree with all the decisions and judgments made by the judiciary, it nevertheless respected the right of the judiciary to make pronouncements on matters of law. *Parliamentary Debates*, 21 November 1989.
56. Dumbutshena, 1990, p.319.
57. Dumbutshena also believes that the independence of the judiciary was maintained: Dumbutshena, 1990, at p.317.
58. *Smith v Mutasa NO*, Unreported, Supreme Court of Zimbabwe SC 152/89. The incident threatened to provoke a constitutional crisis when the five judges of the Supreme Court issued a statement attacking the Speaker for 'the contempt with which [he] holds the Supreme Court and his utter disregard of the rule of law'.
59. *Parliamentary Debates*, 21 November 1989.
60. Indeed the Constitution of Zimbabwe (Amendment) Act No. 11 of 1990 specifically provides for judicial independence: see Hatchard, 1991, p.98.
61. See Article 12 of the United Nations Guidelines on the Independence of the Judiciary.
62. See the earlier discussion on the case.
63. See Hayson and Plasket, 1984, p.303.
64. For example see *Dempsey v Minister of Law and Order* 1986 (4) SA 530 (C); *Hurley v Minister of Law and Order* 1985 (4) SA 709 (D) and *Radebe v Minister of Law and Order* 1987 (1) SA 586 (W).
65. Mureinik, 1986, at p.618.
66. See Davis and Corder, 1988, p.281.
67. *Law Society of Lesotho v Minister of Defence* [1988] LRC (Const) 226.
68. For a useful discussion on this role as well as that of the appellate judiciary in the protection of individual freedoms, see the Suraj Report, 1983, in Baxi, p.179 *et seq*.
69. What constituted a 'technical error' was never defined and was the sole matter for the President. See the discussion by Zimba, 1984, p.123.
70. *Parliamentary Debates*, 16 July 1986.
71. For example, Denis Granger (see Chapter 6) and Kembo Mohadi have not received any payment. Mohadi was a ZAPU MP who successfully sued the government over allegations that he was beaten and partially drowned whilst in police custody in 1985. See, 1986–87 ACR B908.
72. Cf *In re Mhora & the Minister of Home Affairs* 1990 (2) ZLR 236. The State Liabilities Act does not prevent an action being brought against or damages being obtained from the arresting or detaining officer in his own capacity. The problem here is that it is highly unlikely that the individual will have the resources to pay the damages.
73. See Chapter 7 for details.
74. Nyerere, 1966, pp.298–9.
75. Article 2.
76. Article 4. This is without prejudice to judicial review or to mitigation or commutation by competent authorities of sentences imposed by the judiciary, in accordance with the law.
77. *Parliamentary Debates*, 25 July 1989.
78. See n.15 above. It must be said that a limited location of the state of emergency does not entirely solve the problem of the improper use of the detention laws. During the Rhodesian days there was a geographically limited state of emergency and in practice persons who the authorities wished to detain but who were outside the relevant areas were taken into an 'emergency' area and there issued with a detention notice. Cf the infamous English case of *Larsonneur* (1933) 149 LT 542.
79. It is a noticeable feature of the vernacular weekly paper *Kwayedza* that virtually no political news is carried. The paper remained almost silent as regards the corrupt practices perpetrated by some senior government ministers and revealed in the Sandura Commission Report in 1989. The death of Senior Minister Nyagumbo by suicide following the Report's adverse findings against him was reported in *Kwayedza* as having occurred 'after a long illness'. It appears that there was a deliberate policy to starve Zimbabweans of accurate news reporting.
80. Emergency Powers (Control of Omnibuses etc) Regulations 1984 SI 295B/84. Curiously, the regulations were made by the Acting Minister of Transport whilst the substantive holder was absent.
81. Justice McNally in *S v Zimvumi*, Unreported, High Court of Zimbabwe HC-H-355-84 at p.2. A fine of Zimb $75 was substituted but not before the accused had served fourteen days in prison. See also *S v Makamba*, Unreported, Supreme Court of Zimbabwe SC 129/85. In another curious case in 1987, a white Zimbabwean was convicted of using an ash tray inscribed 'Ian Smith UDI November 11 1965'. The object was on his desk in a private office. He was convicted of 'using an item in a public place' connected with the UDI period and contrary to Emergency Powers (Prohibition of Objectionable Souvenirs) Order 1981 GN 785/81. The Supreme Court

quashed the conviction on the grounds that the office did not constitute a public place: *S v De Bruyn* 1987 (2) ZLR 288.

82. For a useful discussion on the issue of the scope of the criminal law, see Williams, 1961, pp.601–4 and Hall, 1960, p.35 *et seq.*

83. See Chapter 6.

84. See Chapter 7.

85. See Chapter 9.

13 Safeguarding Individual Freedoms: National & International Institutions

In the previous chapter it was seen that the development of effective constitutional, legislative and judicial safeguards for individual freedoms are possible even during a state of emergency. These are complemented by two other safeguards, the first of which is the office of the ombudsman.

Individual Freedoms and the Ombudsman[1]

The classic definition of the ombudsman comes from the International Bar Association:

> An office provided for by the constitution or by action of the legislature or parliament and headed by an independent, high-level public official who is responsible to the legislature or parliament, who receives complaints from aggrieved persons against government agencies, officials, and employees or who acts on his own motion, and who has the power to investigate, recommend corrective action, and issue reports.[2]

Thus the aim of the office is the pursuit of administrative justice in a manner which is confidential, informal and flexible. Any person who claims to have suffered injustice at the hands of a government official may complain to the ombudsman and ask for an investigation into the matter. If the case is accepted, an investigation is undertaken in private and free of charge. As a permanent independent statutory (and often constitutionally established) institution, the office is potentially a most effective investigatory body operating within – although not being a part of – government. This is because wide-ranging investigative powers give an ombudsman unique access to government documents and officials and allows for the development of personal contacts with high-ranking government officials which can often swiftly resolve a complaint. In addition, government officials are often co-operative once it is realised that the office is also an important protection for them against unfounded, malicious or unfair attacks.

In recent years the number of countries which have introduced the office has increased markedly. Between 1966 and 1990 over eighty national and provincial offices were set up worldwide including several in Africa. In 1965 in Tanzania the report of the Presidential Commission on the Establishment of a One Party State examined the reasons for the establishment of such an office, and these remain relevant for many African nations:

> In a rapidly developing country it is inevitable that many officials, both of Government and of the ruling Party, should be authorised to exercise wide discretionary powers. Decisions taken by such officials can, however, have the most serious consequences for the individual, and the Commission is aware that there is already a good deal of

> public concern about the danger of abuse of power. We have, therefore, given careful thought to the possibility of providing some safeguard for the ordinary citizen.[3]

This frank admission as to weaknesses in government structures was complemented by the recognition that the office of the ombudsman could play a useful role in preventing abuses of power. As a result, in 1966 Tanzania became the first African country to establish the office under the name of the Permanent Commission of Enquiry (PCE).[4] It was then followed by Ghana where the Expediting Committee of the National Liberation Council assumed similar powers to those of an ombudsman and later other Commissions were periodically appointed to investigate specific sectors of public administration.[5] The 1969 Constitution specifically created the office of ombudsman with the legislature being required to enact detailed provisions relating to jurisdiction and operations. The ombudsman had not commenced operations when the Constitution was rendered inoperative in 1972 so it was not until the passing of the Ombudsman Act in 1980 that the institution became fully established.[6] In Mauritius the Constitutions of 1967 and 1968 provided for the establishment of the office and the first ombudsman was appointed in 1970. The next African country to establish the office was Zambia where the 1973 Constitution of Zambia provided for the establishment of a Commission for Investigations (CFI).[7] This began operations in 1974. Significantly, the CFI has always operated under a state of emergency but there is no evidence to suggest that this has hampered the work of the Commission. In The Sudan the institution was established by the 1973 Constitution which stipulated that 'a Committee formed of members of the Peoples' Assembly shall exercise administrative control . . . and shall be responsible to the Assembly'.[8] This led to the passing of the Peoples' Assembly Committee for Administrative Control Act of 1974. The 1973 Constitution was repealed after the army takeover in April 1985 and the committee dissolved. The 1985 Constitution does not provide for the re-establishment of such a body and there is no apparent intention to do so.[9] In Nigeria, Kaduna State was the first to establish the office in 1974. Following the recommendations of the Public Service Review Commission later that year, a national network of Public Complaints Commissions (PCC) was established in 1975.[10] The national headquarters is in the federal capital with the capital of each of the twenty-one states serving as the PCC headquarters at the state level. At present Nigeria is the only African country with this organisational structure. In 1983 the office was established in Swaziland,[11] whilst the most recent additions to the list are the Inspector-General of Government in Uganda in 1986 and the Namibian Ombudsman in 1990.[12]

In Zimbabwe, provision for the establishment of an ombudsman was originally made in the short-lived 1979 Constitution of Zimbabwe–Rhodesia (the Z–R Constitution) but never implemented. The Constitution of Zimbabwe makes general provision for the office[13] whilst the Ombudsman Act 1982 (the Act)[14] provides a detailed scheme of operation. The office opened on 1 September 1982, complaints from the public were received as from 1 January 1983 and it then became fully operational on 1 May 1983.

All complaints to the Zimbabwean Ombudsman must be lodged in writing with supporting documentation. In practice those unable to write out their complaint are assisted by staff at the office. Complaints must be made within twelve months from the date on which the person aggrieved first had notice of the act complained of unless the ombudsman considers it proper to extend this period in a particular case. In practice many extensions have been granted, particularly in cases where the complainant was previously unaware of the existence of the office. A complaint is not investigated if it is vexatious or trivial; if the complainant has adequate redress through other channels; or where the President has certified that the investigation is not in the interests of security.[15] All proceedings are in private and the Act gives extensive investigative powers. The ombudsman can order the production of documents and compel government officials to supply information. He/she can also summon and examine witnesses at a formal inquiry and has the power to have them committed for contempt. In practice only one formal inquiry has been held, due partly to time constraints but more especially due to the cooperation received from the relevant public bodies. Most cases are dealt with by correspondence although investigating officers have often visited government offices to peruse documents or to hold direct consultations with officials. Indeed the ombudsman has emphasised the importance of the policy of persuasion rather than confrontation.[16]

Jurisdiction

(i) Protecting Individual Freedoms

In Zimbabwe, the ombudsman may investigate action taken by any government body which has allegedly caused injustice to an individual in consequence of maladministration. The complaint will be upheld if the act was either contrary to law, based wholly or partly on a mistake of law or fact, or unreasonably delayed or otherwise unjust or manifestly unreasonable.[17] The meaning of the term 'maladministration' is nowhere defined but a number of broad meanings have been postulated in other jurisdictions. For example, the Investigator-General in Zambia has stated that:

> the abuse of authority or maladministration about which my office is concerned may take various forms, e.g. corruption, bribes, favouritism, tribalism, harshness, misleading a member of the public as to his rights, failing to give reasons when under a duty to do so, using power for wrong purposes, failing to reply to correspondence or causing unreasonable delay in doing desired public acts.[18]

The list provides some useful guidelines and emphasises the desirability of retaining some flexibility by continuing the practice of identifying maladministration merely by the use of actual examples.

The ombudsman may investigate any government Ministry and any force or service maintained and controlled by the State, other than the defence forces, the police and prison service.[19] The exclusion of the security services from investigation is crucial because, in practice, these bodies are frequently responsible for some of the worst violations of individual freedoms. This raises the key question of whether the ombudsman has a role to play in this area.

As noted in earlier chapters, the investigation of violations of individual freedoms by members of the security forces is notoriously difficult given the penchant for governments to keep such matters veiled in secrecy, particularly during a state of emergency. For example, in Chapter 6, it was seen that in response to allegations that members of the Zimbabwean security forces were involved in breaches of individual freedoms, the government sought to prevent widespread publicity of such actions by the use of indemnity regulations and the imposition of an information blackout. It also showed itself unwilling to hold a public judicial inquiry into the activities of the security forces.[20] Sometimes the judicial system is also unable to assist victims. This is neatly illustrated by the Zimbabwean case of *Tshuma*.[21] Here relatives sought information concerning the whereabouts of nine men who were allegedly abducted by members of the security forces in Matabeleland three years earlier and never seen again. The High Court was unable to assist when the police denied all knowledge of the incident and thus the relatives were unable to discover the fate of the men. This is the sort of case where an investigation by the ombudsman into the activities of the security forces on that occasion, including interviews with officers and access to relevant documentation, might have assisted the relatives by, at the very least, determining whether security personnel were involved in the incident.

In this respect, Zimbabwe can learn a lesson from other African countries, and in particular Uganda and Namibia. In Uganda, the Inspector-General of Government may conduct and inquire or order an investigation into any allegation of a violation of human rights, and this includes the power to investigate cases of detention or torture. Similarly in Namibia the ombudsman has the duty to investigate complaints from any inhabitant of Namibia concerning violations of fundamental rights by government officials (both national and local).[22] It is significant that both offices may investigate the very evils and abuses which plagued the countries for so long. Indeed, in Uganda, where complaints of human rights violations by members of the security forces were once commonplace, the Inspector-General of Government recently appointed a former high-ranking army officer to investigate complaints against members of the security forces on the basis that his personal contacts and knowledge would assist any inquiries into any future complaints. Assuming this is not a mere window-dressing exercise, the appointment may result in genuine accountability of the security forces. In Namibia the widespread human rights abuses perpetrated during the colonial era by the South African administration are well documented and need not be examined here.[23] The work of the ombudsman is intended to help ensure such abuses are never repeated. It is interesting to note that in Zambia, Nigeria, Ghana and Tanzania the ombudsman has always had jurisdiction over the activities of the security forces.[24] Although some of these countries have experienced acute security problems, there is no indication that this jurisdiction has led to any security violations or excessive number of complaints,[25] and such jurisdiction has been welcomed.[26] The importance of such a jurisdiction is illustrated by the fact that in Zambia, for example, complaints against the police have often accounted for over 25 per cent of all cases received.[27]

In Zimbabwe the prohibition on such investigations was defended on the grounds that they 'might have the result of inhibiting the activities of [the security forces] much to the detriment of the State'.[28] It was further argued that there would be too many complaints for the ombudsman to deal with as any prisoner or person arrested would be inclined to 'rush to the ombudsman and complain'.[29] Why an investigation into abuses of individual freedoms should 'inhibit' security forces operations is only explicable on the basis that such activity was potentially unlawful and government was anxious to conceal such actions.

There are several advantages to an investigation by the ombudsman into allegations against the security forces which, hopefully, will make the Zimbabwean government and other African States realise that this is a suitable alternative avenue for a citizen to pursue a grievance. Firstly, individuals can have their allegations fully examined by a body which has wide-ranging investigative powers including the right to inspect all relevant documents and to question all those involved. However the confidential procedure prevents the investigation turning into a potential 'trial by the [Western] media'. As Gering has noted, the *modus operandi* of the ombudsman is often more appropriate for the protection of detainees and the handling of complaints involving State security, than are those of the courts.[30] Secondly, practice has shown that the ombudsman is even-handed in his consideration of cases and objectively determines each complaint. Thus a government need have no fear of a vendetta against it. Indeed the patient development of an excellent working relationship with government officials enhances the potential for the carrying out of meaningful investigations. Thirdly, the ombudsman can reinforce public confidence by an impartial and independent examination of complaints. This will reflect well on the government for it will show itself prepared to protect its citizens against abuses of individual freedoms. Of course, much will depend upon the 'independence' of the ombudsman himself and the extent to which government is prepared to allow him to operate in sensitive areas. However, this is a problem for all bodies investigating such matters. Fourthly, fear of publicity and reprisals against aggrieved persons is a very real possibility and may dissuade many from taking legal action. Further, even if a judicial determination of the matter is attempted, it is often impossible to adduce sufficient evidence to satisfy a court. The flexible and confidential investigative powers of the ombudsman overcomes such problems. An illustration of the potential of this jurisdiction came in 1985 when the ombudsman received a complaint from a man who claimed he was detained by the police and held overnight at a police station following a dispute over a tenancy agreement with his tenant, a police officer. Although unable to investigate the case as such, the ombudsman did express serious doubts as to the good faith of the arresting officers and concluded that the police action was unwarranted. The matter was referred to the matter to Police General Headquarters which later accepted that there was substance in the complainant's grievance and advised the ombudsman that disciplinary action against the offending officers would be taken.[31] Without the intervention of the ombudsman, the complainant would have had no practical remedy. In the absence of the necessary jurisdiction, the Zimbabwean ombudsman has made efforts to assist either through informal channels or by directing the complainant to the correct body. Thus, in cases involving a complaint against the police, the case is forwarded to the relevant Ministry and Commissioner of Police for comment. In a number of cases the police have actively assisted in dealing with the matter. For example, following a complaint alleging failure to prosecute certain persons, the police made the relevant documents available to the ombudsman and the explanation for their decision was passed on to the complainant.[32] A similar procedure has been adopted with the army. In one case, an elderly couple drove their car through an unmarked army check point. They were stopped and as a 'punishment' were forced to push the car back to the check point. Army headquarters was unwilling to assist them. However the ombudsman considered that this action was merely endorsing the application of 'rough justice' against the couple. His letter to the Secretary for Defence resulted in an apology being tendered to the couple.[33] Again the ombudsman was the only person in a position to render any practical assistance to the complainants.

The restrictions on jurisdiction meant that the Zimbabwean ombudsman played little part in the protection of individual freedoms during the state of emergency. The Ombudsman Act does permit the President to make regulations providing for the ombudsman to have jurisdiction over the defence, police and prisons organisations and it is vital that the jurisdiction is so extended to permit the carrying out of investigations in the future. In February 1985, the ombudsman was appointed as a member of a Commission of Inquiry into the activities of the Commissioner of the Zimbabwe Republic Police and has also sat as chairman of the detainees review tribunal. These appointments perhaps reveal an increasing confidence in the office and, hopefully, will lead to an expansion of the jurisdiction to the security forces.

Another area currently excluded from investigations is the activities of political parties. Tanzania was the first African nation to give the ombudsman jurisdiction over, in this case, the sole political party TANU (now CCM). This lead was followed by Zambia. An increasing number of complaints are being received by the Zimbabwean Ombudsman against members of the ruling party, some of which have affected individual freedoms, for example apparent concerted violence by elements of the ruling party against political opponents. If this trend continues, it is desirable to follow the lead set by Tanzania and Zambia, although whether such a move is politically acceptable is debatable.[34]

(ii) Independent Investigations

The majority of the people in most African countries still suffer from ignorance of their legal rights and remain extremely susceptible to governmental abuses of power.[35] This means that an ombudsman must be in a position to take immediate action where necessary in order to protect the rights of citizens. As is recognised in Uganda, this means that the ombudsman must be able to undertake investigations on his/her own initiative. As the IGG has noted 'the Inspectorate does not just wait for complaints to be brought to it, but it also goes out to unearth corruption and maladministration whether the public complains or not'.[36] Such a jurisdiction is especially important in cases where urgent action is required for it is clearly unacceptable to predicate action solely upon the receiving of a complaint from a citizen. This is so particularly when transportation and communication problems often make it impossible for a citizen to contact the office in order to lodge an urgent complaint. Nigeria, Namibia and Mauritius also give the ombudsman power to instigate independent investigations when it is considered desirable to do so. Regrettably, the Zimbabwean legislation does not permit such activity. It is difficult to understand the reason for this restriction and it can only be presumed that the decision was based on a desire to 'wait and see' how well the institution operated in practice. In his First Annual Report in 1983, the ombudsman indicated a desire to have such a power, particularly in urgent cases where his immediate intervention might resolve a dispute and this point has been reiterated regularly since. The 1989 Report of the Public Service Commission also supported this view. Such a power is clearly necessary if it is to become the hoped for 'people oriented' institution.[37] Surprisingly, the recommendation of the Public Service Commission was not accepted by government on the grounds that 'the office is fully committed to dealing with its present work load'.[38] Of course this merely begs the question as to why virtually no new resources have been given to the ombudsman since 1983, despite a much increased workload.

Of course the expansion of the office into this field does not exclude or diminish the operation of non-governmental human rights agencies. Both bodies can undertake meaningful investigations into alleged human rights abuses using their different *modus operandi* although there is no doubt that the access of the ombudsman to government documentation and personnel can play a decisive role in determining the truth of the matter. In this respect, the perceived need for an investigative body 'independent' of government is perhaps overstated.[39] Certainly the ombudsman must fulfil certain criteria if the office is to be credible (see below). If this is done, then impartial and effective investigations can result.

(iii) An Advisory Function

There is a continuing lack of access to justice for the many indigent people in Africa. The complexity of the legal process, the absence of effective legal aid schemes and/or the non-availability of lawyers invariably prevents the majority of citizens enforcing their legal rights. This is particularly serious as regards constitutional rights and protections for it is clear that these are only of any real value if they are enforceable in practice. It is recognised in both Namibia and Uganda that the ombudsman has a useful role to play here. In the former, the ombudsman may provide legal assistance or advice to those seeking to enforce or protect a fundamental right through the courts.[40] In the latter, it is considered that because legal procedures are frequently lengthy, complex and expensive, the law courts are not always a suitable venue for many complainants to bring their cases. Accordingly the IGG may investigate complaints despite the availability of a judicial remedy. To give the ombudsman a responsibility in this field is both imaginative and appealing. A legal assistance and advice function is certainly not a substitute for a more formal legal aid scheme but it does represent a practical interim solution for dealing with the problems of access to justice. Zimbabwe faces similar problems concerning access to justice and citizens would certainly benefit if such a jurisdiction were given to the ombudsman.

(iv) Encouraging Systemic Improvements in Administration
The original ombudsman model includes the power to pursue long-term investigations. This is extremely useful because it makes it possible for research to be undertaken into recurring problems of administration. Thus the objectives of the Commonwealth Ombudsman in Australia include:

> identifying legislative, policy and procedural deficiencies, and encouraging systemic improvements to overcome those deficiencies; and contributing to advice to the Government on the adequacy, effectiveness and efficiency of the various means of review of administrative action'.[41]

In some jurisdictions, provision is also made for the ombudsman to publish special reports on investigations which are likely to be of general interest to the public. These functions can serve as a vehicle for investigating broad government policy. Such powers are presently not available to any African ombudsman but clearly such a jurisdiction would certainly encourage systemic improvements in government and consequently in the protection of individual freedoms.

(v) Overview
The precise scope of the jurisdiction inevitably varies from country to country. However, the real significance of the office of the ombudsman is that it is a flexible institution with unique advantages over other organs of government accountability. Thus it offers a further practical means of protecting the rights of citizens at all levels. Given adequate powers, the office can not only benefit those who are victims of incompetent and thoughtless officials but also those who have been victims of deliberate abuses of power and the like.

Implementation of Recommendations

The ombudsman concept does not involve the exercise of any judicial or quasi-judicial function for the incumbent has no enforcement powers and can only make recommendations to rectify an injustice. In Zimbabwe, as in most other African countries, if a complaint is not informally resolved after an investigation, any recommendation by the ombudsman for action is passed to the Head of State who determines the appropriate action. This is frequently a time-consuming, cumbersome and unsatisfactory process.[42] A true guardian of citizens' rights needs adequate powers in order to seek an appropriate and speedy remedy for breaches of those rights. In other words, the ability to take 'effective' action is the key to the success of the ombudsman.

This is recognised in Namibia where the ombudsman has the 'duty and power to take appropriate action to call for the remedying, correction and reversal of instances of ['maladministration', abuse of power etc] through such means as are fair, proper and effective'.[43] This means that well as the usual role of making recommendations for action to the Head of State, the Namibian Ombudsman has other key powers. Thus he/she may take direct action by bringing proceedings for an interdict or other suitable remedy 'to secure the termination of the offending action or conduct or the abandonment or alteration of the offending procedures'.[44] This means, for instance, that the ombudsman can afford citizens direct, speedy and effective protection from abuses of power by intransigent government officials and members of the security forces. This is especially significant in cases requiring urgent action and complements the independent investigatory power. In addition the ombudsman may challenge the validity of any statutory provision if the offending action or conduct 'is sought to be justified by subordinate legislation or regulation which is grossly unreasonable or otherwise ultra vires'.[45] This power represents another major advance as it means that subordinate legislation becomes subject to critical review. In view of the limited scrutinising role played by most African legislatures and the proliferation of subordinate legislation including emergency regulations, such a jurisdiction could transform the manner in which such regulations are used/abused.[46] The wide-ranging investigations of the ombudsman may well also uncover criminal conduct on the part of government officials. In such circumstances the Namibian Ombudsman may refer the matter to the Prosecutor-General with a view to prosecuting the offender(s). This is an unusual power in the African context and is significant because government officials and members of the security forces could face criminal proceedings without the need to obtain presidential approval.[47] Such a power is welcome in that it gives the office an important new weapon when tackling of abuses of power. It remains unclear as to whether such a reference will be made public. Although confidentiality of proceedings and anonymity of the parties is traditionally one of the strengths of the office, the value of the reference procedure is certainly enhanced by an announcement of the fact accompanied by full details. This also has the benefit of making a presidential intervention in the matter politically more difficult.

These remedial procedures go well beyond those available to the 'traditional' ombudsman. They are perhaps controversial in that they circumvent the role of the President who has, hitherto, always controlled the outcome of cases. However the new procedures are a necessary corollary to the enhanced jurisdiction of the ombudsman. The aim is not the replacement of the presidential role – for this will remain relevant and appropriate in many cases – but the provision of realistic alternative procedures aimed at the more effective and efficient protection of individual freedoms. In this respect, they deserve adoption in both Zimbabwe and other African States.

Terms and Conditions of Service

It is important that practical safeguards for an incumbent exist for an able and impartial ombudsman may remain prone to executive pressure unless his/her appointment is accompanied by appropriate conditions of service. Ideally these should be similar to members of the judiciary with the incumbent enjoying security of tenure and the like. In practice most African Ombudsmen are short-term appointees. This constant change of office-holder potentially undermines the effectiveness of the office by ensuring that the incumbent never becomes too 'effective' or popular.[48] There is thus a need to establish a more permanent position such that an able individual can pursue a career in this field and (hopefully) develop a meaningful institution. The mechanism may vary from country to country although the Namibian approach, where the conditions of service are virtually identical to those of judges, is probably the most satisfactory.[49] This point is followed to some extent in Zimbabwe. The ombudsman holds office for five years and is eligible for re-appointment for further terms of up to three years each.[50] His/her salary is paid out of the Consolidated Revenue Fund and is above that of a permanent secretary.[51]

It follows that the removal from office of the ombudsman is not a matter for the exercise of independent presidential action. Here the approach in Zimbabwe is commendable in that the ombudsman cannot be removed from office except for medical reasons or for misbehaviour and in doing so the President is required to act on the advice of a tribunal consisting of three persons, of which at least two must be experienced lawyers.[52]

The Ombudsman in Practice

The operation of the ombudsman in many African countries is somewhat disappointing. Indeed relatively few cases are ever investigated. For example, in Tanzania the PCE is currently dealing with over 3,000 complaints per year, whilst in Mauritius barely 200 cases are dealt with annually.[53] Many of the problems relate to poor organisation/funding and the hostile attitude of some government officials. For example, in Zambia, where an average of only around 550 cases per year are investigated, many of the difficulties are caused by budgetary and staffing constraints which have prevented an adequate service being given to the public so that many cases are not disposed of for many years.[54] In Nigeria, the most populous country in sub-Saharan Africa, an average of just 6,000 cases are handled annually.[55] The reluctance of citizens to bring complaints is largely due to the ineffectiveness of the office caused by recalcitrant officials. As Akanle notes: 'Since its inception in 1975, one Commissioner after another has expressed indignation at the lascivious apathy of public officers when treating inquiries from, and investigations by the Commissioners'.[56]

The need to develop an effective office in Zimbabwe is clearly essential. Efforts were made at the outset to publicise the office by the extensive use of the mass media. Interviews in English and the vernacular languages were given and 5,000 posters in English, Shona and Ndebele were distributed nationwide to all courts and government offices. Some press coverage continues, mainly through the occasional reporting of case summaries in the two national newspapers. The office is slowly becoming more popular with the number of complaints received rising from 414 in 1983 to 979 in 1987 and 896 in 1988. A striking feature of the figures is that between 1985 and 1987, out of 1,592 cases completed, 739 (46 per cent) of the complaints were not sustained.[57] This is important as it shows that the ombudsman is also an important protection for public officials against unfounded, malicious, and unfair attacks on them and this has generally led to their full cooperation with investigating officers.

It is disturbing to note that virtually all complaints come from urban areas with the majority of complainants being civil servants.[58] This means that those most whose individual freedoms are most at risk e.g. the poor, illiterates and those living in the rural areas, have failed to make use of the institution. The immediate cause of this is that the office is wholly based in Harare. Resource problems have prevented investigation officers visiting most other urban or rural areas. This is a sharp contrast to Tanzania, for example, where during the first year of operation the Permanent Commission of Enquiry spent 215 days travelling 16,096 miles to virtually every part of the country advising people as to their rights under the new law. Clearly, therefore, the effectiveness of the office depends upon the provision of adequate funding and other resources.

Overview

This chapter has shown that the institution of the ombudsman is a useful import to Africa. It operates in multi-party States such as Zimbabwe, in one-party States such as Tanzania and (formerly) Zambia and under military governments such as in Nigeria and Ghana. It has withstood many pressures including states of emergency and military coups.[59] The office clearly has the potential to play an effective role in the protection of individual freedoms.

The perceived need for an 'independent' body to investigate such matters is perhaps overstated,[60] so long as adequate safeguards on its powers and operations are present.

The introduction of the ombudsman in Zimbabwe signified an apparent willingness on the part of government to develop a more open administration and to make the public service accountable to the people. As Professor de Smith has rightly pointed out, 'an ombudsman cannot be bought off the peg: he must be made to measure'.[61] This means that the ombudsman in Zimbabwe needs some re-organisation if it is to be in a position to protect individual freedoms. In this regard, other African jurisdictions give some useful pointers as to how to achieve this goal.

At present, there are several obstacles to the achievement of this goal in Zimbabwe. It is argued that the office of the ombudsman can and must be developed into an effective guardian of individual freedoms, especially during a state of emergency when other safeguards are potentially less effective. This means, in particular, that it must have jurisdiction to investigate complaints against members of the security forces. As noted earlier, comparable bodies in Africa all have jurisdiction over the security forces and there is nothing to suggest that this has in any way compromised security or led to an excessive number of complaints. In fact the Inspector-General of Government in Uganda has been quite successful in dealing with cases of unlawful detention in Kampala.[62] Now is the time to expand the jurisdiction in this direction.

To make the expanded jurisdiction meaningful, other changes are necessary. One is to ensure that the ombudsman has jurisdiction in a case 'where it is not reasonable to expect [the complainant] to resort to any court of law'.[63] This 'double-lock' system of a judicial/ombudsman protection of individual freedoms is a very sound approach, particularly as the majority of citizens do not have the means to resort to the judicial system. Another change is to empower the ombudsman to recommend a pecuniary or other remedy against the security forces following the sustaining of a complaint against them. Inevitably, this will be subject to presidential approval, although a refusal to comply with a recommendation should be reported to parliament. The failure of government to make adequate resources available or to expand the powers of the ombudsman raises the question of whether it is merely paying lip service to the policy that 'the public service should be the servant and not the master of the people'.[64] As a former Commonwealth Ombudsman rightly notes:

> I do not think it is an overstatement to say that an Ombudsman's office not properly budgeted, not properly staffed, not sufficiently independent and not properly backed by those who brought it into being, amounts to nothing more than a front and a facade. The public may well be led to believe that they have a crutch on which to lean when in fact they have nothing at all.[65]

A State that allows its citizens no protection on the grounds of national security is a dangerous place. State security is not absolute and the ombudsman can operate as the link between the citizen and the State in such matters. As Frank asserts, '. . . the right to complain, the right to be heard, the right to have corrective action taken if one has suffered harm from government, are human rights'.[66] Whether the office of the ombudsman in Zimbabwe can protect these rights remains to be seen.

Non-Governmental Organisations

National non-governmental organisations can also make a crucial contribution both in the formulation of human rights standards and in the implementation of such standards. They contribute to the supervision of the observation of individual freedoms by calling attention to violations, by gathering information and by helping victims of such violations.[67] Zimbabwe is fortunate in that there are two such organisations involved in the development and safeguarding of individual freedoms.

The first is the Catholic Commission for Justice and Peace. The Catholic Church has a tradition for taking a critical stand against abuses of individual freedoms in the country. During the Smith regime, the Church, spearheaded by the outspoken Bishop Donal Lamont, was virtually the only voice raised against the government. In 1971 the Justice and Peace Commission was founded which was the first formal, structured commitment to social justice by the Catholic hierarchy.[68] By its creation, the Bishops in Rhodesia proclaimed that the struggle for African rights was an integral function of the Church. Its work to protect individual freedoms continued throughout the 1980s. It campaigned vigorously against the state of emergency and sought to highlight and investigate alleged breaches of human rights. Through its newsletter (which is published in all three official languages) its annual report and other public statements, the Commission continues to provide a vital watchdog function at the grassroots level. It also monitored the use of emergency regulations, provided independent advice and assistance to citizens involved in human rights cases and provided legal assistance to detainees appearing before the detainees review tribunal. It was frequently criticised by government for its stance on human rights abuses and at one stage its two leading figures were detained.[69] Nevertheless, it remained the one local body which sought to monitor such abuses.

In January 1990, its increasing criticism of the continued state of emergency led to the chairman of the Commission sending an open letter to all Members of Parliament urging them to 'consider very carefully whether there are valid grounds for prolonging further the State of Emergency'.[70] The sensitivity of government to such criticism was evident when, in Parliament, the Minister of Home Affairs reacted angrily, describing the action as 'unacceptable interference in the manner that hon. members deliberate on important issues' and adding that the letter 'implies that it is doubting the hon. members ability to arrive at a sound judgment without being influenced by the Commission'.[71] It is curious that the minister appeared to overlook the fact that Members of Parliament are representatives of the people whose duty it is to listen and consider to their views. In view of the fact that the vast majority of Members of Parliament had unquestioningly voted for renewals of the state of emergency in the past, it was also crucial that there was some public questioning of the policy.

Overall, the work of the Commission shows that an independent human rights organisation operating locally can make a telling contribution towards the protection of individual freedoms even during a state of emergency. As the work of the Commission shows, such bodies are flexible enough to broaden their mandate to be both reactive and proactive and to deal with both individual cases and systemic problems.[72]

The second organisation is the Legal Resources Foundation. This is an autonomous, charitable and educational Trust established in July 1984. Its objectives include the improvement of access to legal and information services for all sections of the population. As Donovan points out: 'Ignorance ensures that ordinary people remain unaware of the basic rights to which they are entitled. Poverty means that even if the hurdle of ignorance is overcome, ordinary people cannot afford to pursue the remedies which are available'.[73] The emergency and other security laws were a legal minefield for the best informed citizen. *A fortiori* a poorly educated population can become objects of oppression. Thus the move to publicise rights nationwide is a considerable step forward.

To date the Foundation has made rapid progress. Thus it has undertaken a programme of public legal education which includes grassroots legal literacy programmes and a legal education programme in senior schools, using pamphlets produced by its in-house publications unit. There is also a pilot project for the training of para-legal staff who are able to act as an advice and referral agency in the rural areas. This promises to greatly improve knowledge about basic rights amongst the rural population. The Foundation is also responsible for the training programme for police and other security personnel.[74] Crucially, the Foundation has also established offices in three other urban areas so that (unlike the ombudsman) its services are truly nationwide.

The Legal Publications Unit of the Foundation, which is the only legal publisher in the country, is central to its operation. Since its establishment in 1988, the unit has produced a wide range of publications including a short guide to cases on emergency powers. It also produces a regular Bulletin of Zimbabwean Law and has recently completed the onerous task of bringing the Zimbabwe Law Reports up to date. Such work is a major contribution to the protection of individual freedoms. Easy access to legislation, delegated legislation and case law ensures that the work of government and the courts is open to public scrutiny and comment.

The considerable contribution to the protection of individual freedoms made by the Catholic Commission and the Legal Resources Foundation illustrate the impact which non-governmental organisations can have in practice. In this respect they are excellent models for Africa.

Institutions at the International Level

The protection of human rights at the national level is the main and undoubtedly the best guarantee for the protection and promotion of human rights. As the earlier discussion has shown, much work is still necessary if national institutions are to play an effective role in this regard. This raises the question as to whether international institutions can play a useful role here. In the African context, clearly the African Charter on Human and Peoples' Rights must be considered. The more so because the Charter was ten years old on 21 October 1991 and this date represents the fifth anniversary of its coming into force and the establishment of the Commission.

The relevant provisions of the Charter itself have been discussed throughout the book and need not be further considered here. Whilst it is not intended to undertake a detailed analysis, a few comments are appropriate concerning the operation of the African Commission itself.[75] The duties of the Commission under the Charter are to protect and promote human rights by its interpretation of the Charter; by documentation, studies and seminars; by disseminating information; and by encouraging local and national institutions concerned with human rights. It is also empowered to formulate principles and rules upon which African governments can base their legislation. At present, the Commission is operating under considerable difficulties as a result of, for example, non-co-operation from State parties; lack of funding; inability of commissioners to undertake meaningful investigations; and problems with the terms of the Charter itself. The difficulties are epitomised by the problems surrounding Article 62 of the Charter. This obliges State parties to submit every two years 'a report on the legislative or other measures taken with a view to giving effect to the rights and freedoms recognized and guaranteed by the present Charter'. Extensive guidelines for reporting were produced by the Commission. Initial reports were due by 21 October 1988 i.e. two years after the Charter came into effect and these were to be followed by periodic reports every two years. By October 1991 of the forty African countries to ratify the charter, only seven have produced even initial reports.[76] Despite its obligation to do so, Zimbabwe has never submitted any report.

The inevitable conclusion is that the African Commission has failed to play any effective role in the protection of individual freedoms. Here is not the appropriate place to undertake an analysis of what steps are required to remedy this situation. However, it should be noted that Zimbabwean NGOs have a role in at least ensuring that Charter obligations are taken seriously by the Zimbabwean government. Such action includes persuading commissioners to meet and consult with them during national visits, and taking appropriate steps to encourage the production of adequate national reports by the Zimbabwean government.

Notes

1. In this chapter the general descriptive term 'ombudsman' is used although a number of countries have adopted different terminologies. For a general discussion on the ombudsman in Africa see Hatchard, 1986, p.255 and 1991c, p.937. I was somewhat troubled by the gender connotation of the word and considered using either 'ombudsperson' or 'ombuds'. I was informed that most words in Swedish are in the neuter gender and thus 'ombudsman' can be either male or female. In any case, the word 'man' cannot be simply dropped or replaced as it would change the meaning altogether.
2. Resolution adopted in Vancouver in 1974 and amended in West Berlin in 1980.
3. Report of the Presidential Commission, p.32.
4. See Norton, 1973, p.603.
5. For example the Commission of Inquiry into Bribery and Corruption of 1970. See Werlin, 1972, p.247. For a background to the ombudsman in Ghana see Ocran, 1978, pp.90–115.
6. This was in accordance with article 110 of the Constitution of Ghana 1979.
7. Detailed provisions are set out in the Commission for Investigations Act (Cap 183).
8. Article 181, Constitution of The Sudan 1973.
9. I am grateful to Ahmed Shawky of Cairo University at Khartoum for this information.
10. Federal Republic of Nigeria, Public Service Review Commission, Main Report 1974, Lagos, pp.50–51. See now, Public Complaints Commission Decree 1975.
11. See King's Proclamation (Amendment)(No. 2) Decree, Regent's Decree 2 of 1983, para 16. For a note on its establishment see (1984) 17 *Comparative and International Law Journal of Southern Africa*, p.111. For details of its failure and abolition see Ayee, 1988, p.8.
12. See Inspector-General of Government Statute 1988 (Uganda) and Article 90 of the Namibian Constitution and Ombudsman Act 1990. South Africa has not introduced an ombudsman but one is operating in the South African homeland of Bophuthatswana: see St Paul, 1989, p.219.
13. Sections 107, 108 and 110, Constitution of Zimbabwe.
14. As amended by the Ombudsman (Amendment) Acts 1985 and 1988.
15. Section 9, Ombudsman Act 1982.
16. First Annual Report of the Zimbabwean Ombudsman, p.6.
17. Section 16, Ombudsman Act 1982.
18. Frederick Chomba in an address to the Third Annual Conference of the Institute of Personnel Management, Lusaka, 20 March 1975.
19. Section 108(2) Constitution of Zimbabwe and sections 8 and 10 and schedule 1, Ombudsman Act 1982. Also specifically excluded are the President and his staff; the Cabinet Office and judicial officers; the Attorney-General and his law officers in relation to legal advice given to the State or legal proceedings, including prosecutions conducted on behalf of the State: section 9 and schedule 2 Ombudsman Act 1982.
20. As noted in Chapter 2, the report of the inquiry headed by Justice Dumbutshena into the Entumbane incident was never published.
21. Unreported, High Court of Zimbabwe, 1987.
22. The only 'officials' specifically excluded are judges and judicial officers. Does this mean the ombudsman can investigate a complaint against the President or Prime Minister?
23. See, for example, SWAPO, 1981, especially section 1 and Fact Papers on Southern Africa series from the International Defence and Aid Fund for Southern Africa.
24. There was some confusion over the exact terms of the legislation in Nigeria with the Chief Public Complaints Commissioner stating in 1977 that the commission was not empowered to entertain complaints against the security forces: see Sule, 1977, p.316. Akanle has convincingly demonstrated that this approach was the result of an incorrect reading of the relevant legislation: see Akanle, 1978, p.73. In The Sudan there was a separate complaints institution in the office of the Inspector-General of the Army.
25. See generally, International Commission of Jurists, 1978. In fact the Z-R Constitution gave the ombudsman jurisdiction over the prison service.
26. See, for example, Martin, 1977, p.247.
27. On one occasion, a senior police officer in the Zambia Police Force demanded free entrance to a dance at a restaurant for himself and his six companions. This was refused and he accordingly sent members of the National Police Force to stop the dance and close the restaurant. The investigation concluded that there had been a very

serious abuse of authority and the President directed that the officer be dismissed from the Force: Case 216/75, Annual Report of the Commission for Investigations, 1975.
28. Minister of Justice, *Parliamentary Debates*, 18 June 1982. He also pointed out that originally the jurisdiction of the Parliamentary Commissioner for Administration in the United Kingdom was similarly restricted. He omitted to add that later a separate Police Complaints Authority was established to handle complaints from the public.
29. Minister of Justice, *Parliamentary Debates*, 18 June 1982. Provisions precluding an investigation on grounds of security and on matters which the ombudsman considers frivolous, vexatious or trivial are already contained in the Ombudsman Act: see section 9(3)(c) and (d).
30. Gering, 1974, pp.287–9.
31. Case OMB/C/221/85 referred to in the 1985 Annual Report of the Ombudsman, p.50.
32. Case OMB/C/132/85.
33. OMB/C/125/85.
34. Of course, as Zimbabwe is a multi-party state, such a jurisdiction would also extend to other political groups.
35. See, for example, the Report of the Secretary-General on the implementation of the Declaration of Basic Principles of Justice for Victims of Crime and Abuse of Power, United Nations Document E/AC.57/1990/3, 15 December 1989, paras 56.
36. *General Information on the Office of the Inspector-General of Government*, above, p.7
37. First Annual Report of the Zimbabwean Ombudsman, Harare, 1983, p.6.
38. Minister of State for the Public Service discussing the recommendation made for such an expansion in the Report of the Public Service Review Commission 1989: see *Parliamentary Debates*, 1 November 1989.
39. Cf the argument put forward by Carver, 1989, p.391.
40. Article 25(2) Namibian Constitution.
41. Commonwealth and Defence Force Ombudsman Annual Report 1989–90, p.2
42. See Hatchard, above at p.258
43. Article 91(e) Namibian Constitution.
44. Article 91(e)(dd) Namibian Constitution.
45. Article 91(e)(ee) Namibian Constitution.
46. The only comparable power is in Nigeria where the Public Complaints Commissioner may refer cases to the Supreme Military Council for action where it is felt that the existing laws or administrative regulations are inadequate: see Decree No. 31 of 1975 as amended by Decree No. 21 of 1979.
47. In Nigeria the Public Complaints Commissioner may recommend that a person be prosecuted if it is discovered that a crime has been committed or where the conduct of a person should be subject to disciplinary action. Decree No. 31 of 1975 as amended by Decree No. 21 of 1979.
48. Perhaps there is also a fear that the ombudsman might pose a political threat to the government. His/her knowledge of the working of government through access to officials and sensitive official documents could be of considerable use to political rivals.
49. This includes the provision that the ombudsman shall hold office until the age of sixty-five years. Indeed the President may extend the retiring age to seventy years: Article 90(2) Namibian Constitution.
50. Section 4(1)(1a) Ombudsman Act 1982 as inserted by the Ombudsman Amendment Act 1988. This was in response to concern voiced by the present incumbent as to the tenure of the office.
51. Section 5, Ombudsman Act 1982.
52. Section 110, Constitution of Zimbabwe.
53. See Sewgobind, 1980.
54. For example, in the 1982 report, the Investigator-General reported that there were still eight cases outstanding dating back to 1975. In The Sudan only some 200 cases a year were dealt with, which was probably due to the institution being understaffed and without an adequate budget: see ICJ report, n.25, above.
55. Statistics of the Nigerian Public Complaints Commission: e.g. 8,357 cases were handled in 1976 and 5,225 in 1979. By 1989 the number had only risen to 13,457. See generally, Adamolekun, 1983, p.147 *et seq*.
56. Akanle, above, at p.70.
57. i.e. the ombudsman determined that the complainant did not suffer an injustice resulting from an alleged act of maladministration.
58. Typically the complaints relate to claims for salary, pension or other benefits; or disputes over unfair dismissal from the Public Service.
59. For example, in Ghana, section 14 of the Provisional National Defence Council (Establishment) Proclamation 1981, specifically stated that the office of ombudsman, as established under the 1979 Constitution, shall continue as before despite the suspension of the Constitution by the Council.
60. Cf the argument put forward by Carver, above n.39.
61. Mauritius Legislative Assembly Sessional Paper No. 2 of 1965, para.39.
62. See Carver, above, p.378. To date, there have been no investigations into killings by members of the security forces in rural areas.
63. This system is used in Zambia.
64. Minister of Justice in *Parliamentary Debates*, 17 June 1982.
65. Arthur Maloney, QC, former Ombudsman of Ontario quoted in Abedin, 1986, p.323. For a somewhat similar view see Jacomy-Millette, 1974, p.146.
66. Frank, 1976, p.122.
67. See Baehr, 1991, p.15.
68. See Linden, 1980. For an account of the approach of the Anglican Church during the UDI period, see Thomas, 1985, p.113.

69. See Chapter 6. Some government Ministers clearly regarded the organisation as ZAPU dominated, pointing out that the Director, Nicholas Ndebele, was the ZAPU legal adviser at Lancaster House whilst the Chairman, Michael Auret, was a member of ZAPU.
70. Open letter to Parliamentarians and Senators dated 10 January 1990.
71. *Parliamentary Debates*, 17 January 1990.
72. This point was recognised by the experiences of several NGOs, including the CCJP: see Steiner, 1991, pp.10–11.
73. Donovan, I. 'The Lawyers Role in the Protection of Human Rights in Zimbabwe'. Address to the Law Society of Zimbabwe, 1986. Ian Donovan was one of the founders of the LRF.
74. See Chapter 6 for details.
75. For a detailed account see, for example, D'sa, 1985, p.77 *et seq*. Ringera (p.15) also argues that one of the reasons for the limitations on the operation of the Charter is that it represents the maximum concessions African States were willing to make on their jealously guarded sovereignties.
76. For a useful account of the problems the Commission faces in fulfilling its functions see Benedek, 1991, pp.216–19.

14 Back to the Future: Reflections on the State of Emergency in Zimbabwe

The protection of individual freedoms during a state of emergency is a challenge to every nation for without them emergency powers are liable to turn a State into a dictatorship. This is a problem which has plagued Africa since the first 'winds of change' swept across the continent. The second 'winds/gales of change' are now bringing with them a fresh commitment to constitutionalism and to the development of new democratic institutions. Thus it is a good moment to reflect on the problems posed by the use of emergency and quasi-emergency powers. In this respect, Zimbabwe offers an excellent case-study with lessons which are applicable continent wide.

In 1980 the Government of Zimbabwe inherited a nation virtually torn apart by a long and vicious bush war and where a tiny white minority had used every means possible to retain political domination. The use of wide-ranging emergency regulations together with other security legislation and a non-justiciable Declaration of Rights had created a legal framework which effectively eliminated individual freedoms. The new nation itself faced serious political, security and economic challenges from both within and without. The fact that it was possible to establish a non-racial, independent and relatively economically healthy nation in the face of these challenges was a considerable achievement for which the government must take great credit. Indeed the practical implementation of the policy of national reconciliation is one which is almost unique in Africa. This was linked to a commitment to constitutionalism despite the fact that the government bitterly disliked many features of the independence Constitution which was imposed by Britain.

Despite these positive features, the previous discussion indicates that the Zimbabwean experience raises several vital policy issues. The first, and perhaps fundamental, issue concerns the actual declaration/retention of a state of emergency. In the case of Zimbabwe, the key question is whether its retention up to 1990 actually assisted government in tackling its problems. There is little evidence to suggest that this was the case. At the risk of being over-simplistic, the dissident question, which was for long the major reason for the retention of the state of emergency, was essentially a political problem which required a political solution – as the results of the Unity Agreement dramatically showed. In addition the increased powers given to the security forces were often abused and instead of helping to resolve the unrest in Matabeleland led to the alienation of a sizeable section of the population and to serious abuses of individual freedoms. This starkly illustrates the fact that the declaration/retention of a state of emergency is not a panacea for all national ills. It creates its own problems such that it must be utilised sparingly and only as a last resort. In this respect the Zimbabwean experience highlights the wisdom and importance of Article 4 of the International Covenant on Civil and Political Rights. It follows that any such declaration must inevitably be temporary, must be of the last resort and that governments have a duty to terminate it at the earliest possible moment.[1] Otherwise the 'Permanence of the Temporary' will prevail, with all its attendant ills.[2] This is a point which the Government of Zimbabwe (as well as many other African governments) seemingly overlooked or simply ignored.

A related issue concerns the reasons propounded for the continued state of emergency. In Zimbabwe these included increasing crime; security threats from South Africa; internal unrest; re-structuring of the economy; economic problems and industrial unrest. It was argued in earlier chapters that, based on Article 4 of the International Covenant (which was the declared basis of the state of emergency in Zimbabwe), these reasons did not justify the retention of the state of emergency. At best reliance on them demonstrated a lack of understanding as to the grounds for proclaiming a state of emergency. At worst they illustrated a desire to use emergency powers to circumvent the normal constitutional process and to rule by decree.

This raises the question of what safeguards are possible to prevent unwarranted emergency proclamations. The Zimbabwean (and the Rhodesian) experience demonstrates that effective safeguards enshrined in domestic law are problematical. As was noted earlier, the six-monthly extension process had some value for it at least permitted some public debate on the issue. Even so, the consent of the legislature was always a foregone conclusion. Indeed, despite the existence of a multi-party system the dominance of the ruling party in Parliament ensured that any objective analysis by parliamentarians as to the need for the continued state of emergency was rare indeed. This one-party domination is likely to continue despite the decision of government to retain the present multi-party State.[3] It remains to be seen whether the political changes throughout Africa will encourage a more assertive role for the legislature. Similarly, the effectiveness of constitutional and judicial safeguards in this respect is limited. Even so, the attempt by some African countries, such as Nigeria and Tanzania,[4] to specify the grounds for an emergency proclamation at least has the merit of directing attention to the need for the declaration in the first place. In this respect, the introduction of a similar provision into other African Constitutions would be helpful.

The shortcomings of domestic safeguards underscore the importance of international safeguards in this field. Today many international human rights documents ensure that international bodies maintain reviewability over a State's determination as to what constitutes a public emergency.[5] This is in recognition of the basic principle that the proclamation of a state of emergency is not a purely internal matter for a State but one which is open to international scrutiny. Regrettably, Zimbabwe, together with several other African nations, has shown little interest in such documents and, by the end of 1990, had not ratified either of the International Covenants.[6] Clearly this is a situation which must be rectified rapidly. Regrettably the African Charter does not specifically provide for a review of State action in this field by the African Commission on Human and Peoples' Rights. Whilst arguably it is possible for the Commission to do so where the State concerned is party to the ICCPR,[7] a specific power would remove all doubt. In this respect it is hoped that eventually the Commission will operate along similar lines to the European model. This would place a duty on a State to report to the Commission the fact of a declaration or renewal of a state of emergency together with the reasons therefor and the steps being taken to end the emergency. In response the Commission would have the power to give an opinion as to whether or not the crisis constituted a public emergency. This procedure has the merit of not only objectively legitimising the emergency declaration in appropriate cases but also of ensuring that pressure is exerted upon governments to end the state of emergency if the reasons are rejected and to help end 'permanent' states of emergency.

The third issue concerns the use of emergency regulations. The Zimbabwean experience illustrates that there is a real danger that wide-ranging regulations are used to deal with issues far removed from the stated reasons for the state of emergency. In order to control their use/abuse, it is vital that regulations are limited to areas directly connected with the emergency. This is another reason for requiring governments to give a clear and unambiguous statement as to the reasons for the emergency. Coupled with this is the need to ensure that regulations have a limited life and require specific parliamentary approval. Such principles should be enshrined into the national constitution and be reinforced by a willingness on the part of the judiciary to enforce it.

The fourth issue concerns the protection of individual freedoms. Throughout the book it was argued that, especially during a period of public emergency, an effective constitutional framework is necessary to ensure that an acceptable and realistic balance is maintained between the needs of the State and the protection of individual freedoms. Whilst international standards and norms remain influential, domestic safeguards can play a decisive role here. In this respect a justiciable Declaration of Rights which contains adequate protections for individual freedoms is a prerequisite. Some areas in the present Constitution of Zimbabwe need strengthening in this regard and these were discussed in Chapter 12. The critical point here is that there is always a danger that these freedoms will be abrogated or amended by government in such a manner as to render them ineffective. Indeed it was seen in earlier chapters that, on occasions, the State sought to interpret the Constitution in a manner which would have rendered certain individual freedoms entirely nugatory just at the time when they were most needed. Because of the vital importance of the individual freedoms enshrined in the Constitution, it is argued that they should be protected from any further abrogation.

One approach is based on the doctrine of the 'basic structure' or 'essential features' of the Constitution which has received the support of courts in both India and Bangladesh.[8] This states that a constitution stands on certain fundamental principles which are its structural pillars. If these pillars are demolished or even damaged, the constitutional edifice will fall. Consequently, any law which has that effect must be pronounced invalid by the judiciary. Whilst an attractive argument in theory, the all too clear danger is that such a judicial pronouncement will lead to a damaging confrontation between the judiciary and government.[9] Thus in practice it is a doctrine which is fraught with danger and should be avoided at all costs by the courts in Africa. The issue is not without importance because clear support for the doctrine was given by the Chief Justice of Zimbabwe, the Honourable Mr Justice A.R. Gubbay, at the opening of the 1991 Legal Year.[10] It is hoped that the courts in Zimbabwe do not seek to adopt the doctrine.

The best approach is to provide a clear constitutional provision which specifically prevents the abrogation of individual freedoms, whilst permitting a strengthening of such freedoms. This was recognised by the drafters of the Namibian Constitution who accordingly enshrined the principle in Article 25(1) which states:

> Save in so far as it may be authorised to do so by this Constitution, Parliament, or any other subordinate legislative authority, shall not make any laws, and the Executive and the agencies of government shall not take any action which abolishes or abridges the fundamental rights and freedoms conferred by this Chapter, and any law or action in contravention thereof shall to the extent of the contravention be invalid . . .[11]

The enactment of such a provision to protect individual freedoms in all African constitutional documents is highly desirable. In the case of Zimbabwe, such a provision would be particularly timely in view of the fact that amendments to the Declaration of Rights now require only a two-thirds parliamentary majority and there are indications of government willingness to weaken individual freedoms.[12]

The final issue concerns the use of quasi-emergency legislation. This is used in several African states to give the government greatly increased security powers without having to declare a state of emergency. The problem is well illustrated in the case of Zimbabwe for, despite the ending of the state of emergency, other wide-ranging security legislation remains in force. The powers contained in these statutes, and in particular the Law and Order (Maintenance) Act are anachronistic (and many are, arguably, unconstitutional) and remain a threat to the full exercise of individual freedoms. Indeed in many respects it is difficult to differentiate between LOMA and the hated Internal Security Act of South Africa. The failure of the Zimbabwean government to repeal all repressive colonial legislation contrasts markedly with the position in Mozambique where all such legislation was swept away after independence. As such, the words of the late Samora Machel are applicable continent wide:

> This State, this power, these laws, are not neutral techniques or instruments which can be equally well used by the enemy or by us. We cannot serve the masses by governing with State powers designed to oppress the masses.

Overall, the Zimbabwean experience shows that the protection of individual freedoms during a state of emergency is a complex undertaking involving a range of safeguards each of which can make a unique contribution. The basis for such protection is the existence of an enforceable constitutional document backed up by the active co-operation of the legislature, judiciary and other bodies such as statutory human rights bodies and non-governmental organisations. This is then reinforced by the adherence of the State to its international human rights obligations.

Of course, at the end of the day, the degree of governmental respect for the rule of law and the protection of individual freedoms during a state of emergency rests on the attitude of the governors themselves.[13] Perhaps the fundamental lesson is therefore that governors have got to work at developing respect for individual freedoms themselves. This is indeed a challenge for many African States. Zimbabwe illustrates some of the difficulties involved in attaining this objective but also shows that it is one which can be achieved.

Notes

1. See Commonwealth Advisory Group, above, p.75
2. A phrase used by Mathews and Albino in their article 'The Permanence of the Temporary: An Examination of the 90 and 180 Day Detention Laws' (1966) 83, *South African Law Journal*, p.16.
3. Whilst a multi-party state is the ideal, it should not be thought that this, in itself, is necessarily an effective safeguard against governmental abuse of power. The overwhelming parliamentary majority for ZANU(PF) prevents any effective role for opposition parties. In this regard it is likely that Zimbabwe will follow the pattern of multi-party democracy in Botswana which is characterized by complete political domination by the Botswana Democratic Party. See Molutsi, 1990, p.3.
4. See Chapter 2.
5. See Buergenthal, 1981, pp.72–9.
6. As at October 1990, the other Commonwealth African countries not to have ratified the covenants are: Botswana; Ghana; Lesotho; Malawi; Namibia; Nigeria; Seychelles; Sierra Leone; and Swaziland.
7. See Gittleman, 1984, p.164.
8. See especially *Kesavananda v State of Kerala* AIR [1973] SC 1461 (India) and *Anwar Hossain Chowdhury v Bangladesh* [1989] 41 Dhaka Law Reports (AD) 165 (Bangladesh). For a review of the Indian decision see Morgan, 1981, p.307.
9. Indeed following the application of the doctrine in the *Kesavananda* case in India, the retirement of the Chief Justice was announced (as he had reached retirement age). The government then departed from the established practice of appointing the longest-serving puisne judge as Chief Justice. The three most senior judges, all of whom were members of the majority in *Kesavananda*, were superseded by the most senior member of the minority in the case. The choice was regarded as too much of a coincidence and the three superseded judges promptly resigned.

See Morgan, 1981, at pp.335–7.
10. For the full text of the speech see *Legal Forum*, March 1991, p.3.
11. In an effort to avoid a potential confrontation, rather than declaring a law or action invalid, Article 25(1)(a) empowers a court to allow the particular body concerned to correct any defect in the impugned law or action within a specified period during which time such law or action remains valid.
12. As opposed to a 100 per cent majority for ten years after independence. Thus in 1991 a constitutional amendment overturned the landmark and internationally acclaimed decision of the Supreme Court of Zimbabwe, *A Juvenile v The State* 1990 (4) SA 151 (SC) which proclaimed that corporal punishment for juveniles was unconstitutional: see section 5, Constitution of Zimbabwe Amendment (No. 11) Act.
13. Zimba, 1984, p.208.

APPENDIX

I Constitution of Zimbabwe: Chapter 3

The Declaration of Rights

11. Whereas every person in Zimbabwe is entitled to the fundamental rights and freedoms of the individual, that is to say, the right whatever his race, tribe; place of origin, political opinions, colour, creed or sex, but subject to respect for the rights and freedoms of others and for the public interest, to each and all of the following namely:

(a) life, liberty, security of the person and the protection of the law;
(b) freedom of conscience, of expression and of assembly and association; and
(c) protection for the privacy of his home and other property and from the compulsory acquisition of property without compensation;

and whereas it is the duty of every person to respect and abide by the Constitution and the laws of Zimbabwe, the provisions of this Chapter shall have effect for the purpose of affording protection to those rights and freedoms subject to such limitations of that protection as are contained herein, being limitations designed to ensure that the enjoyment of the said rights and freedoms by any person does not prejudice the rights and freedoms of others or the public interest.

12. (1) No person shall be deprived of his life intentionally save in execution of the sentence of a court in respect of a criminal offence of which he has been convicted.

(2) A person shall not be regarded as having been deprived of his life in contravention of subsection (1) if he dies as the result of the use, to such extent and in such circumstances as are permitted by law, of such force as is reasonably justifiable in the circumstances of the case:

(a) for the defence of any person from violence or for the defence of property;
(b) in order to effect a lawful arrest or to prevent the escape of a person lawfully detained;
(c) for the purpose of suppressing a riot, insurrection or mutiny or of dispersing an unlawful gathering; or
(d) in order to prevent the commission by that person of a criminal offence;

or if he dies as the result of a lawful act of war.

(3) It shall be sufficient justification for the purposes of sub-section (2) in any case to which that subsection applies if it is shown that the force used did not exceed that which might lawfully have been used in the circumstances of that case under the law in force immediately before the appointed day.

13. (1) No person shall be deprived of his personal liberty save as may be authorized by law in any of the cases specified in sub-section (2).

(2) The cases referred to in sub-section (1) are where a person is deprived of his personal liberty as may be authorized by law:

(a) in consequence of his unfitness to plead to a criminal charge or in execution of the sentence or order of a court, whether in Zimbabwe or elsewhere, in respect of a criminal offence of which he has been convicted;

(b) in execution of the order of a court punishing him for contempt of that court or of another court or tribunal or in execution of the order of Parliament punishing him for a contempt;

(c) in execution of the order of a court made in order to secure the fulfilment of an obligation imposed on him by law;

(d) for the purpose of bringing him before a court in execution of the order of a court or an officer of a court or before Parliament in execution of the order of Parliament.

(e) upon reasonable suspicion of his having committed, or being about to commit, a criminal offence;

(f) in execution of the order of a court or with the consent of his parent or guardian, for the purposes of his education or welfare during a period beginning before he attains the age of twenty-one years and ending not later than the date when he attains the age of twenty-three;

(g) for the purpose of preventing the spread of an infectious or contagious disease;

(h) if he is, or is reasonably suspected to be, of unsound mind, addicted to drugs or alcohol, or a vagrant, for the purpose of his care, treatment or rehabilitation or the protection of the community; or

(i) for the purpose of preventing his unlawful entry into Zimbabwe or for the purpose of effecting his expulsion, extradition or other lawful removal from Zimbabwe or the taking of proceedings relating thereto.

(3) Any person who is arrested or detained shall be informed as soon as reasonably practicable, in a language that he understands, of the reasons for his arrest or detention and shall be permitted at his own expense to obtain and instruct without delay a legal representative of his own choice and hold communication with him.

(4) Any person who is arrested or detained:

(a) for the purpose of bringing him before a court in execution of the order of a court or an officer of a court; or

(b) upon reasonable suspicion of his having committed, or being about to commit, a criminal offence;

and who is not released, shall be brought without undue delay before a court; and if any person arrested or detained upon reasonable suspicion of his having committed or being about to commit a criminal offence is not tried within a reasonable time, then, without prejudice to any further proceedings that may be brought against him, he shall be released either unconditionally or upon reasonable conditions, including in particular such conditions as are reasonably necessary to ensure that he appears at a later date for trial or for proceedings preliminary to trial.

(5) Any person who is unlawfully arrested or detained by any other persons shall be entitled to compensation therefore from that other person or from any person or authority on whose behalf or in the course of whose employment that other person was acting:

Provided that

(a) any judicial officer acting in his judicial capacity reasonably and in good faith; or

(b) any other public officer, or person assisting such public officer, acting reasonably and in good faith and without culpable ignorance or negligence;

may be protected by law from liability for such compensation.

14. (1) No person shall be held in slavery or servitude or required to perform forced labour.

(2) For the purposes of subsection (1), 'forced labour' does not include

(a) any labour required in consequence of the sentence or order of a court;
(b) labour required of any person while he is lawfully detained which, though not required in consequence of the sentence or order of a court

(i) is reasonably necessary in the interests of hygiene or for the maintenance or management of the place at which he is detained; or
(ii) is reasonably required for the purposes referred to in section 13(2)(f) or (h);

(c) any labour required of a member of a disciplined force in pursuance of his duties as such or any labour required of any person by virtue of a written law in place of service as a member of such force;
(d) any labour required by way of parental discipline; or
(e) any labour required by virtue of a written law during a period of public emergency or in the event of any other emergency or disaster that threatens the life or well being of the community, to the extent that the requiring of such labour is reasonably justifiable in the circumstances of any situation arising or existing during that period or as a result of that other emergency or disaster, for the purpose of dealing with that situation.

15. (1) No person shall be subjected to torture or to inhuman or degrading punishment or other such treatment.

(2) No treatment reasonably justifiable in the circumstances of the case to prevent the escape from custody of a person who has been lawfully detained shall be held to be in contravention of subsection (1) on the ground that it is degrading.

(3) No moderate corporal punishment inflicted

(a) in appropriate circumstances upon a person under the age of eighteen years by his parent or guardian or by someone **in loco parentis** or in whom are vested any of the powers of his parent or guardian; or
(b) in execution of the judgement or order of a court, upon a male person under the age of eighteen years as a penalty for breach of any law;

shall be held to be in contravention of subsection (1) on the ground that it is inhuman or degrading.

(4) The execution of a person who has been sentenced to death by a competent court in respect of a criminal offence of which he has been convicted shall not be held to be in contravention of subsection (1) solely on the ground that the execution is carried out in the manner prescribed in section 315 (2) of the Criminal Procedure and Evidence Act [**Chapter 59**] as that section existed on the 1st October, 1990.

16. (1) No property of any description or interest or right therein shall be compulsorily acquired except under the authority of a law that

(a) requires the acquiring authority to give reasonable notice of the intention to acquire the property, interest or right to any person owning the property or having any other interest or right therein that would be affected by such acquisition;
(b) requires that the acquisition is reasonably necessary in the interests of defence,

public safety, public order, public morality, public health, town and country planning, the utilization of that or any other property for a purpose beneficial to the public generally or to any section thereof or, in the case of land that is under-utilized, the settlement of land for agricultural purposes;

(c) requires the acquiring authority to pay promptly adequate compensation for the acquisition;

(d) requires the acquiring authority, if the acquisition is contested, to apply to the High Court or some other court before, or not later than thirty days after, the acquisition for an order confirming the acquisition; and

(e) enables any claimant for compensation to apply to the High Court or some other court for the prompt return of the property if the court does not confirm the acquisition and for the determination of any question relating to compensation, and to appeal to the Supreme Court.

(2) [Repealed]

(3) Where any person, by virtue of a law, contract or scheme relating to the payment of pensions benefits, has a right, whether vested or contingent, to the payment of pensions benefits or any commutation thereof or a refund of contributions, with or without interest, payable in terms of such law, contract or scheme, any law which thereafter provides for the extinction of or a diminution in such a right shall be regarded for the purposes of subsection (1) as a law providing for the acquisition of a right in property.

(4) Nothing contained in or done under the authority of any law shall be held to be in contravention of subsection (1) to the extent that the law in question authorizes the taking of possession of property compulsorily during a period of public emergency or in the event of any other emergency or disaster that threatens the life or well-being of the community or where there is a situation that may lead to such emergency or disaster and makes provision that

(a) requires the acquiring authority promptly to give reasonable notice of the taking of possession to any person owning or possessing the property;

(b) enables any such person to notify the acquiring authority in writing that he objects to the taking of possession;

(c) requires the acquiring authority to apply within thirty days of such notification to the High Court or some other court for determination of its entitlement to take possession;

(d) requires the High Court or other court to order the acquiring authority to return the property unless it is satisfied that the taking possession is reasonably justifiable, in the circumstances of any situation arising or existing during that period or as a result of that other emergency or disaster or that may lead to such emergency or disaster, for the purpose of dealing with that situation;

(e) requires

(i) when possession is no longer reasonably justifiable as referred to in paragraph (d), wherever possible, the prompt return of the property in the condition in which it was at the time of the taking of possession; and

(ii) the payment within a reasonable time of fair compensation for the taking of possession and, where appropriate, for the failure to return the property in accordance with subparagraph (i) or for any damage to the property; and

(f) enables any claimant for compensation to apply to the High Court or some other court for the prompt return of the property and for the determination of any question relating to compensation, and to appeal to the Supreme Court.

(5) [Repealed]

(6) [Repealed]

(7) Nothing, contained in or done under the authority of any law shall be held to be in contravention of subsection (1) to the extent that the law in question makes provision for the acquisition of any property or any interest or right therein in any of the following cases

(a) in satisfaction of any tax or rate;
(b) by way of penalty for breach of any law, including any law of a foreign country which, by or in terms of an Act of Parliament, is recognized or applied for any purpose in Zimbabwe, whether under civil process or after conviction of an offence, or forfeiture in consequence of a breach of the law or in pursuance of any order referred to in section 13 (2) (b);
(c) upon the removal or attempted removal of the property in question out of or into Zimbabwe in contravention of any law;
(d) as an incident of a contract, including a lease or mortgage, which has been agreed between the parties to the contract, or of a title deed to land fixed at the time of the grant or transfer thereof or at any other time with the consent of the owner of the land;
(e) in execution of the judgment or order of a court in proceedings for the determination of civil rights or obligations;
(f) by reason of the property in question being in a dangerous state or prejudicial to the health or safety of human, animal or vegetable life or having been constructed or grown on any land in contravention of any law relating to the occupation or use of that land;
(h) as a condition in connexion with the granting of permission for the utilization of that other property in any particular manner;
(i) by way of the taking of a sample for the purposes of a law;
(j) where the property consists of an animal, upon its being found trespassing or straying;
(k) for so long only as may be necessary for the purpose of any examination, investigation, trial or inquiry;
(l) in the case of land, for so long only as may be necessary for the purpose of the carrying out therein of

(i) work for the purpose of the conservation of natural resources of any description; or
(ii) agricultural development or improvement which the owner or occupier of the land has been required, and has without reasonable or lawful excuse refused or failed, to carry out;

(m) in consequence of any law requiring copies of any book or other publication published in Zimbabwe to be lodged with the National Archives or a public library;
(n) for the purposes of, or in connexion with, the prospecting for or exploitation of minerals, mineral oils, natural gases, precious metals or precious stones which are vested in the President on terms which provide for the respective interests of the persons affected;
(o) for the purposes of, or in connection with, the exploitation of underground water or public water which is vested in the President on terms which provide for the respective interests of the persons affected;

except so far as that provision or, as the case may be, the thing done under the authority thereof is shown not to be reasonably justifiable in a democratic society.

(8) Nothing contained in or done under the authority of any law shall be held to be in contravention of subsection (1) to the extent that the law in question makes provision for the acquisition of any property or any interest or right therein in any of the following cases

(a) for the purpose of the administration, care or custody of any property of a deceased person or a person who is unable, by reason of any incapacity, to administer it himself, on behalf and for the benefit of the person entitled to the beneficial interest therein;

(b) by way of the vesting or administration of any property belonging to or used by or on behalf of an enemy or an organization which is, in the interests of defence, public safety or public order, proscribed or declared by a written law to be an unlawful organization;

(c) by way of the administration of moneys payable or owing to a person outside Zimbabwe or to the government of some other country where restrictions have been placed by law on the transfer of such moneys outside Zimbabwe;

(d) as an incident of

(i) a composition in insolvency accepted or agreed to by a majority in number of creditors who have proved claims and by a number of creditors who proved claims represent in value more than fifty *per centum* of the total value of proved claims; or

(ii) a deed of assignment entered into by a debtor with his creditors;

(e) by way of the acquisition of the shares, or a class of shares, in a body corporate on terms agreed to by the holders of not less than nine-tenths in value of those shares or that class thereof.

(9) Nothing in this section shall affect the making or operation of any law in so far as it provides for

(a) the orderly marketing of any agricultural produce or mineral or any article or thing prepared for market or manufactured therefore in the common interests of the various persons otherwise entitled to dispose of that property or for the reasonable restriction of the use of any property in the interests of safeguarding the interests of others or the protection of lessees or other persons having rights in or over such property; or

(b) the taking of possession or acquisition in the public interest of any property or any interest or right therein where that property, interest or right is held by a body corporate established directly by law for a public purpose in which no moneys have been invested other than moneys provided from public funds.

(c) Nothing in this section shall affect the making or operation of any Act of Parliament in so far as it provides for the extinction of any debt or other obligation gratuitously assumed by the State or any other person.

(10) In this section:
'acquiring authority' means the person or authority compulsorily taking possession of or acquiring the property or the interest or right therein;
'agricultural purposes' includes forestry, fruit-growing and animal husbandry, including the keeping of poultry, bees or fish;
'land' includes anything permanently attached to or growing on land;
'pensions benefits' means any pension, annuity, gratuity or other like allowance

(a) which is payable from the Consolidated Revenue Fund to any person;

(b) for any person in respect of his service with an employer or for any spouse, child or dependant of such person in respect of such service;

(c) for any person in respect of his ill-health or injury arising out of and in the course of his employment or for any spouse, child or dependant of such person upon the death of such person from such ill-health or injury; or

(d) for any person upon his retirement on account of age or ill-health or other termination of service;

'piece of land' means a piece of land registered as a separate entity in the Deeds Registry.

17. (1) Except with his own consent or by way of parental discipline, no person shall be subjected to the search of his person or his property or the entry by others on his premises.

(2) Nothing contained in or done under the authority of any law shall be held to be in contravention of subsection (1) to the extent that the law in question makes provision

(a) in the interests of defence, public safety, public order, public morality, public health or town and country planning;

(b) without derogation from the generality of the provisions of paragraph (a), for the enforcement of the law in circumstances where there are reasonable grounds for believing that the search or entry is necessary for the prevention, investigation or detection of a criminal offence, for the seizure of any property which is the subject-matter of a criminal offence, for the seizure of any property which is the subject-matter of a criminal offence or evidence relating to a criminal offence, for the lawful arrest of a person or for the enforcement of any tax or rate;

(c) for the purposes of a law which provides for the taking of possession or acquisition of any property or interest or right therein and which is not in contravention of section 16;

(d) for the purpose of protecting the rights and freedoms of other persons;

(e) that authorizes any local authority or any body corporate established directly by or under an Act of Parliament for a public purpose to enter on the premises of any person in order to inspect those premises or anything therein for the purpose of any tax or rate or in order to carry out work connected with any property of that authority or body which is lawfully on those premises; or

(f) that authorizes, for the purpose of enforcing the judgment or order of a court in any civil proceedings, the search of any person or property by order of a court or the entry upon any premises by such order;

except so far as that provision or, as the case may be, the thing done under the authority thereof is shown not to be reasonably justifiable in a democratic society.

(3) A law referred to in subsection (2) which makes provision for the search of the person of a woman shall require that such search shall, unless made by a medical practitioner, only be made by a woman and shall be conducted with strict regard to decency.

18. (1) Every person is entitled to the protection of the law.

(2) If any person is charged with a criminal offence, then, unless the charge is withdrawn, the case shall be afforded a fair hearing within a reasonable time by an independent and impartial court established by law.

(3) Every person who is charged with a criminal offence

(a) shall be presumed to be innocent until he is proved or has pleaded guilty;

(b) shall be informed as soon as reasonably practicable, in a language that he understands and in detail of the nature of the offence charged;

(c) shall be given adequate time and facilities for the preparation of his defence;

(d) shall be permitted to defend himself in person or, save in proceedings before a local court, at his own expense by a legal representative of his own choice;

(e) shall be afforded facilities to examine in person or, save in proceedings before a local court, by his legal representative the witnesses called by the prosecution before the court and to obtain the attendance and carry out the examination of witnesses to testify on his behalf before the court on the same conditions as those applying to witnesses called by the prosecution; and

(f) shall be permitted to have without payment the assistance of an interpreter if he cannot understand the language used at the trial of the charge;

and except with his own consent, the trial shall not take place in his absence unless he so conducts himself as to render the continuance of the proceedings in his presence impracticable and the court has ordered him to be removed and the trial to proceed in his absence.

(4) When a person is tried for any criminal offence, the accused person or any person authorized by him in that behalf shall, if he so requires and subject to payment of such reasonable fee as may be prescribed by law, be given within a reasonable time after judgment a copy for the use of the accused person of any record of the proceedings made by or on behalf of the court.

(5) No person shall be held to be guilty of a criminal offence on account of any act or omission that did not, at the time it took place, constitute such an offence, and no penalty shall be imposed for any criminal offence that is severer in degree or description than the maximum penalty that might have been imposed for that offence at the time when it was committed.

(6) No person who shows that he has been tried by a competent court for a criminal offence upon a good indictment, summons or charge upon which a valid judgment could be entered and either convicted or acquitted shall again be tried for that offence or for any other criminal offence which he could have been convicted at the trial for that offence, save

(a) where a conviction and sentence of the High Court or of a court subordinate to the High Court are set aside on appeal or review on the ground that evidence was admitted which should not have been admitted or that evidence was rejected which should have been admitted or on the ground of any other irregularity or defect in the procedure; or

(b) otherwise upon the order of the High Court in the course of appeal or review proceedings relating to the conviction or acquittal.

(7) No person shall be tried for a criminal offence if he shows that he has been pardoned for that offence.

(8) No person who is tried for a criminal offence shall be compelled to give evidence at the trial.

(9) Every person is entitled to be afforded a fair hearing within a reasonable time by an independent and impartial court or other adjudicating authority established by law in the determination of the existence or extent of his civil rights or obligations.

(10) Except in the case of a trial such as is referred to in subsection (14) or with the agreement of all the parties thereto, all proceedings of every court and proceedings for the determination of the existence or extent of any civil right or obligation before any other adjudicating authority, including the announcement of the decision of the court or other authority, shall be held in public.

(11) Nothing in subsection (10) shall prevent -

(a) the court or other adjudicating authority from excluding from the proceedings, except the announcement of its decision, persons other than the parties thereto and their legal representatives to such extent as the court or other authority

(i) may by law be empowered so to do and may consider necessary or expedient in circumstances where publicity, would prejudice the interests of justice, or in interlocutory proceedings, or in the interests of public morality, the welfare of persons under the age of twenty-one years or the protection of the private lives of persons concerned in the proceedings; or

(ii) may by law be empowered or required so to do in the interests of defence, public safety, public order or the economic interests of the State;

or

(b) the court from excluding from proceedings preliminary to trial in respect of a criminal offence persons other than the accused person and his legal representative when so required by law, unless the accused person otherwise requests.

(12) Notwithstanding anything contained in subsection (4), (10) or (11), if in any proceedings before such court or other adjudicating authority as is referred to in subsection (2) or (9), including any proceedings by virtue of section 24, a certificate in writing is produced to the court or other authority signed by a Minister that it would not be in the public interest for any matter to be publicly disclosed, the court or other authority shall make arrangements for evidence relating to that matter to be heard *in camera* and shall take such other action as may be necessary or expedient to prevent the disclosure of that matter.

(13) Nothing contained in or done under the authority of any law shall be held to be in contravention of

(a) subsection (2), (3) (e) or (9) to the extent that the law in question makes reasonable provision relating to the grounds of privilege or public policy on which evidence shall not be disclosed or witnesses are not competent or cannot be compelled to give evidence in any proceedings;
(b) subsection (3) (a) to the extent that the law in question imposes upon any person charged with a criminal offence the burden of proving particular facts;
(c) subsection (3) (e) to the extent that the law in question imposes reasonable conditions which must be satisfied if witnesses called to testify on behalf of an accused person are to be paid their expenses out of public funds;
(d) subsection (6) to the extent that the law in question authorizes a court to try a member of a disciplined force for a criminal offence notwithstanding any trial and conviction or acquittal of that member under the appropriate disciplinary law, so, however, that any court so trying such a member and convicting him shall in sentencing him to any punishment take into account any punishment awarded him under that disciplinary law; or
(e) subsection (8) to the extent that the law in question authorizes a court, where the person who is being tried refuses without just cause to answer any question put to him, to draw such inferences from that refusal as are proper and to treat that refusal, on the basis of such inferences, as evidence corroborating any other evidence given against that person.

(14) In the case of a person who is held in lawful detention, the provisions of subsection (2) shall not apply in relation to his trial for a criminal offence under the law regulating the discipline of persons held in such detention, save that the case of such person shall be afforded a fair hearing within a reasonable time, and the person or authority conducting the trial shall be regarded as a court for the purposes of this section.

(15) For the purposes of this section, a local court shall not be regarded as not being an independent and impartial court by reason of

(a) the fact that a member of the court has an interest in the proceedings because of his position in the tribal society; or
(b) the traditional or customary tribal practices and procedures

19. (1) Except with his own consent or by way of parental discipline, no person shall be hindered in the enjoyment of his freedom of conscience, that is to say, freedom of thought and of religion, freedom to change his religion or belief, and freedom, whether alone or in community with others, and whether in public or in private, to manifest and propagate his religion or belief through worship, teaching, practice and observance.

(2) Except with his own consent or, if he is a minor, the consent of his parent or guardian, no person attending any place of education shall be required to receive religious instruction or to take part in or attend any religious ceremony or observance if that instruction, ceremony or observance relates to a religion other than his own.

(3) No religious community shall be prevented from making provision for the giving by persons lawfully in Zimbabwe of religious instruction to persons of that community in the course of any education provided by that community, whether or not that community is in receipt of any subsidy, grant or other form of financial assistance from the State.

(4) No person shall be compelled to take any oath that is contrary to his religion or belief or to take any oath in a manner that is contrary to his religion or belief.

(5) Nothing contained in or done under the authority of any law shall be held to be in contravention of subsection (1) or (3) to the extent that the law in question makes provision

(a) in the interests of defence, public safety, public order, public morality or public health;
(b) for the purposes of protecting the rights and freedoms of other persons, including the right to observe and practise any religion or belief without the unsolicited intervention of persons professing any other religion or belief; or
(c) with respect to standards or qualifications to be required in relation to places of education, including any instruction, not being religious instruction, given at such places; except so far as that provision or, as the case may be, the thing done under the authority thereof is shown not to be reasonably justifiable in a democratic society.

(6) References in this section to a religion shall be construed as including references to a religious denomination and cognate expressions shall be construed accordingly.

20. (1) Except with his own consent or by way of parental discipline, no person shall be hindered in the enjoyment of his freedom of expression, that is to say, freedom to hold opinions and to receive and impart ideas and information without interference, and freedom from interference with his correspondence.

(2) Nothing contained in or done under the authority of any law shall be held to be in contravention of subsection (1) to the extent that the law in question makes provision

(a) in the interests of defence, public safety, public order, the economic interests of the State, public morality or public health;
(b) for the purpose of

(i) protecting the reputations, rights and freedoms of other persons or the private lives of persons concerned in legal proceedings;
(ii) preventing the disclosure of information received in confidence;
(iii) maintaining the authority and independence of the courts or tribunals or Parliament;

(iv) regulating the technical administration, technical operation or general efficiency of telephony, telegraphy, posts, wireless broadcasting or television or creating or regulating any monopoly in these fields;

(v) in the case of correspondence, preventing the unlawful dispatch therewith of other matter;

or

(c) that imposes restrictions upon public officers; except so far as that provision or, as the case may be, the thing done under the authority thereof is shown not to be reasonably justifiable in a democratic society.

(3) No religious denomination and no person or group of persons shall be prevented from establishing and maintaining schools, whether or not that denomination, person or group of persons is in receipt of any subsidy, grant or other form of financial assistance from the State.

(4) Nothing contained in or done under the authority of any law be held to be in contravention of subsection (3) to the extent that the law in question makes provision

(a) in the interests of defence, public safety, public order, public morality, public health or town and country planning; or

(b) for regulating such schools in the interests of persons receiving instruction therein;

except so far as that provision or, as the case may be, the thing done under the authority thereof is shown not to be reasonably justifiable in a democratic society.

(5) No person shall be prevented from sending to any school a child of whom that person is parent or guardian by reason only that the school is not a school established or maintained by the State.

(6) The provisions of subsection (1) shall not be held to confer on any person a right to exercise his freedom of expression in or on any road, street, lane, path, pavement, sidewalk, thoroughfare or similar place which exists for the free passage of persons or vehicles.

21. (1) Except with his own consent or by way of parental discipline, no person shall be hindered in the enjoyment of his freedom of assembly and association, that is to say, his right to assemble freely and associate with other persons and in particular to form or belong to political parties or trade unions or other associations for the protection of his interests.

(2) The freedom referred to in subsection (1) shall include the right not to be compelled to belong to an association.

(3) Nothing contained in or done under the authority of any law shall be held to be in contravention of subsection (1) to the extent that the law in question makes provision

(a) in the interests of defence, public safety, public order, public morality or public health;

(b) for the purpose of protecting the rights or freedoms of other persons;

(c) for the registration of companies, partnerships, societies or other associations of persons, other than political parties, trade unions or employers' organizations; or

(d) that imposes restrictions upon public officers;

except so far as that provision or, as the case may be reasonably justifiable in a democratic society.

(4) The provisions of subsection (1) shall not be held to confer on any person a right to exercise his freedom of assembly or association in or on any road, street, lane, path, pavement, side-walk, thoroughfare or similar place which exists for the free passage of persons or vehicles.

22. (1) No person shall be deprived of his freedom of movement, that is to say, the right to move freely throughout Zimbabwe, the right to reside in any part of Zimbabwe, the right to enter and to leave Zimbabwe and immunity from expulsion from Zimbabwe.

(2) Any restriction on a person's freedom of movement that is involved in his lawful detention shall not be held to be in contravention of subsection (1).

(3) Nothing contained in or done under the authority of any law shall be held to be in contravention of subsection (1) to the extent that the law in question makes provision

(a) for the imposition of restrictions on the freedom of movement of persons generally or any class of persons that are required in the interests of defence, public safety, public order, public morality or public health;
(b) for the imposition of restrictions on the acquisition or use of land or other property in Zimbabwe;
(c) for the imposition of restrictions by order of a court on the movement or residence within Zimbabwe of any person or on any person's right to leave Zimbabwe

(i) in consequence of his having been found guilty of a criminal offence under the law of Zimbabwe or for the purpose of ensuring that he appears before a court for trial for such a criminal offence or for proceedings preliminary to trial;
(ii) for proceedings relating to his extradition or lawful removal from Zimbabwe; or
(iii) for the purpose of ensuring that he appears before a court as a witness for the purposes of any criminal proceedings;

(d) for the imposition of restrictions on the movement or residence within Zimbabwe of persons who are neither citizens of Zimbabwe nor regarded by virtue of a written law as permanently resident in Zimbabwe or for excluding or expelling from Zimbabwe any person who is not a citizen of Zimbabwe;
(e) for the imposition of restrictions by order of a court on the right of any person to leave Zimbabwe that are required for the purpose of ensuring that he appears before a court or other adjudicating authority as a party or a witness or to secure the jurisdiction of the court or other adjudicating authority for the purposes of any civil proceedings, or
(f) for the imposition of restrictions on the residence within Communal Land of persons who are not tribespeople to the extent that such restrictions are reasonably required for the protection of the interests of tribespeople or their well-being;

except, in the case of any provision referred to in paragraphs (a) to (e), so far as that provision or, as the case may be, the thing done under the authority thereof is shown not to be reasonably justifiable in a democratic society.

(4) The provisions of subsection (3) (a) shall not be construed as authorizing a law to make provision for preventing any person from leaving Zimbabwe or excluding or expelling from Zimbabwe any person who is a citizen of Zimbabwe.

23. (1) Subject to the provisions of this section

(a) no law shall make any provision that is discriminatory either of itself or in its effect; and
(b) no person shall be treated in a discriminatory manner by any person acting by virtue of any written law, or in the performance of the functions of any public office or any public authority.

(2) For the purposes of subsection (1), a law shall be regarded as making a provision that is discriminatory and a person shall be regarded as having been treated in a discriminatory manner if, as a result of that law or treatment, persons of a particular description by race, tribe, place of origin, political opinions, colour or creed are prejudiced

(a) by being subjected to a condition, restriction or disability to which persons of another such description are not made subject; or
(b) by the according to persons of another such description of a privilege or advantage which is not accorded to persons of the first-mentioned description;

and the imposition of that condition, restriction or disability or the according of that privilege or advantage is wholly or mainly attributable to the description by race, tribe, place of origin, political opinions, colour or creed of the persons concerned.

(3) Nothing contained in any law shall be held to be in contravention of subsection (1) (a) to the extent that the law in question relates to any of the following matters

(a) adoption, marriage, divorce, burial, devolution of property on death or other matters of personal law;
(b) the application of African customary law in any case involving Africans or an African and one or more persons who are not Africans where such persons have consented to the application of African customary law in that case;
(c) restrictions on entry into or employment in Zimbabwe or on the enjoyment of services provided out of public funds in the case of persons who are neither citizens of Zimbabwe nor regarded by virtue of a written law as permanently resident in Zimbabwe;
(d) qualifications, not being qualifications, specifically relating to race, tribe, place of origin, political opinions, colour or creed, for service as a public officer or as a member of a disciplined force or for service with any public authority or any body corporate established directly by or under an Act of Parliament for a public purpose;
(e) the appropriation of public revenues or other public funds; or
(f) the according to tribespeople to the exclusion of other persons of rights or privileges relating to Communal Land.

(4) The provisions of subsection (1)(b) shall not apply to

(a) anything that is expressly or by necessary implication authorized to be done by section 75(2), 94(2) or 98(2), or by any provision of a law that is referred to in subsection (3); or
(b) the exercise of any discretion relating to the institution, conduct or discontinuance of civil or criminal proceedings in any court vested in any person by or under this Constitution or any other law.

24. (1) If any person alleges that the Declaration of Rights has been, is being or is likely to be contravened in relation to him (or, in the case of person who is detained, if any other person alleges such a contravention in relation to the detained person), then, without prejudice to any other action with respect to the same matter which is lawfully available, that person (or that other person) may, subject to the provisions of subsection (3), apply to the Supreme Court for redress.

(2) If in any proceedings in the High Court or in any court subordinate to the High Court any question arises as to the contravention of the Declaration of Rights, the person presiding in that court may, and if so requested by any party to the proceedings shall, refer the question to the Supreme Court unless, in his opinion, the raising of the question is merely frivolous or vexatious.

(3) Where in any proceedings such as are mentioned in subsection (2) any such question as is therein mentioned is not referred to the Supreme Court, then without prejudice to the right to raise that question on any appeal from the determination of the court in those proceedings, no application for the determination of that question shall lie to the Supreme Court under subsection (1).

(4) The Supreme Court shall have original jurisdiction

(a) to hear and determine any application made by any person pursuant to subsection (1) or to determine without a hearing any such application which, in its opinion, is merely frivolous or vexatious; and
(b) to determine any question arising in the case of any person which is referred to it pursuant to subsection (2);

and may make such orders, issue such writs and give such directions as it may consider appropriate for the purpose of enforcing or securing the enforcement of the Declaration of Rights:

Provided that the Supreme Court may decline to exercise its powers under this subsection if it is satisfied that adequate means of redress for the contravention alleged are or have been available to the person concerned under other provisions of this Constitution or under any other law.

(5) If in any proceedings it is alleged that anything contained in or done under the authority of any law is in contravention of section 16, 17, 19, 20, 21 or 22 and the court decides, as a result of hearing the parties, that the provision of the law concerned is reasonably justifiable in a democratic society on such of the grounds mentioned in section 16(7), 17(2), 19(5), 20(2) and (4), 21(3) or 22(3) (a) to (e), as the case may be, as are relied upon by the other party without proof to its satisfaction, it shall issue a rule nisi calling upon the responsible Minister to show cause why that provision should not be declared to be in contravention of the section concerned.

(6) If in any proceedings it falls to be determined whether any law is in contravention of the Declaration of Rights, the Attorney-General shall be entitled to be heard by the court on that question and if in any such proceedings any law is determined by the court to be in contravention of the Declaration of Rights, then, whether or not he has exercised his right to be heard in those proceedings, the Attorney-General shall have the like right with respect to an appeal from that determination as if he had been a party to the proceedings.

(7) Where any law is held by a competent court to be in contravention of the Declaration of Rights, any person detained in custody under that law shall be entitled as of right to make an application to the Supreme Court for the purpose of questioning the validity of his further detention, notwithstanding that he may have previously appealed against his conviction or sentence or that any time prescribed for the lodging of such an appeal may have expired.

(8) A written law may confer upon the Supreme Court powers additional to those conferred by this section for the purpose of enabling the Supreme Court more effectively to exercise the jurisdiction conferred upon it by this section.

[Subsection as amended by section 13 of Act No 25 or 1981]

(9) A written law may make provision with respect to the practice and procedure

(a) of the Supreme Court in relation to the jurisdiction and powers conferred upon it by or under this section; and
(b) of subordinate courts in relation to references to the Supreme Court under subsection (2);

including provision with respect to the time within which any application or reference shall or may be made or brought.

25. Notwithstanding the foregoing provisions of this Chapter, an Act of Parliament may in accordance with Schedule 2 derogate from certain provisions of the Declaration of Rights in respect of a period of public emergency or a period when a resolution under section 31J(6) is in effect.

26. (1) In this Chapter, unless the context otherwise requires -
'child' includes a stepchild and a lawfully adopted child and 'parent' and cognate expressions shall be construed accordingly;
'Court' means any court of law in Zimbabwe, including a tribal court, but does not, except for the purposes of section 12 or 14, include a court established by or under a disciplinary law;
'legal representative', means a legal practitioner who is lawfully in Zimbabwe;
'parental discipline' includes school or other quasi-parental discipline.

(2) Subject to the provisions of subsection (3), nothing contained in or done under the authority of any written law shall be held to be in contravention of the Declaration of Rights to the extent that the law in question

(a) is a law with respect to which the requirements of section 52 were applicable and were complied with;
[(b)–(d) Repealed by CZAA No 7 s20]

(3) [Repealed]

(4) For the purposes of this section, the reference

(a) [Repealed]
(b) in subsection (2) to a written law includes any instrument having the force of law;

(5) In relation to any person who is a member of a disciplined force of Zimbabwe, nothing contained in or done under the authority of the disciplinary law of that force shall be held or be in contravention of any of the provisions of the Declaration of Rights, other than sections 12, 14, 15, 16 and 23.

(6) In relation to any person who is a member of a disciplined force that is not a disciplined force of Zimbabwe and who is present in Zimbabwe under arrangements made between the Government and the government of some other country or an international organization law of that force shall be held to be in contravention of the Declaration of Rights.

(7) No measures taken in relation to a person who is a member of a disciplined force of a country with which Zimbabwe is at war or with which a state of hostilities exists and no law, to the extent that it authorizes the taking of any such measures, shall be held to be in contravention of the Declaration of Rights.

Chapter 4

31J. (1) The President may at any time, by proclamation in the *Gazette*, declare in relation to the whole of Zimbabwe or any part thereof that

(a) a state of public emergency exists; or
(b) a situation exists which, if allowed to continue, may lead to a state of public emergency.

(2) A declaration under subsection (1), if not sooner revoked, shall cease to have effect at the expiration of a period of fourteen days beginning with the day of publication of the proclamation in the *Gazette* unless, before the expiration of that period, the declaration is approved by resolution of Parliament.

Provided that, if Parliament is dissolved during the period of fourteen days, the declaration, unless sooner revoked, shall cease to have effect at the expiration of a period of thirty days beginning with the day of publication of the proclamation in the *Gazette* unless, before the expiration of that period, the declaration is approved by resolution of Parliament.

(3) Where a declaration under subsection (1)

(a) is not approved by resolution under subsection (2), the President shall forthwith, after Parliament has considered the resolution and failed to approve it or, if Parliament has not considered the resolution, on the expiration of the appropriate period specified in subsection (2), by proclamation in the *Gazette*, revoke the declaration;
(b) is approved by resolution under subsection (2), the declaration shall, subject to the provisions of subsection (4), continue in effect for a period of six months beginning with the day of publication of the proclamation in the *Gazette*:

Provided that, where Parliament has in the resolution under subsection (2) specified that the declaration shall continue in effect for a period of less than six months, the President shall, by proclamation in the *Gazette*, make provision that the declaration shall, subject to the provisions of subsection (4), be revoked on the expiration of the period so specified.

(4) If Parliament resolves that it considers it expedient that a declaration under subsection (1) should be continued for a further period not exceeding six months, the President shall forthwith, by proclamation in the *Gazette*, extend the declaration for such further period as may be so resolved.

(5) Notwithstanding any other provision of this section, Parliament may at any time

(a) resolve that a declaration under subsection (1) should be revoked; or
(b) whether in passing a resolution under subsection (2) or (4) or subsequently, resolve that a declaration under subsection (1) should relate to such lesser area as Parliament may specify;

and the President shall forthwith, by proclamation in the *Gazette*, revoke the declaration or provide that the declaration shall relate to such lesser area, as the case may be.

(6) Without prejudice to the provisions of subsections (1) to (5), Parliament may at any time resolve in relation to the whole of Zimbabwe or any part thereof that a situation exists which

(a) if allowed to continue, may lead to a state of public emergency; and
(b) may require the preventive detention of persons in the interests of defence, public safety or public order.

(7) A resolution under subsection (6) shall, subject to the provisions of subsection (8) and unless Parliament has specified that it shall have effect for a period of less than one year, have effect for a period of one year beginning with the day on which it is passed.

(8) Parliament may continue a resolution under subsection (6) for a further period, not exceeding one year.

(9) Notwithstanding any other provision of this section, Parliament may at any time resolve

(a) that a resolution under subsection (6) shall cease to have effect; or
(b) that a resolution under subsection (6) shall relate to such lesser area as Parliament may specify.

(10) A declaration under subsection (1) or a resolution under subsection (6) may be continued in accordance with this section notwithstanding that it has previously been continued.

(11) No resolution under subsection (2), (4), (6) or (8) shall be deemed to have been duly passed unless it receives the affirmative votes of more than one-half of the total membership of Parliament.

(12) Where Parliament passes a resolution under subsection (6), (8) or (9), the Secretary to Parliament shall forthwith cause to be published in the *Gazette* a notice of such resolution and the effect thereof.

Schedule 2 (Section 25 & 31J)

Savings in the Event of Public Emergencies

1. (1) Nothing contained in any law shall be held to be in contravention of section 13, 17, 20, 21 or 23 to the extent that the law in question provides for the taking, during a period of public emergency, of action for the purpose of dealing with any situation arising during that period, and nothing done by any person under the authority of any such law shall be held to be in contravention of any of the said provisions unless it is shown that the action taken exceeded anything which, having due regard to the circumstances prevailing at the time could reasonably have been thought to be required for the purpose of dealing with the situation.

(2) Nothing contained in any law shall be held to be in contravention of section 13 to the extent that the law in question provides for preventive detention, during a period when a resolution under section 31J(6) is in effect, in the interests of defence, public safety or public order, and nothing done by any person under the authority of any such law shall be held to be in contravention of section 13 unless it is shown that the action taken exceeded anything which, having due regard to the circumstances prevailing at the time, could reasonably have been thought to be required for the purpose of dealing with the situation.

(3) Where a declaration under section 31J (1) or a resolution under section 31J(6) applies only in relation to a part of Zimbabwe, the law in question shall not provide for the taking of action or for preventive detention, as the case may be in relation to any place outside that part.

2. (1) Where a person is detained under any law providing for preventive detention

(a) he shall be informed as soon as reasonably practicable after the commencement of the detention, and in any case not later than seven days thereafter, in a language that he understands of the reasons for his detention and shall be permitted at his own expense to obtain and instruct without delay a legal representative of his own choice and to hold communication with him;

(b) his case shall be submitted not later than fourteen days (or during a period of public emergency thirty days) after the commencement of the detention for review by a tribunal established under subparagraph (4) and shall be reviewed by such tribunal forthwith; and thereafter his case shall be reviewed by such tribunal at intervals of thirty days (or during a period of public emergency one hundred and eighty days) from the date on which his case was last reviewed;

(c) at the hearing of his case by the tribunal he shall be permitted to appear in person or at his own expense by a legal representative of his own choice; and

(d) if the tribunal orders, either because he satisfies the tribunal that new circumstances have arisen or because the tribunal considers it to be desirable, that his case should be submitted to the tribunal for review before the expiration of thirty days (or during a period of public emergency one hundred and eighty days) from the previous review, the case shall be submitted for review when so ordered by the tribunal.

(2) On any such review, the tribunal may make recommendations concerning the necessity or expedience of continuing the detention to the authority by which it was ordered and that authority shall be obliged to act in accordance with any such recommendation unless, during a period of public emergency, the President otherwise directs; and where the President so directs, the authority shall cause to be published in the *Gazette* a notice that he has so directed.

(3) A person who has been detained under any law providing for preventive detention and who has been released from detention in consequence of a report of a tribunal established under subparagraph (4) that there is, in its opinion, insufficient cause for his detention shall not again be detained by virtue of such law within the period of one hundred and eighty days from his release on the same grounds as those on which he was originally detained.

(4) A tribunal for the purposes of this paragraph shall be established by law and shall consist of

(a) a chairman, who shall be a person who is or has been a judge of the Supreme Court or the High Court or is qualified under section 82 to be appointed as such; and

(b) two other persons, one of whom

(i) is or has been a judge of the Supreme Court or the High Court or is qualified under section 82 to be appointed as such;

(ii) has been a magistrate in Zimbabwe for not less than seven years; or

(iii) is and has been for not less than seven years, whether continuously or not, qualified to practise as a legal practitioner in Zimbabwe.

(4a) In computing, for the purposes of subparagraph (4)(b)(iii), the period during which any person has been qualified to practise as a legal practitioner in Zimbabwe, any period during which he was qualified to practise as an advocate or attorney in Zimbabwe shall be included.

(5) No law providing for preventive detention during a period when a resolution under section 31J(6) is in effect shall authorize the detention of a person for a period longer than fourteen days unless the Minister designated for the purpose has issued an order providing for the preventive detention of that person.

(6) The reference in subparagraph (1)(b) to a period of fourteen or thirty days in relation to a first review includes a reference to any lesser periods that amount in the aggregate to fourteen or thirty days respectively:

Provided that no two such lesser periods shall be aggregated for this purpose if the period between the expiration of the first and the commencement of the second is more than fourteen or thirty days, as the case may be.

(7) For the purposes of subparagraph (3), a person shall be deemed to have been detained on the same grounds as those on which he was originally detained unless a tribunal established under subparagraph (4) has reported that, in its opinion, there appear *prima facie* to be new and reasonable grounds for the detention, but the giving of any such report shall be without prejudice to the provisions of subparagraphs (1) and (5).

APPENDIX
II Emergency Powers Act: Chapter 83

(as amended by the Emergency Powers Amendment Act 1986, the Constitution of Zimbabwe Amendment (No. 7) Act and the Constitution of Zimbabwe Amendment (No. 9) Act)

1. This Act may be cited as the Emergency Powers Act (*Chapter 83*).

2. In this Act—
'essential service' includes:

(a) any hospital service;
(b) any transport service;
(c) any service relating to the generation, supply or distribution of electricity;
(d) any service relating to the supply and distribution of water;
(e) any sewerage or sanitary service;
(f) any service relating to the production, supply, delivery or distribution of food, fuel and coal;
(g) any fire brigade;
(h) coal mining;
(i) communications;

and any other service declared by the President, by notice in the *Gazette*, to be an essential service for the purposes of this Act.

'Minister' means the Minister of Home Affairs or any other Minister to whom the President may from time to time assign the administration of this Act.

3. (1) Where a declaration in terms of subsection (1) of section 31J of the Constitution has been made and so long as that declaration is in force, it shall be lawful for the President to make such regulations as appear to him to be necessary or expedient for all or any of the following

(a) the public safety;
(b) the maintenance of public order;
(c) the maintenance of any essential service;
(d) the preservation of the peace;
(e) making adequate provision for dealing with any circumstances which

  (i) have arisen or, in his opinion, are likely to arise, whether such circumstances relate to the maintenance of any essential or other service or otherwise; and
  (ii) in his opinion, will interfere with the peace, order and good government;

(f) making adequate provision for terminating the state of emergency;

in Zimbabwe or that part of Zimbabwe, as the case may be.

(2) Regulations made in terms of subsection (1) of section three may make provision for

(a) the summary arrest, detention or restriction of the movements of any person whose arrest, detention or restriction of movement, as the case may be, appears to the Minister to be expedient in the public interest;
(b) the deportation and exclusion from Zimbabwe of any person who is not a citizen of Zimbabwe;
(c) the removal from one part of Zimbabwe to some other part of Zimbabwe of any person whose removal appears to the Minister to be expedient in the public interest;
(d) the regulation and control of persons employed or engaged in any trade, business, occupation, profession, calling or industry in Zimbabwe;
(e) the taking possession or control on behalf of the State of any property or undertaking;
(f) the regulation and control of companies registered in or persons carrying on business in Zimbabwe, including the suspension or discharge of persons employed by any such company or other person or, in the case of a company or association, concerned with the management thereof;
(g) the acquisition on behalf of the State of any property other than land;
(h) the entering and search of any premises;
(i) the assistance to be afforded to persons affected by a natural disaster;
(j) the payment of compensation and remuneration to persons affected by any regulations or order made under this section;
(k) the arrest of any person contravening or offending against any regulations or order made under this section;
(l) the penalties to be imposed for any contravention or failure to comply with any provision of any regulations or order made under this section.

(3) Regulations made under subsection (1) may

(a) be published in the same *Gazette* as the declaration in terms of subsection (1) of section 31J of the Constitution;
(b) provide for empowering such authorities or persons as may be specified in the regulations to make orders for any of the purposes for which such regulations are authorized by this section to be made and may contain such incidental and supplementary provisions as appear to the President to be necessary or expedient for the purposes of the regulations.

(4) It is declared that, notwithstanding anything to the contrary contained in any law

(a) the provisions of section 19 of the Interpretation Act [*Chapter1*] shall apply in relation to this section;
(b) notwithstanding the enumeration of the specific powers of subsection (2), the President may make such regulations in terms of subsection (1) as appear to him to be necessary or expedient whether or not such regulations relate to any of the matters specified in subsection (2) and whether or not such regulations are inconsistent with the provisions of subsection (2).

(5) Regulations made in terms of subsection (1) of section three may provide for the continuation in force thereunder of any notice, order, direction, permit, licence or other thing whatsoever, including, for the removal of doubt, the detention or restriction of movement of any person, which was issued, authorized, done or continued in force under regulations in force immediately before the publication of those regulations

(6) Every regulation made under this Act by the President shall be laid before Parliament as soon as may be after it is made.

(7) If Parliament, within the next twenty-eight days on which it has sat after such regulation as aforesaid is laid before it, resolves that the regulation be annulled, the regulation shall thereupon cease to have effect except in regard to things previously done or omitted to be done, without prejudice, however, to the making of another regulation.

4. (1) Any regulation shall have effect, notwithstanding anything inconsistent therewith contained in any law.

(2) So far as [it] appears to the President to be necessary for the purposes of the regulations, regulations may provide for amending any law, for suspending the operation of any law, and for applying any law, with or without modification.

5. Where any law has been amended, suspended or modified by a regulation, then, notwithstanding the provisions of section 15 of the Interpretation Act, such law shall, with effect from the expiration or repeal of such regulation, have effect as if such amendment, suspension or modification had never been made.

6. (1) Where a resolution in terms of subsection (6) of section 31J of the Constitution has been passed and so long as that resolution is in effect it shall be lawful for the President to make such regulations as appear to him to be necessary or expedient for

(a) the preventive detention of any person in the interests of defence, public safety or public order;
(b) empowering any Minister designated in the regulations to issue orders for the preventive detention of any person;
(c) empowering any police officer or other person in the employment of the State to arrest and detain any person for a period not exceeding fourteen days, pending the issue of an order referred to in paragraph (b);
(d) the procedure for the review of cases of detained persons by a tribunal established in accordance with paragraph 2 of Schedule 2 of the Constitution to review such cases;
(e) the treatment and discipline of detained persons and the places where they may be detained;
(f) the penalties that may be imposed for any contravention of the regulations.

(2) The provisions of subsections (3), (4), (5), (6) and (7) of section three, and sections four and five shall apply, *mutatis mutandis*, in relation to the regulations made in terms of subsection (1).

7. (1) Whenever a resolution passed in terms of subsection (6) of section 31J of the Constitution becomes or is effective upon the expiry or revocation of a declaration in terms of subsection (1) of that section, any regulations that were made in terms of section three and were in force immediately before the revocation or expiry of the declaration shall, to the extent that they relate to the matters referred to in subsection (1) of section six, continue in force as if they had been made whilst a resolution in terms of subsection (6) of section 31J of the Constitution was in effect.

(2) Whenever a declaration in terms of subsection (1) of section 31J of the Constitution becomes or is effective upon the expiry or revocation of a resolution passed in terms of subsection (6) of that section, any regulations that were made in terms of section 6 and were in force immediately before the expiry or revocation of the resolution shall continue in force as if they had been made whilst a declaration in terms of subsection (1) of section 31J of the Constitution was in effect.

APPENDIX

III Emergency Powers Regulations: Zimbabwe

Table of Cases

Table of Statutes

Bibliography

Abedin, N. (1986) 'Transplantation of the Ombudsman Institution in Developed and Developing Countries', *The Round Table* p.333.

Adamolekun, L. (1983) 'Nigeria' in Caiden, G. (ed.) *International Handbook of the Ombudsman*, Westport, Greenwood.

Advisory Committee on Law Reform (1982) *Aspects of Capital Punishment*, Harare, Government Printers (Zimbabwe).

Africa Watch (1989) *Zimbabwe: A Break with the Past?*, New York.

Africa Watch (1990) *Malawi*, New York.

African Conference on the Rule of Law: A Report of the Proceedings (1961) Geneva, International Commission of Jurists.

Agbakoba, O. and Fagbohunlu, T. (1991) 'Nigeria's State Security (Detention of Persons) Decree No. 2 of 1984: Exploding the Myth of Judicial Impotence', vol.1, *Journal of Human Rights Law and Practice*, p.45.

Akanle, O. (1978) 'Self-Restraint or Abdication? A Note on the Investigatory Powers of the Nigerian Public Complaints Commissioner', vol.10, *Zambia Law Journal*, p.70.

Allen, C.K. (1965) *Law and Orders*, London, Stevens.

Amnesty International, *Annual Reports 1980–90*, London.

Amnesty International (1984) *Torture in the 1980s*, Oxford, Robertson.

Amnesty International (1988) *Malawi: Human Rights Violations 25 Years After Independence*, London.

Amnesty International (1989) *Uganda: The Human Rights Record 1986–1989*, London.

An-Na'im, A. (1986) 'Detention in the Sudan : The Use and Abuse of Legal Powers', vol.17, *Columbia Human Rights Law Review*, p.159.

Austin, R. (1968) *The Character and Legislation of the Rhodesia Front since UDI*, unpublished.

Ayee, J. (1988) 'The Ombudsman Experience in the Kingdom of Swaziland: A Comment', *Verfassung und Recht in Ubersee*, p.8.

Baehr, P. (1991) 'Human Rights: A Common Standard of Achievement?', vol.9, *Netherlands Quarterly of Human Rights*, p.15.

Baker, C. (1983) 'Conducting the Elections in Zimbabwe 1980' in vol.2, *Public Administration and Development*, p.45.

Basu, D. (1983) *Constitutional Law*, third edition, Delhi, Jain.

Baxi, U. *et al* (1987) *The Right to be Human*, New Delhi, Lancer International.

Baxter, L. (1984) *Administrative Law*, Cape Town, Juta.

Benedek, W. (1991) 'The 9th Session of the African Commission on Human and Peoples' Rights', vol.12, *Human Rights Law Journal*, p.216

Black, D. (1911) *Constitutional Law*, New Haven, Yale University Press.

Bonner, D. (1985) *Emergency Powers in Peacetime*, London, Sweet and Maxwell.

Buergenthal, T. (1981) 'To Respect and to Ensure: State Obligations and Permissible Derogations' in Henkin, L. (ed.) *The International Bill of Rights: The Covenant on Civil and Political Rights*, New York, Columbia University Press.

Carty, A. (1986) 'Human Rights in a State of Exception: The ILA and the Third World' in T. Campbell *et al* (eds), *Human Rights: From Rhetoric to Reality*, Oxford, Blackwell.

Carver, R. (1990) 'Called to Account: How African Governments Investigate Human Rights Violations', vol.89, *African Affairs*, p.391.

Catholic Commission for Justice and Peace (1975) *The Man in the Middle*, pamphlet.

Centre for the Independence of Judges and Lawyers (1989) *The Harassment and Persecution of Judges and Lawyers 1988–1989*, Geneva.

Chirkin, V. (1985) *Constitutional Law and Political Institutions*, Moscow, Progress.

Chowdhury, S. (1989) *Rule of Law in a State of Emergency*, London, Pinter.

Christie, R. (1983) 'The Executive and Judiciary in Zimbabwe', vol.100, *South Africa Law Journal*, p.297.

Cilliers, J. (1985) *Counter-Insurgency in Rhodesia*, London, Croom Helm.

Cliffe, L. (1984) 'Nationalist Politics in Zimbabwe: The 1980 Elections and Beyond' in vol.18, *Review of African Political Economy*, p.29.

Coldham, S. (1991) '*DPP v Daudi Pete*', vol.35, *Journal of African Law*, p.205.

Cole, B, (1988) *Sabotage and Torture*, Amanzimtoti, Three Knights.

Commonwealth Advisory Group (1991) *Put Our World to Rights*, London, Commonwealth Human Rights Initiative.

Conboy, K. (1978) 'Detention without Trial in Kenya', vol.8, *Georgia Journal of International and Comparative Law*, p.441.

Cottrell, J. (1991) 'The Constitution of Namibia: An Overview', vol.35, *Journal of African Law*, p.46.

Cross, R and Tapper, C. (1990) *Cross on Evidence*, London, Butterworths.

Davis, D and Corder, H. (1988) 'The Long March: Administrative Law in the Appellate Division', vol.4, *South African Journal on Human Rights*, p.281.

D'Sa, R. (1985) 'Human and Peoples' Rights: Distinctive Features of the African Charter', vol.29, *Journal of African Law*, p.77.

Duchcek, I. (1973) *Rights and Liberties in the World Today: Constitutional Promise and Reality*, Santa Barbara, ABC–Clio.

Dumbutshena, E. (1990) 'The Role of Law in a Constitutional Democracy with Particular Reference to the Zimbabwe Experience', vol.5, *South African Journal of Human Rights*,3 p.11.

Ebiasah, J. (1979) 'Protection of the Human Rights of Political Detainees: The Contradictions and Paradoxes in the African Experience', vol.22, *Howard Law Journal*,2 p.49.

Edgar, G. (1971) *Craies on Statute Law*, seventh edition, London, Sweet and Maxwell.

Eze, O. (1984) *Human Rights in Africa*, Lagos, Macmillan.

Federal Republic of Nigeria (1974) *Public Service Review Commission, Main Report*, Lagos, Government Printer.

Feltoe, G.(1975) 'Legalising Illegalities', *Rhodesia Law Journal*, p.121.

Feltoe, G. (1983) *Law, Ideology and Coercion in Southern Rhodesia*, unpublished M.Phil thesis.

Feltoe, G. (1986) 'Extenuating Circumstances: A Life and Death Issue', vol.4, *Zimbabwe Law Review*, p.42.

Feltoe, G (1988) 'The Policy in Relation to the Reporting of the Presence of Dissidents', unpublished research paper, University of Zimbabwe.

Feltoe, G. and Lewin, P. (1987) 'Remedies for Unlawful Interference with Personal Liberty in Zimbabwe', vol.5, *Zimbabwe Law Review*, p.26

Flower, K. (1987) *Serving Secretly*, London, Murray.

Foster, D. (1987) *Detention and Torture in South Africa*, London, James Currey.

Frank, B. (1976)'The Ombudsman and Human Rights Revisited', vol.6, *Israel Yearbook on Human Rights*, p.122.

Frederikse, J. (1984) *None But Ourselves: Masses v the Media in the Making of Zimbabwe*, Gweru, Mambo and James Currey, London.

Geldenhuys, D. (n.d.) *Some Foreign Policy Implications of South Africa's 'Total National Strategy'*, Braamfontein, South African Institute of International Affairs.

General Information on the Office of the Inspector-General of Government (1987) Kampala, Government Printers.

Georges, T. (1967) 'The Court in the Tanzanian One Party State' in G. Sawyerr (ed.), *East African Law and Social Change*, Nairobi, East African Publishing House.

Gering, L. (1974) 'Legal Institutions and Human Needs', vol.37, *Tydsk Rif Vir Hedendaagse Romeins–Hollandse Reg*, p.274.

Ghai, Y. and McAuslan, P. (1970) *Public Law and Political Change in Kenya*, Nairobi, Oxford University Press.

Gittleman, A. (1984) 'The Banjul Charter on Human and Peoples' Rights: A Legal Analysis' in Welch, C. and Meltzer, R. (eds), *Human Rights and Development in Africa*, Albany, State University of New York.

Groves, H. (1961) 'Emergency Powers' in *Journal of the International Commission of Jurists* Winter 1961, p.1.

Gubbay, A. Speech (1991), vol. 3 (1) *Legal Forum*, p.3.

Gutto, S. and Makamure, K. (1985) 'Judicial Subversion in the Guise of Legality', vol.3, *Zimbabwe Law Review*, p.119.

Hall, J. (1960) *General Principles of Criminal Law*, New York, Wiley.

Hartman, S. (1981) 'Derogation from Human Rights Treaties in Public Emergencies', vol.22, *Harvard International Law Journal*, p.1.

Hatchard, J. (1985) 'Detention without Trial and Constitutional Safeguards in Zimbabwe', vol.29, *Journal of African Law*, p.38.

Hatchard, J. (1986) 'The Ombudsman in Africa with Special Reference to Zimbabwe', vol.35, *International and Comparative Law Quarterly*, p.255.

Hatchard, J. (1988) 'Bail and Public Security in Some African Jurisdictions', vol.37, *International and Comparative Law Quarterly*, p.952.

Hatchard, J. (1989a) 'The Implementation of Safeguards on the Use of Emergency Powers: A Zimbabwean Perspective', vol.9, *Oxford Journal of Legal Studies*, p.116.

Hatchard, J. (1989b) 'The Constitution of Malawi', *Constitutiones Africae*, vol.2, Brussels, Bruyant.

Hatchard, J. (1990) 'Emergency Powers in the United Kingdom' in Gardner, J. (ed.), *United Kingdom Law in the 1990's*, London, National Council of Civil Liberties.

Hatchard, J. (1991a) 'The Constitution of Zimbabwe: Towards a Model for Africa?', vol.35, *Journal of African Law*, p.79.

Hatchard J. (1991b) 'The Ombudsman in Africa Revisited', vol.40, *International and Comparative Law Quarterly*, p.937.

Hatchard, J. (1992) 'Paying the Price for Being in the Front Line: Destabilisation in Southern Africa' in Ben-David, S. (ed.), *Victimology: Selected Papers*, Jerusalem, World Society of Victimology.

Hatchard, J. and Slinn, P. (1989) 'Towards an African–Zimbabwe Constitution' in *Third World Legal Studies*, p.78.

Hatchard, J. and Slinn, P. (1990) 'Namibia: Independence and Beyond', vol.10, *International Affairs*, p.137.

Hayson, N. and Plasket, C. (1984) 'The War Against the Law: Judicial Activism in the Appellate Division', vol.4, *South African Journal on Human Rights*, p.303.

Higgins, R. (1978) 'Derogations under Human Rights Treaties', vol.48, *British Yearbook of International Law*, p.281.

Hodder-Williams, R. (1983) *Conflict in Zimbabwe: The Matabeleland Problem*, London, Institute for the Study of Conflict.

Howard, R. (1986) *Human Rights in Commonwealth Africa*, New Jersey, Rowman and Littlefield.

International Commission of Jurists (1961) *Ghana's Preventive Detention Act*, Geneva, ICJ.

International Commission of Jurists (1978) *Follow-Up Mission to the Dar es Salaam Seminar on Human Rights*, Geneva, ICJ.

International Commission of Jurists (1983) *States of Emergency: Their Impact on Human Rights*, Geneva, ICJ.

International Defence and Aid Fund (1979) *Political Prisoners in Rhodesia 1979*, London.

International Law Association, (1980) *Report of the 59th Conference*, Belgrade.

Jacomy-Millette, A. (1974) 'Is the Institution of the Ombudsman Applicable to Africa? Legislation and First Results', vol.8, *Canadian Journal of African Studies*, p.146.

Kieh, G. (1980) 'Setting the Stage: Historical Antecedents to the Liberian 1979 Riots', vol.12, *Liberian Studies Journal*, p.203.

Klieman, T. (1978) 'Emergency Powers and Liberal Democracy in Britain', vol.16, *Journal of Commonwealth and Comparative Politics*, p.190.

Lawyers Committee for Human Rights (1986) *Zimbabwe: Wages of War*, New York.

Liebenow, J. (1986) *African Politics: Crises and Challenges*, Bloomington, Indiana University Press.

Linden, I. (1980) *The Catholic Church and the Struggle for Zimbabwe*, London, Longman.

Lule, H. (1982) 'Human Rights Violations in Uganda under Obote', *Munger Africana Library Notes*, November.

Machan, H. (1975) *Human Rights and Human Liberties: The Radical Reconstruction of the American Political Tradition*, Chicago.

Maisels, I. and de Villiers, J. (1981) 'Report to the Medical Association of South Africa by the Ad Hoc Committee Appointed to Consider Certain Ethical Issues' Supplement to the *South African Medical Journal*, 22 August.

Mangan B. (1988) 'Protecting Human Rights in National Emergencies: Shortcomings in the European System', vol.10, *Human Rights Quarterly*, p.372.

Marks, S. (1982) 'Principles and Norms of Human Rights Applicable in Emergency Situations: Underdevelopment, Catastrophes and Armed Conflicts' in Vasak and Alston (eds), vol. 1, *The International Dimensions of Human Rights*, Paris, UNESCO.

Martin, R. (1974) *Freedom and the Law in Tanzania*, Dar es Salaam, Oxford University Press.

Martin, R. (1977) 'The Ombudsman in Zambia', vol.15, *Journal of Modern African Studies*, p.239.

Mathews, A. (1971) *Law, Order and Liberty in South Africa*, Cape Town, Juta.

Mathews, A. (1986) *Freedom, State Security and the Rule of Law: Dilemmas of the Apartheid Society*, Cape Town, Juta.

Mathews, A. and Albino, R. (1966) 'The Permanence of the Temporary: An Examination of the 90 and 180 Day Detention Laws', vol.83, *South African Law Journal*, p.16.

Mbao, M. (1989a) 'Extension of Powers of Preventive Detention to Economic Crimes in Zambia', vol.33, *Journal of African Law*, p.116.

Mbao, M. (1989b) 'Emergency (Essential Supplies and Services) Regulations 1988 of Zambia', vol.33, *Journal of African Law*, p.126.

Michelson Institute, (1987) *Zambia: Country Study and Norwegian Aid Review*, Oslo.

Molutsi, P. (1990) 'Political Parties and Democracy in Botswana', vol.3, no.7, *Southern Africa*.

Morgan, D. (1981) 'The Indian Essential Features Case', vol.30, *International and Comparative Law Quarterly*, p.307.

Mubako, S. (1983–84) 'Fundamental Rights and Judicial Review: The Zambian Experience', vol.1, no.2, *Zimbabwe Law Review*, p.125.

Mugabe, R.G. (1984) 'The Parliament of Zimbabwe and Some Aspects of the Constitution', vol.65, *The Parliamentarian*, p.4.

Mumma, A. (1988) 'Preservation of Public Security through Executive Restraint of Personal Liberty', *Verfassung und Recht in Ubersee*, p.445.

Mureinik, E. (1986) 'Administrative Law in South Africa', vol.103, *South Africa Law Journal*, p.615.

Mwaanga, V. (1986) *The Other Society: A Detainee's Diary*, Lusaka, Fleetfoot.

Niesewand, P. (1973) *In Camera: Secret Justice in Rhodesia*, London, Weidenfeld and Nicolson.

Norton, P. (1973) 'The Tanzanian Ombudsman', vol.22, *International and Comparative Law Quarterly*, p.603.

Nyagumbo, M. (1980) *With the People*, London, Allison and Busby.

Nyerere, J. (1966) *Freedom and Unity*, Dar es Salaam, Oxford University Press.

Nyerere, J. (1968) *Freedom and Socialism*, Oxford, Oxford University Press.

Ocran, T. (1978) *Law in Aid of Development*, Tema, Ghana Publishing Corporation.

Ojo, A. (1987) *Constitutional Law and Military Rule in Nigeria*, Ibadan, Evans.

Ojo, O. and Sesay, A. (1986) 'The Organisation of African Unity and Human Rights: Prospects for the 1980's and Beyond', vol.8, *Human Rights Quarterly*, p.89.

Orucu, C. (1986) 'The Core of Rights and Freedoms: The Limits of Limits' in Campbell, T. (ed.), *Human Rights: From Rhetoric to Reality*, Oxford, Blackwell.

Palley, C. (1966) *Constitutional History of Southern Rhodesia*, Oxford, Clarendon Press.

Peter, C.M. (1990) *Human Rights in Africa*, New York, Greenwood Press.

Presidential Commission on the Establishment of a Democratic One Party State (1965) Dar es Salaam, Government Printer.

Read, J.S. (1973) 'Bills of Rights in the Third World: Some Commonwealth Experiences' in vol.6, *Verfassung und Recht in Ubersee*, p.21

Reyntjens, F. (1991) 'The Winds of Change, Political and Constitutional Evolution in Francophone Africa, 1990–1991', vol.35, *Journal of African Law*, p.44.

Riekert, J. (1985) 'The Silent Scream: Detention Without Trial, Solitary Confinement and Evidence in South African Security Law Trials', vol.1, *South African Journal of Human Rights*, p.245.

Ringera, A. (1984) 'The African Charter on Human and Peoples' Rights: A Comment', vol.3, *The Advocate (Nairobi)*, p.15.

Rose Innes, L. (1963) *Judicial Review of Administrative Action in South Africa*, Cape Town, Juta.

Rossiter, C. (1948) *Constitutional Dictatorship: Crisis Government in the Modern Democracies*, Princeton, Princeton University Press.

Rudolph, H. (1984) *Security, Terrorism and Torture: Detainees Rights in South Africa and Israel*, Cape Town, Juta.

Scarman, L. (1974) *English Law: The New Dimension*, London, Stevens.

Scarman, L. (1987) 'Human Rights in an Unwritten Constitution' *Denning Law Journal*, p.129.

Seidman, R. (1987) 'Drafting for the Rule of Law', vol.12, *Yale Journal of International Law*, p.84.

Seidman, R. *et al*, (n.d.) 'The Law and Practice of Bail in Zimbabwe', unpublished research paper, University of Zimbabwe.

Sewgobind, R. (1980) *The Mauritian Ombudsman*, Occasional Paper No.8, Alberta, International Ombudsman Institute.

Shaidi, W. (1988) *The Old Brick Lives*, Gweru, Mambo.

Stockholm International Peace Research Institute (1987) *World Armaments and Disarmament Yearbook 1987*, Stockholm.

Sithole, M. (1986) 'The General Elections: 1979–85' in I. Mandaza (ed.), *Zimbabwe: The Political Economy of Transition 1980–1986*, Dakar, Codesria.

Skelton, G. (1980) 'Standards of Procedural Due Process under International Law vs. Preventive Detention in Selected African States', vol.2, *Houston Journal of International Law*, p.319.

Steinberg, R. (1987) 'Judicial Independence in States of Emergency: Lessons from Nicaragua's Popular Anti-Somocista Tribunals', vol.18, *Columbia Human Rights Law Review*, p.359.

Steiner, H. (1991) *Diverse Partners: Non-Governmental Organizations in the Human Rights Movement*, Cambridge, Harvard Law School Human Rights Program.

St Paul, A. (1989) 'L'Ombudsman au Bophuthatswana', vol.43, *Revue Juridique et Politique*, p.219.

Sule, A. (1977) 'The Nigerian Public Complaints Commission, vol.3, *Commonwealth Law Bulletin*, p.312.

Swainson, N (1978) 'State and Economics in Post-Colonial Kenya, 1963-78', vol.12, *Canadian Journal of African Studies*, p.357.

SWAPO, (1981) *To Be Born a Nation: The Liberation Struggle for Namibia*, London, Zed Press.

Thomas, N. (1985) 'Church and State in Zimbabwe', vol.27, *Journal of Church and State*, p.113.

Tordoff, W. (1977) 'Residual Legislatures: The Cases of Tanzania and Zambia', vol.15, *Journal of Commonwealth and Comparative Politics*, p.235.

United States Department of State (1982) *Country Reports on Human Rights Practices for 1981*, Washington D.C.

van Maarseveen, H (1978) *Written Constitutions: A Computerized Comparative Study*, Oceana, New York, 1978.

Webster, D. and Friedman, T. (1989) 'Repression and the State of Emergency: June 87–March 89', *South African Review*, p.21.

Weisfelder, R. (1984) 'Human Rights in Southern Africa' in Welch, C. and Meltzer, R. (eds), *Human Rights and Development in Africa*, Albany, State University of New York.

Weitzer, R. (1984) 'In Search of Regime Protection', vol.22, *Journal of Modern African Studies*, p.529.

Werlin, H. (1972) 'The Roots of Corruption', vol.10, *Journal of Modern African Studies*, p.247.

Williams, C. (1982) 'Placing the Burden of Proof' in L. Waller and G. Campbell (eds), *Well and Truly Tried*, Sydney, Law Book Co.

Williams, G. (1961) *Criminal Law: The General Part*, London, Stevens.

Woods, D. (1978) *Biko*, New York, Paddington Press.

Wrobel, B. (1986) 'Intimidation, Political Freedom and the Common Roll' in M. Arnold, *Zimbabwe: Report on the 1985 General Elections*, Washington D.C. Human Rights Law Group.

Young, I. (1969) *Rhodesia and Independence: A Study in British Colonial Policy*, London, Dent.

Zimba, L. (1984) *The Zambian Bill of Rights*, Nairobi, East African Publishing House.

Zimmerli, C. (1971) 'Human Rights and the Rule of Law in Southern Rhodesia', vol.20, *International and Comparative Law Quarterly*, p.239.

Zvogbo, E. (1976) 'The Abuse of Executive Prerogative', vol.6, Winter 1976, *Issue* , p.38.

Index